The Schoolroom

THE SCHOOLROOM

A Social History of
Teaching and Learning

Dale Allen Gyure

History of Human Spaces

An Imprint of ABC-CLIO, LLC
Santa Barbara, California • Denver, Colorado

Library of Congress Cataloging-in-Publication Data

Names: Gyure, Dale Allen, author.
Title: The schoolroom : a social history of teaching and learning / Dale
    Allen Gyure.
Description: Santa Barbara, California : ABC-CLIO, LLC, 2018. | Series: History
    of human spaces | Includes bibliographical references and index.
Identifiers: LCCN 2018015124 (print) | LCCN 2018019928 (ebook) | ISBN
    9781440850387 (eBook) | ISBN 9781440850370 (alk. paper)
Subjects: LCSH: Education—Social aspects—United States—History. |
    Classrooms—United States—History. | Schools—United States—Furniture,
    equipment, etc.—History.
Classification: LCC LC191.4 (ebook) | LCC LC191.4 .G96 2018 (print) | DDC
    306.43/2—dc23
LC record available at https://lccn.loc.gov/2018015124

ISBN: 978-1-4408-5037-0 (print)
       978-1-4408-5038-7 (ebook)

22 21 20 19 18   1 2 3 4 5

This book is also available as an eBook.

Greenwood
An Imprint of ABC-CLIO, LLC

ABC-CLIO, LLC
130 Cremona Drive, P.O. Box 1911
Santa Barbara, California 93116-1911
www.abc-clio.com

This book is printed on acid-free paper ∞
Manufactured in the United States of America

CONTENTS

PREFACE

What factors shaped the development of classroom spaces? How are schoolrooms influenced by teaching techniques or educational philosophies? How do today's school buildings compare with the past? Schools are salient features of American lives: between the ages of 5 and 18, the average American probably spends more time in a school building than any other single place outside the home. But we know very little about the history of our school buildings or the development of the classrooms within them or the objects used in those classrooms. These spaces and objects influence the behaviors of students and teachers and reflect changing educational ideologies. *The Schoolroom: A Social History of Teaching and Learning* is the first book-length account of the material culture and architectural design of schoolrooms. Currently there is no comparable work that seeks to read the physical spaces or material objects of the classroom as reservoirs of information about American educational history. *The Schoolroom* explains how classrooms and school buildings reached their current form, describing how educators teamed with architects to shape the spaces of learning in response to curricular and pedagogical fashions, population shifts, cultural expectations, and a concern for children's health. It also reveals the little-known histories of ubiquitous educational objects like blackboards, school desks, and computers.

The Schoolroom is intended for students and readers who are curious about material culture or educational or architectural history, in addition to general readers interested in American history. The book begins by chronicling the American schoolroom from its colonial beginnings to the present day, examining the various factors that have influenced classroom design and use. Then the story shifts to the school building—the place where schoolrooms reside—and its own development. These two chapters give the reader a sense of how education's spatial environments have reflected and sometimes inspired changes in teaching and curriculum. The book's final chapters delve into the origins of important objects used in schoolrooms, from blackboards to computers, and the ancillary physical spaces like corridors and lockers that interact with the schoolroom. Readers will come away from *The Schoolroom* with a better understanding of the intertwined stories of educational spaces, objects, methods, and theories and the impact on all of them from cultural or societal influences.

INTRODUCTION

Universal public education, such as we see in the United States and most other developed countries in the 21st century, is a rather new phenomenon in human history. Long before mass education became the norm, learning took place either privately or on a very small scale under restrictive conditions. In Europe and England, for example, before the settlement of the North American colonies, education was a limited matter, largely in the hands of religious organizations and almost exclusively for boys.

Europeans began to embrace the formal education of children as part of the Protestant Reformation in the 16th century. Prior to this, the Roman Catholic Church that dominated the continent offered reading and writing instruction for monks and future priests, and churches were some of the earliest centers of learning, but outside of the Church there was very little in the way of organized education. The major tenets of Protestantism—salvation through faith alone, the supremacy of holy scripture, and a direct relationship with God without the intercession of human organizations—combined to bring a new emphasis on reading the Bible. As a first step toward understanding God's requirements, worshippers needed to be able to read the scriptures. Thus, the earliest attempts at public education focused on reading over writing, and, in particular, the ability to read Latin was emphasized. On the European continent, education would remain in the hands of Protestant and Catholic churches until the public school movement of the late 19th century, with a notable exception being Frederick the Great's institution of widespread public education in Prussia beginning in 1763 (although even then churches provided most of the teachers and schools).

The most extensive opportunities for children's education appeared in England, where schools for boys predated the Reformation by centuries. These schools tended to attract boys whose parents were unable to educate them at home, and they catered to commoners, since the nobles were able to afford private tutors for their offspring. Typically the schools were affiliated with religion in some way, taking place in religious buildings and taught by monks, friars, and priests. A change began to occur in the 14th century with an increasing number of schools endowed by wealthy individuals to teach Latin grammar to children and with the beginnings of the English college system. King Henry VIII's conflict with the Roman Catholic Church eventually led to his closing of monasteries and friaries, thus providing more existing buildings that might be utilized for educational purposes. This move coincided with a growing interest in expanding the number of schools. According to historian Malcom Seaborne, by 1660, "a whole network of schools had been set up, covering not only the principal towns but many villages and hamlets as well" (Seaborne 1971, 33).

The system that developed in England from the Anglo-Saxon period on mostly aimed at teaching Latin grammar, described by historian Nicholas Orme as "the chief concern of formal schooling" (Orme 2006, 86). The main reason for learning to read was to learn Latin, the official language of prayer in Western Europe. Pupils began their studies by learning the alphabet and various songs. Until the late 14th century, song schools contrived for these purposes thrived throughout the kingdom. Once the student mastered the alphabet, he moved on to grammar. In these grammar schools, boys learned how to read, compose, write, and speak Latin. Beyond Latin, some students were instructed in the less important languages of French and English. Successful completion of grammar school marked the end of most students' educational experiences, although a few would advance to further study in areas pertaining to business (such as letter writing, accounting, and study of the common law) or to the university, where they encountered liberal arts subjects divided into the trivium (grammar, rhetoric, and logic) and the quadrivium (arithmetic, music, geometry, and astronomy). Below the university level, these subjects were rarely taught.

Schools in the Middle Ages and early Renaissance period occupied numerous different kinds of buildings, few of which were purpose built; those that were specially designed as schools were often on the grounds of a church or college. Most were utilitarian, rectangular buildings with nondescript exteriors that gave no indication of the activities inside. Inside, the schoolrooms of this era tended toward uniformity. A large oblong space was the most essential feature, usually with a single door for access on one of the short sides and small windows placed high on the walls to deter students from looking outside. The teacher, called a master, sat in a large chair (sometimes under a canopy) at one end of the room, and the students sat on benches along the sidewalls. Over time, these benches were used to segregate the students according to achievement level, or "form." The term may have been borrowed from the choir areas of medieval churches, which were rectangular areas for singers near the altar that included tiered seats also called forms. Originally the educational forms were simply the students' benches. By the 16th century, form became synonymous with what we now call "grade." Students of the same ability occupied a single form, separated from those who were more or less advanced. Eventually English schools evolved a common standard of six forms, although this was never universal. In some schools the master taught the upper forms, while the lower forms were overseen by the master's assistant, known as an usher—a word derived from the Latin *hostiarius*, or "doorkeeper." This indicated the usher's prime responsibility in the classroom—controlling access into or out of the room via his seat next to the lone doorway.

Students sat on the forms and held their books or manuscripts in their laps. Popular before the invention of the printing press, manuscripts were hand-written documents copied by monks or former students. By the 13th century, handheld tablets made from a piece of wood with parchment nailed on supplemented instruction, especially for less advanced students. These tablets evolved into hornbooks by the 16th century, with a thin, transparent sheet of animal horn laid over the parchment for protection. When not working on their own, students approached the master (never vice versa) for individualized instruction. At other times, the master called on boys individually to be questioned or examined. Most of the educational process was conducted through memorization and recitation, wherein the student was evaluated on his ability to memorize particular bits of information. Since writing played little or no part in this process, most schoolrooms were devoid of desks, although in some instances the master had a desk to hold his materials.

In summary, education was a rare commodity in pre-17th-century Europe and the British Isles. Access to education generally was restricted to boys of at least the middle class and above, learning tended to be limited to learning Latin grammar and basic reading skills, and there was little preparation for any particular job or profession. Students endured rudimentary pedagogical techniques that emphasized their ability to memorize and recall information in physical surroundings usually comprised of a simple rectangular room and a series of wooden benches. This classroom model would migrate to the English colonies in the 1600s, forming the physical basis for the origins of the American schoolroom and the iconic one-room frontier schoolhouse.

CHRONOLOGY

1635 Boston Latin School is opened as the first Latin grammar school in the colonies for boys who will occupy the upper echelons of society.

1636 Harvard College is established, the first institution of higher education in the colonies.

1647 The Massachusetts General Court issues the Old Deluder Satan Act to stimulate literacy as a weapon against evil; the law requires every town within the colony with at least 50 families to hire a schoolmaster to teach reading and writing and every town with at least 100 families to open a Latin grammar school.

1690 The *New England Primer*, which will become the most widely used textbook in New England, is published in Boston.

1787 The Land Ordinance of 1787 is passed by the Confederation Congress to control westward expansion. It divides the Northwest Territory into 640-acre townships; every township must reserve one section of land for education.

1805 The Quaker-operated Free School Society in New York opens the first monitorial school in the United States. Based on the ideas of British educators Joseph Lancaster and Dr. Andrew Bell, the system utilizes superior students to teach their peers and emphasizes organization and control. Monitorial schools enjoyed widespread popularity before their eventual demise by the 1850s.

1821 Boston English High School opens, the nation's first public high school.

1827 Massachusetts creates a law requiring each town with more than 500 families to establish a public high school.

1828 The faculty of Yale College publishes the "Yale Report," a defense of classical liberal-arts education and the faculty-psychology / mental-discipline approach over specialized training.

1832 The New England Association of Farmers, Mechanics and Other Workingmen publicly condemns the practice of child labor.

1836 William Holmes McGuffey publishes the first *McGuffey Reader*, which will become one of the most influential and popular textbooks in 19th-century America.

Massachusetts requires children under age 15 working in factories to attend school at least three months out of the year.

1837 Massachusetts forms the nation's first state board of education. Horace Mann is appointed its secretary.

1839 The first state-funded normal (teacher-training) school opens in Lexington, Massachusetts.

1842 Henry Barnard publishes the first edition of *School Architecture: Or Contributions to the Improvement of School-Houses in the United States.*

1844 Horace Mann's *Seventh Annual Report* as secretary of education for Massachusetts argues for graded schools and better-quality schoolhouses.

1847 The first graded school in the United States—the Josiah Quincy Grammar School—opens in Boston. It divides students by age into cohorts, resulting in smaller class sizes and more curricular control.

1852 Massachusetts enacts the nation's first mandatory-attendance law, requiring all children—whether employed or not—to attend school for part of the year. By 1918, all states will pass similar legislation.

1856 A private kindergarten school begins operation in Watertown, Wisconsin. St. Louis would open the nation's first publicly funded kindergarten program 14 years later.

1857 The National Teachers Association (now the National Education Association) is formed in Philadelphia.

1859 The first patent is issued for a combination desk, which joins chair and desk into one unit.

1867 The federal government creates the U.S. Department of Education. Henry Barnard is appointed to be the first commissioner of education.

1874 The Michigan Supreme Court rules that the city of Kalamazoo may legally levy taxes to support the formation of a public high school, legitimizing publicly funded education in the United States.

1893 The National Education Association's (NEA) Committee on Secondary School Studies (Committee of Ten) issues a report establishing a standard secondary-school curriculum—oriented toward college preparation—for use throughout the country.

1895 A similar NEA Committee on Elementary Education (Committee of Fifteen) reaffirms the traditional structure of the elementary curriculum and its emphasis on lectures, recitations, and memorization.

1896 In *Plessy v. Ferguson*, the U.S. Supreme Court decides that a Louisiana law requiring racial segregation on railroad cars does not violate the Constitution, essentially legalizing discrimination. As a result, numerous Southern states enact "separate but equal" laws requiring racial segregation in public schools.

1905 Samuel Parker Moulthrop, a school principal in Rochester, New York, invents the first mass-marketed adjustable, movable combination desk.

1908 The first open-air school in the nation, in Providence, Rhode Island, adopts the nascent European practice of providing schools with no walls for tubercular students, allowing them to have continual access to fresh air.

1909 Columbus, Ohio, opens the United States' first junior high school.

1910 The Rochester, New York, public schools become the first to use motion pictures for educational purposes.

1911 The first Montessori school in the United States opens in Tarrytown, New York.

1917 The federal Smith-Hughes Act provides federal funding for agricultural and vocational education in public schools.

1918 A report by the National Education Association's Commission on the Reorganization of Secondary Education (the Cardinal Principles report) reverses the Committee of Ten's emphasis on college preparation, instead emphasizing that the public high school's purpose is to train students for adult life rather than college attendance.

1920 The Department of Commerce begins to issue licenses for educational radio stations.

1923 The first public school in the United States to broadcast lessons over the radio is Haaren High School in New York City.

1928 Sidney Pressey receives the first patent for his "Machine for Intelligence Tests," the first viable teaching machine.

1929 Oak Lane Country Day School, near Philadelphia, designed by William Lescaze and George Howe, is the first modernist school building in the United States.

1935 Richard Neutra's Corona Avenue School opens in Bell, California, near Los Angeles, and becomes the nation's first widely publicized modern-style school building.

1938 The Fair Labor Standards Act sets the first federal standards for child labor, covering minimum ages of employment and hours of work.

1939 Ernest J. Kump Jr.'s Acalanes High School (Lafayette, California) is a notable early example of the finger plan.

1940 The Crow Island School, the most architecturally celebrated school in American architectural history, opens in Winnetka, Illinois.

1942 The New York Museum of Modern Art's traveling exhibition *Modern Architecture for the Modern School* begins a four-year tour of the country, celebrating the functional superiority and pedagogical opportunities offered by the nation's first generation of modern schools.

1946 Congress approves the National School Lunch Act, establishing a system of subsidies to schools to provide low-cost or free school lunches to qualified students.

1953 Perkins & Will's Heathcote Elementary School (Scarsdale, New York) introduces the cluster plan.

1954 In the landmark case *Brown v. Board of Education of Topeka*, the U.S. Supreme Court overturns *Plessy v. Ferguson*, ruling that "separate educational facilities are inherently unequal," thus establishing the basis for an end to legal discrimination in public education (although de facto discrimination continues).

1957 Federal troops are required to enforce the integration of nine black students at Arkansas's Little Rock Central High School.

The Sputnik satellite, launched by the Soviet Union, initiates the space race and raises fears that the United States has fallen behind in the sciences, with potential repercussions for national security.

Michigan's Carson City Elementary School, designed by Louis C. Kingscott & Associates, has over 12,000 square feet of classroom space with no interior walls.

1958 The Sputnik scare inspires the passage of the National Defense Education Act, which increases federal funding for science, mathematics, and foreign-language education.

A joint effort funded by the Ford Foundation and including the American Institute of Architects and Columbia University Teachers College creates the Educational Facilities Laboratories, a nonprofit corporation that researches the relationship between education and architecture.

1965 Congress enacts the Elementary and Secondary Education Act to provide federal support for low-income students as part of President Lyndon Johnson's War on Poverty. Johnson had been a teacher early in his career.

Project Head Start, a federal preschool education initiative for low-income children, is given an eight-week summer trial. It will grow to become one of the most successful educational programs in American history.

1971 Intel Corporation releases the first microprocessor, which will revolutionize computing and lead to the development of microcomputers.

1975   The Education for All Handicapped Children Act requires all public schools receiving federal aid to comply with regulations concerning equal access for the disabled.

1978   The National Energy Act establishes grants for schools and other institutions willing to incorporate energy-conservation measures.

1984   Apple Inc. begins to sell the Macintosh, a mass-market personal computer that includes software specifically designed for teachers.

1990   The Americans with Disabilities Act requires equal, barrier-free access to public and private facilities and bans discrimination against disabled people.

2002   The No Child Left Behind Act, signed by President George W. Bush, reshapes the landscape of American education, emphasizing mass testing to gauge student achievement and penalizing schools that fail to meet yearly progress goals.

2016   Sandy Hook Elementary School opens on the site of a school massacre in 2012 that killed 26 children and adults. The building represents a new era in school design, deftly melding educational and security concerns in a peaceful natural setting.

Chapter 1

THE SCHOOLROOM

The schoolroom is the material heart of American education and always has been. Since the earliest days of education in the North American colonies—when the school was *nothing but* a classroom—it has been the most important element of the school's physical environment. Before the early 20th century, schoolrooms tended toward similarity in terms of size, shape, and purpose; there was little modification except for the desire to accommodate the necessary number of students. Schoolrooms also were authoritarian spaces where educators exerted tight control over student learning and behavior. With new insights into learning theory and developmental psychology, however, came adjustments, initially seen in progressive educators' experiments with informal room arrangements and smaller-scale furniture in kindergartens and lower grades. Schoolrooms for these youngest children soon began to break out of the traditional rectangular box form by adding alcoves or partially separated work areas, and many ground-level rooms included patios or outdoor play areas immediately accessible from the main activity space. In the postwar era, classrooms forged a closer relationship with the outdoors. They also began to appear in almost every conceivable shape, from hexagons and octagons to circles and ovals. Meanwhile, advances in lighting and ventilation practices—two areas that had always dominated the architectural side of classroom design—virtually eliminated the health concerns of previous generations. Air and temperature regulation reached the point where windowless classrooms were introduced; they remain a polarizing topic to this day. And the open-education movement had a broad and controversial impact on classroom design with its advocacy of rooms without walls. In the 21st century, although security looms larger in educators' minds than before and computer technology introduces continual changes for teachers to explore, the basic schoolroom in America remains remarkably unchanged.

COLONIAL BEGINNINGS

According to historian Jonathan Zimmerman, "For the first two hundred years of European settlement in America, the majority of people who attended school went to a one-room schoolhouse" (Zimmerman 2009, 18). He might have added that they would have done so in circumstances that differed greatly from the romanticized image of the Little Red Schoolhouse. The first schoolrooms in America consisted of any space that could accommodate a teacher and some pupils. Commonly, teachers conducted classes in their own home. The colonies' oldest school, the Boston Latin School, opened in 1635 under such circumstances. On the ever-expanding frontier, a nascent community's largest interior space—often a barn or a church— often served the same purpose. The first structures specifically built to house students probably appeared at the beginning of the 18th century.

Education was an essential component of the colonial experience. Although the many groups migrating to North America had wide-ranging religious beliefs and commercial expectations, they uniformly respected the importance of educating their young, particularly those Protestant sects that settled in New England. Calvinists in particular believed in literacy as a means to understanding and interpreting the word of God through the scriptures, a fundamental skill needed in a world where ignorance could open the door to evil. Reading was a path to salvation. The Massachusetts General Court recognized reading's significance when it passed a law known as the Old Deluder Satan Act in 1647 to stimulate public literacy. The legislation required every town or village in the colony with at least 50 families to hire a schoolmaster to teach reading and writing, and every town with at least 100 families to open a Latin **grammar school**, in order to provide the populace with the weapon needed to thwart Satan in his perpetual attempts to deceive people into sinning. Reading was by far the main focus; writing instruction was not considered as necessary for the average child.

The outstanding characteristic of the colonial and early national period education was its local organization, a trait that would later form the foundation of the American public-school system that continues to this day. Despite legislation like the Old Deluder Satan Act, throughout the colonies the responsibility for educating the young fell upon the community. Citizens banded together to establish schools in towns, cities, and rural landscapes for their children. They found or built the facilities, hired the schoolmaster, and controlled the limited **curriculum**, funding these activities from their own pockets in the absence of any financial support from the colonial government (except in rare instances in New England) or predominant religious factions. Often known as subscription schools, such community-supported forms evolved into **district schools** by the early 1800s and influenced the nascent public system that would later appear. Elsewhere, particularly in cities, private lessons in reading and writing were available through **dame schools**, named for the women who operated them from their own homes.

The history of American education is generally a story of unequal access for minority or lower-income students, continuing into the 21st century, and the roots of this inequity reach back to organized education's earliest days. Despite the efforts of solitary champions like Thomas Jefferson and Daniel Webster, the colonists' and early Americans' commitment to education was far from universal. From the beginning, schooling was considered most appropriate for white boys: girls, blacks, Native Americans, or any other minorities were restricted to varying degrees, often being completely excluded, especially in those areas farthest from New England. In these years, education had already begun to divide into two tracks. Middle- and upper-class white children could avail themselves of the options named above, but poorer or nonwhite children had fewer opportunities. Among the lower socioeconomic groups, church-sponsored schools or tuition-free charity schools were more common. Some black students attended schools in New England, but in the South they were barred from public education: in Southern states, it was a criminal offense to teach slaves to read and write. Free black children relied on abolitionist groups and religious congregations to provide them with basic skills. After the Civil War, the Freedmen's Bureau, formed by the U.S. Congress, established a series of elementary schools for the children of freed slaves. Native American children fared no better. Their education often was limited to so-called Indian schools, where civilizing and Christianizing initiatives took priority over providing quality education.

Whether in a private house or a new, purpose-built school building, the schoolroom's organization, spatial layout, and educational activities were similar across the colonies. The initial generations of schoolhouses were almost universally single-room structures without interior partitions. Some had a small foyer or vestibule area marking the transition from outside to inside, while others were entered directly. There were no indoor toilets. Students sat on benches that identified them with a grade or particular ability level (known as their form). In the earliest schools, these benches, along with a teacher's desk and a fireplace or stove, constituted the entirety of the school's equipment.

Education was a much simpler affair at the beginning. In addition to the lack of desks, most of the materials we associate with elementary schools— like pencils, paper, and books—were absent. Teachers had few amenities to aid their teaching. A common accoutrement was the hornbook, widely used in the colonies by the early 1700s. Hornbooks were paddle-shaped pieces of wood, ivory, bone, leather, or any other hard material on which was laid a small piece of paper or vellum containing a lesson—often the alphabet or basic arithmetic functions—overlaid by a thin, translucent shaving of animal horn for protection. They had been used for centuries in England and parts of Europe and may have been particularly popular in Holland, where the English Pilgrims lived prior to their transatlantic crossings. Hornbooks were cheaper and more durable than books at a time when schools were so underfunded that buildings often had gaps between the wooden boards forming the walls and lacked glass for windows.

At some point in the first century of colonial education, the upper-form students (fourth through sixth forms) began to be supplied with desks. However, because many urban-school systems were bifurcated with separate schools teaching reading and writing, there was little necessity for places to write in the reading (primary) schools. Students often wrote on handheld slates in the age before blackboards. Slates had been part of mass education for centuries, but their popularity increased in the 1800s. An alternative for the youngest children learning the alphabet was the sand table, which allowed them to temporarily trace letters or even words in the sand with their fingers. When writing desks were introduced to schoolrooms, they frequently lined two to three walls, forming an L or U shape around the room. Older students could use them for written work, pivoting on their benches to face the teacher when necessary.

The teacher's desks usually occupied one end of the room, frequently positioned on a platform of some kind that allowed full view of the space. Alternatively, in some cases, the teacher's desk was centrally located if the stove was not. This was the least preferred layout because it meant some students were seated behind the teacher and out of his sight and control.

Before school design became a full-time profession in the mid-19th century, when there was no need for specialized spaces in the building, schoolhouses were built by community members or carpenters and mimicked houses in many ways. Existing evidence indicates that the majority of schoolrooms were rectangular in shape, with squares being the second most common configuration and circular or octagonal schools appearing in rare circumstances. Customarily the room's long sides were at least twice its short sides; most schoolrooms were probably around 30 to 50 feet long and 20 to 25 feet wide. There were few decorations on the walls. Many school buildings were, in fact, log cabins, adding to their primitive ambience. Windows were crucial for letting in light and air, but there were no standards as to their size or location. Wood-burning stoves were

A typical 19th-century, one-room schoolhouse in rural Minnesota. In the 18th century, benches would have been more common than desks. (Library of Congress)

likewise required to make the colder months bearable. But the stoves were notoriously ineffectual; colonial students later reminisced about wearily struggling to remain awake on cold winter days when seated next to it while their classmates on the room's outskirts, particularly near windows, might be shivering at the same time. The shoddy nature of construction in most of these buildings added to the uncomfortable schoolroom atmosphere, with drafts regularly seeping through the crudely assembled walls. Teachers' only means of regulating room temperatures and the amount of fresh air was through manipulating doors and windows.

In these circumstances, teachers tried to provide children with fundamental reading and writing skills so that they might be able to read the Bible and function as an informed citizen. Some of the children from wealthier families or those demonstrating higher intelligence or a capacity for learning might dream of a career in the clergy and be encouraged to learn Latin. Urban schools with larger enrollments and more schoolmasters available began to offer Greek, Latin, and sometimes Hebrew for the advanced students, along with geography, history, and mathematics. While rural schools tended to be smaller, in the larger cities, schoolrooms might hold between 50 and 80 students, spanning numerous grade levels or forms. Teachers—who were all men—dealt with these challenging conditions by implementing a tightly controlled system that stressed memorization achieved through endless drill and **recitation**.

THE 19TH CENTURY

Schoolrooms increased in number throughout the 19th century but changed very little in terms of their size and function until its final decades. During this period, educators recognized the schoolroom's role as the building block of the schoolhouse. They began to take note of the room's effects on students' health and teamed with architects to devise spaces attuned to lighting, ventilation, and hygienic concerns; however, schoolroom designs were not very diverse given the limited curriculums and near-universal pedagogical techniques that dominated the century.

Monitorial Schools

Across the United States, schoolrooms barely differed from their colonial predecessors until a push for reform began to arise in the late 1830s. Prior to this groundswell, however, there was a unique exception—the **monitorial school**. Invented in Great Britain simultaneously by Joseph Lancaster (1778–1838) and Dr. Andrew Bell (1753–1832) as a more efficient means of teaching large numbers of urban children, the monitorial system attracted much attention in this country in the early 19th century. It required a specialized layout in order to work properly and thus became the first instance in this country of architectural space structured by educational requirements.

Monitorial schools succeeded because they established an environment where a single teacher could supervise up to 1,000 students in a single vast, undivided room. Obviously organization and discipline were crucial to their achievement. The teacher's—or master's—desk was elevated on a platform at one end of a rectangular space. Facing him, ranks of equally spaced desks and benches filled the middle of the room, ideally on a gently inclined floor that provided the master with greater visibility of children in the back rows. The monitorial system's salient feature was the use of advanced students, called monitors, to teach their peers. Students were organized by ability level and led by monitors through exercises where they recited memorized lessons.

Each monitor was assigned a small group of students and had a designated area in the aisles along the sidewalls where the students would stand in a semicircle facing the wall. When the cohort finished their recitations, they returned to the desks to continue studying. By subdividing this great mass of children according to a pyramid-like hierarchy of students, assistant monitors, monitors, and head monitor, culminating with the master, these schools let students progress according to their own ability, with the more advanced among them no longer constrained by the master's need to dedicate time to all students in all grades like in the one-room schoolhouse. Monitorial schools fostered competition among students through awards for achievement and a clear structure for advancement. And it further motivated some students to become monitors themselves. The monitorial system had the added benefit of training future teachers, as monitors might acquire years of experience teaching their peers before ever leaving school.

The monitorial system proved attractive because it allowed for unprecedented economies of scale at a time when educating the poor became a high priority for Western educators. It became the most prevalent and successful educational reform in the Western world during the early 19th century. The first American school to adopt Lancaster's ideas, although on a reduced scale, was the Quaker-operated Free School Society in New York, a charity school that began using the Lancaster-Bell method in 1805. Educators in cities like New York, Philadelphia, and Baltimore followed in the next two years, and monitorial schools proved particularly attractive to school administrators in such western frontier cities as Detroit, Louisville, and Pittsburgh. Although none of the American monitorial schools were as large as their London counterparts, enrollments of up to 400 were not uncommon.

As might be expected, the learning atmosphere in these schoolrooms was not ideal. Uninterrupted interior spaces up to 70 to 80 feet long and 30 to 40 feet wide with 20-foot-high ceilings, filled with hundreds of students walking back and forth and simultaneously reciting a variety of lessons, would have generated a cacophony of sounds to challenge even those children with exceptional concentration. And noise was not the only criticism of the monitorial schools. Opponents complained about the inferior nature of education derived from teaching practices aimed at expediency rather than quality. But they would have difficulty faulting the school's orderliness and disciplinary tactics, which proved quite successful. As an instrument of social control, the monitorial school was unmatched. An important component of the system was its ability to instill discipline in its students, an aspect that was just as prized among educators—and more highly regarded by some—as learning the three R's (reading, writing, and arithmetic). The corps of monitors enforced military discipline on students and controlled their movements, utterances, and even access to the equipment allocated for educational purposes, like pencils or books. In their recitation areas, or drafts, students stood in order of achievement, and the highest ranking among them often wore medals or ribbons to signify their status. They moved in unison to and from the drafts at the monitors' commands or a bell's signal. Even cleaning one's slate was a highly regimented activity, performed in a series of steps that concluded with the command "Hands behind!" with one hand grasping the other behind the back. All these disciplinary measures were intended to train students to be self-regulating and to inculcate the qualities of punctuality, obedience, and deference necessary to become productive and morally upright citizens.

Interest in monitorial schools began to wane in America in the 1830s for various reasons, including a shortage of monitors, the method's pedagogical limitations, and the proliferation of new public schools in larger cities. New York, which had been the first major city to adopt monitorial education, was the last to abandon it, continuing until 1853—long after other educators abandoned mutual instruction techniques. Monitorial schools were more than a unique footnote in American educational history, however, because their accommodation of individual abilities would help to inspire the **graded school** model that eventually reshaped schools around the country.

Common Schools

The early 19th century gave rise to frequent efforts among educational reformers and concerned parents to improve the quality of education and expand its reach. These actions produced the **common school** movement, so named because its advocates proposed an unprecedented uniformity among school districts. Common school advocates envisioned a scheme where all children in a given district, region, or even across the country studied a common curriculum under teachers using the same pedagogical techniques. The reformers sought to overcome the uneven quality of education then existing. Common schools, although limited in application, would form the basis for the fledgling public-school scheme that followed them.

The common school movement was strongest in New England, particularly Massachusetts and Connecticut, the historical centers of educational innovation dating back to the colonial era; on the other hand, common schools were rare in the South until after the Civil War. Advocates extolled the common schools' efficiency. Looking into the future, and recognizing the trend toward increasing enrollments, they tried to implement a nearly universal educational system of free public schools supported by local property taxes and overseen by a governing board. Traditional subjects and skills would be supplemented by a heavy dose of education in what historian Carl Kaestle deemed the "native Protestant ideology." This phrase captures the prevailing mind-set of antebellum America's cultural and political leaders, who wanted children trained in a second version of the three R's, consisting of republicanism, Protestantism, and capitalism. Kaestle described the native Protestant ideology's major propositions as follows:

> the sacredness and fragility of the republican party (including ideas about individualism, liberty, and virtue); the importance of individual character in fostering social morality; the central role of personal industry in defining rectitude and merit; the delineation of a highly respected but limited domestic role for women; the importance for character building of familial and social environment (within certain racial and ethnic limitations); the sanctity and social virtues of property; the equality and abundance of economic opportunity in the United States; the superiority of American Protestant culture; the grandeur of America's destiny; and the necessity of a determined public effort to unify America's polyglot population, chiefly through education. (Kaestle 1983, 76–77)

Understanding and appreciating the interconnections among these driving forces was crucial for students in order for them to achieve success and continue what was commonly believed to be the United States' divinely inspired ascendance.

Although the common school movement did not immediately improve the nation's educational situation, it planted seeds that later public-school supporters would sow in the ensuing decades. Common school reformers succeeded in convincing Americans that (a) education should be open to all children (theoretically), (b) that it should be tuition-free, supported by local taxes, and (c) that it was needed to supplement the process of moral development begun with the family and the church. It took some time, however, to make this desire a reality. The country entered the 19th century with a hodgepodge of educational institutions, all unconnected to one another and each liable to have its own curriculum. Municipal governments gradually began to institute tax-supported public schools, forming basic structures of governance and management, which would permit them to assimilate larger numbers of students at a future time when enrollments might grow. The scope of public education extended as well. Public high schools appeared in the 1820s to provide opportunities for older or more advanced students, and in the other direction, the kindergarten proved extremely popular after its introduction later in the century. Within a few decades, public education had matured from sporadic beginnings into a semiorganized system. By 1850, a larger percentage of children under age 15 attended school in the United States than any other country (Zimmerman 2009, 19).

Graded Schools

The common school movement had no direct impact on schoolroom design. Common schools neither introduced new pedagogical techniques nor made unique demands on the schoolroom; anything from a one-room log cabin to a multiroom, multistory building would suffice. But another innovation emerging during the zenith of common schools had a far-reaching influence, eventually reshaping both school systems and individual school buildings by the end of the century. The graded school was a revolutionary invention that first appeared in Boston in 1847. Prior to this time, students were lumped together in one room despite their differences in age and ability, which presented teachers with extraordinary disciplinary and pedagogical challenges. As enrollments increased in larger cities, filling schoolrooms with up to 100 students even in nonmonitorial settings, the situation reached a crisis. Unwilling to adopt the monitorial system that was created for mass education, Boston's educators elected instead to apportion students into smaller, more manageable sections that gathered children of similar ages and achievement levels. The notion of grading schools to increase efficiency had originated, like many 19th-century educational innovations, in the Kingdom of Prussia, which occupied territory now formed by Northern Germany, Denmark, Poland, and the Baltic States.

Like other cities in the colonial era, Boston operated separate reading and writing schools in physically independent buildings. After 1789 these two functions were combined into a single facility, although they continued to exist as independent schools and even had different governing bodies. By the early 19th century, the system evolved into distinct primary and grammar schools. **Primary schools** were for the youngest students, 4- to 7-year-olds who were learning to read. Their origins were in the dame schools present in every city. The primary school typically housed up to 50 students per schoolroom. Frequently educators controlled their sizes in an attempt to keep a domestic scale and not overwhelm the young children. Since women were considered to have natural advantages in nurturing children of this age group, the majority of primary school teachers were female. Grammar schools, for 7- to 13-year-olds who could read, were much larger, including up to 200 pupils in one space. A single male master, occasionally with male assistants, or ushers, was expected to organize and educate these masses. The grammar schools were separated into reading and writing schools, each of which was attended for half a day. Educators found that splitting students in this way allowed them to educate girls and boys—who were segregated—in the same building by rotating them between these two functions. Normally school buildings were three-story brick blocks, with the reading school on the first floor, the writing school in the middle, and a third-floor assembly hall. Students attended one of the schools in the morning and then switched in the afternoon. Because reading and writing schools operated independently, there were two male masters—one for each school—present in the building.

In 1836, the city began to build new grammar schools, with rooms for a primary school in the basement or on the ground floor. This had the effect of unifying different levels of education in the same building while maintaining their independence. Boston's educators were stimulated to consider an adjustment after Horace Mann's (1796–1859) 1844 report. Mann was the initial secretary of the Massachusetts Board of Education, and in his seventh annual report, he expressed a desire for change inspired by a six-month tour of European schools the previous year. In particular, he was impressed—like other American commentators—by Prussia's centralized public-education scheme that incorporated such advanced notions as universal, compulsory education; tax-supported funding; governmental oversight and regulation of teachers and subject matter; division of students into age and ability levels; and small class sizes in dedicated classrooms. This graded system had distinct advantages, perhaps the most significant being the greater control over both curriculum and behavior afforded by decreasing the size of the classroom and its number of students.

Mann proposed the adoption of as many of these methods as possible. In Boston, this "divide and conquer" approach fit well with the existing trend toward combining primary and grammar schools in the same building. Within a few years, Boston's educators developed a new type of school focusing on the small graded single-teacher classroom in partial emulation of the Prussian model. The Josiah Quincy Grammar School (Gridley J. F. Bryant, architect, 1847–1848) was the first of its kind. The four-story brick-walled building's simple floor plan and negligible neoclassical decor reflected contemporary Bostonian trends. The first three floors contained identical layouts: a central hallway extending between the front and back staircases split the floor into two halves, each further subdivided into two classrooms. Classrooms were approximately 31 feet long and 26 feet wide and held 50 to 60 students. This was a noteworthy deviation from normal practice—commonly such rooms were much larger and could seat hundreds of pupils. The grammar schools' traditional bifurcation of reading and writing functions continued at the Quincy School but occurred in smaller spaces on three levels rather than in two massive schoolrooms. The top floor held a single large assembly room that could fit all of the school's students if necessary. An attic space for physical exercise and a basement containing furnaces completed the building.

This concept of smaller, graded classrooms was inspired by the Prussian model, but that was not the only stimulus. Decades of success in the city's primary schools with smaller classrooms and class sizes and female teachers also factored into the graded-school experiment. Additionally, Boston's educators were familiar with the inefficiency of massive grammar-school classrooms and the auditory and visual distractions of up to 200 students performing a variety of different activities in an echoing barnlike space—not to mention the temperature-control and ventilation problems associated with such rooms. To address those challenges, a group of ushers suggested installing partitions, following the lead of educators in other cities who had begun to attach reduced-size recitation rooms to main schoolrooms for similar reasons. And perhaps even more important than these influences was the desire for an authoritative male presence in the schoolhouse. In part, the Quincy School plan was an outgrowth of Boston's confusing public-school organization. At the time, the city supported two coexisting but independent school systems: one controlled the primary schools; the other operated the grammar schools. Although continuing demand for qualified teachers had given women more opportunities for employment in one of the few professions available to them, the stereotype of women as natural nurturers had resulted in their restriction to the primary grades. They were not authorized to teach older children. In an age when the schoolmaster was not only a teacher but also an enforcer of moral discipline and social order, only men were considered appropriate for these roles when it came to the higher grades. Thus, the employees of these two levels differed: primary schools were usually staffed by female teachers supervised by a male master, while grammar-school masters and ushers were all males.

Boston's educators were split between those who believed in this "double-headed" system of independent reading and writing grammar schools in the same building (each with its own male master) and those who advocated consolidating them under a single master for efficiency's sake. Both groups, however, stressed the absolute need for the male overseer in the school building. The Quincy plan offered a solution—reading and writing education in smaller classes in smaller rooms with female teachers and a large assembly room capable of holding the entire student body under the supervision of the master. Students were graded by age and ability. Under this "single-headed" scheme, a male master was in charge of the school, with the female teachers as his assistants. This Quincy arrangement guaranteed the male presence that was deemed essential to proper moral development while shifting most of the grammar-school teaching load—uniquely for the time—to women.

A crucial feature of the Quincy School project was a physical space: the assembly hall. This element of the Quincy School did not derive from Prussian practices but rather from American tradition. Many school buildings of this era contained a large, open room on the top floor for the male master to conduct formal recitations, to gather the entire student body for important events, or for students' families to attend school ceremonies or public exercises. Often, this top floor was identical to those below it except the walls were removed or never installed. Architects placed these rooms on the highest floor, beneath the roof, for structural reasons—the open span created by eliminating interior walls meant there was very little support for anything to be placed above the assembly room. Perhaps more essential, however, was the assembly hall's role in students' moral development. While it may seem counterintuitive to us to view a larger room as easier to control, to antebellum educators the assembly hall allowed one male master to oversee the entire student body. This direct contact with a male authority figure was deemed necessary for maintaining order in the school. Double-headed system advocates worried that such authority would be impossible to exercise in a building subdivided into small classrooms on multiple floors with female instructors. The Quincy School's assembly hall was therefore an integral feature in the origin of the graded-school scheme: it continued its traditional function of accommodating large groups while also providing a space for the male master's authority to be visibly asserted. In this way, the Quincy School building's design guaranteed that propriety would be upheld in Boston's schools through the presence of a male supervisor.

Pedagogy, Mental Discipline, and Moral Education

The graded school's core conception, that there were appropriate levels of education for each child, proved immensely popular, and graded levels eventually would become a foundation of American education. By the time of the Civil War, grade levels were almost universally adopted in those places where there were enough students to form them. Graded schools eventually inspired the demise of the grammar school/primary school dichotomy so that cities like Boston would merge the two into one elementary school. The next step in forming the nascent public-school structure was the invention of public high schools. Their supporters argued that while everyone should receive elementary schooling, the ideal educational system should be constructed as a pyramid with the uppermost level reserved for the most talented children. At the summit would be the high school—the "people's college." Consequently, high schools began to appear in the 1820s in the young nation's larger cities. By the end of the 19th century, the grammar and high schools had been supplemented by public kindergartens, completing an educational scaffolding that has remained unchanged to this day.

A major aspect of this public-education system, however, has been radically transformed since the colonial and early national periods: the classroom techniques used to teach students. At every level of education back then, educators' most important goals for their students were to teach them to think and to develop their moral character, and the means used to achieve these goals were very different from today's **active learning** and casual multimedia practices. Training children to think accurately was accomplished through **passive learning** techniques and so-called **mental discipline**. Advocates claimed mental discipline provided the properly instructed mind with the ability to easily adapt itself to any future endeavor. Two prevalent theories concerning the nature and development of knowledge formed the basis for this outlook. The first was the **faculty theory of psychology**, which held that a number of distinct faculties (reason, memory, emotion, etc.) made up the human mind, and each of these faculties could be strengthened—like a muscle—through exercise. A second influence came from science, whose leading figures explained the accumulation of knowledge as a passive process in which sensory information from the external world impressed upon a receptive mind. These two beliefs combined to have a profound effect on the educational process. Subject matter was less valuable than the techniques used to learn it. The mental-discipline approach developed one's reasoning ability instead of specific skills or a body of knowledge.

Memory was the bedrock of the 18th- and 19th-century education. The traditional methods of instruction associated with the mental-discipline approach remained virtually unchanged for centuries despite the best efforts of educational reformers. In schools across the country, students sat in orderly rows of desks bolted to the floor and facing the teacher. They raised their hands to answer questions and stood when speaking. Historian David Macleod summarized primary-school instructional practices: "By the late nineteenth century, teachers had settled into a routine of marching students through textbooks. Some teachers . . . merely prescribed assignments and checked their completion, commonly by catechizing students. Others . . . organized exercises, unison recitations, and competitions.

A standard 19th-century classroom, Iowa. Schoolrooms featured orderly rows of desks facing the teacher. The desks were arranged so that natural light entered the room from the students, left side, to facilitate right-handed writing. (Carol M. Highsmith Archive, Library of Congress)

A third group . . . actually 'clarified and elaborated' materials for students. Yet all three teaching styles settled for rote reproduction of skills or knowledge" (Macleod 1998, 79). These same techniques would have been used for all grade levels with no adjustment for the students' age or abilities. Students in a grade cohort studied the same texts at the same speed; one either learned or was left behind. In this strict environment, the main vehicle of instruction, as it had been for centuries, was the recitation. Recitation was designed to develop the so-called mind muscle through memorization. Students memorized long poems, multiplication tables, historic events, and geographical locations from textbooks and then recited them to the teacher. Even science education depended on textbooks and recitations rather than laboratory work.

Teachers controlled the recitation process with a steady stream of questions. A study of New York City teachers found, for example, that they asked an average of 2 to 3 questions each minute. In a 45-minute period, teachers could ask from 25 to 200 questions. The author determined that teachers were "drillmasters instead of educators" (Cuban 1993, 36).

Educational critic Dr. Joseph M. Rice reached a similar conclusion. Rice visited elementary schools in 36 cities in the late 19th century to directly observe American education. His investigation provided the first comprehensive evaluation of American teaching. Overall, Rice found both good and bad teaching in the nation's schools, but his judgments tended to be caustic and critical, and his final evaluation was that there was much "ludicrous teaching" in these schools due to "unscientific management." In too many "mechanical" schools, Rice discerned, "the aim of instruction is limited mainly to drilling facts into the minds of the children, and to hearing them recite lessons that they have learned by heart from text-books" (Rice 1893, 9, 20). While Rice examined only elementary schools, we can assume his findings were applicable to **secondary education** as well.

The ubiquitous formal recitation classroom was shaped by broader social and cultural beliefs. A widely held assumption was that public education should include moral training. Good character served a vital twofold purpose: individual morality was the main vehicle for preserving freedom and democracy, and it would anchor American society as it faced the unsettling tides of modernization, industrialization, and immigration. The public-education system created in the 19th century emphasized moral character in the form of discipline and order from the lowest grades up through high school.

The main source for character education was the Christian religion. The dominant Protestant ideology led educators to see nothing incompatible about pairing Christianity and public schools. For example, the National Teachers Association passed a resolution in 1869 declaring that the Bible should be studied by all schoolchildren. In public schools across the country, students began their day with Bible readings, hymns, and prayers. Christianity was enlisted to teach morality in less overt ways as well. Students advanced through an educational world that continually emphasized such Protestant values as industriousness, piety, thrift, self-reliance, and righteousness at every stage. *McGuffey Readers*, the most popular grammar-school books, reinforced these values in countless stories. Students also encountered desirable character traits in science and mathematics textbooks. Almost every subject presented teachers with the opportunity to impart such qualities as honesty, good work habits, obedience to parents and adults, and Christian piety.

Moral development was not limited to the curriculum. Some educators like Rhode Island commissioner of public schools Henry Barnard (1811–1900), who later served as the first U.S. commissioner of education, believed the school building itself could teach valuable lessons about order, organization, and beauty. "Every school-house should be a temple," wrote Barnard, "consecrated in prayer to the physical, intellectual, and moral culture of every child in the community" (Barnard 1848, 55). This was actually a common conviction in the antebellum period: many saw the value of architecture as a material means of reinforcing Protestant-Republican virtues.

Lighting

The schoolroom environment where such beliefs were instilled tended to be somewhat unsophisticated. To the untrained observer, these schoolrooms appear to have been designed only to accommodate recitations and lectures and give the teacher a view of the students. But there was a hidden layer of complexity to some of these schoolrooms, having to do with the proper amount of light and fresh air deemed necessary to keep students healthy. Lighting and ventilation were *the* salient considerations in schoolroom design in the 19th century.

Before artificial lighting became common in urban schoolhouses, architects literally reshaped and reoriented school buildings in an effort to control the amount and direction of natural light entering the classroom. Light was considered essential for maintaining students' eyesight; it was also prized for its alleged germicidal qualities. Efforts to control proper light distribution were founded on decades' worth of "evidence" that poor lighting had damaged students' eyesight. In the 1910s, writers quoted scientific studies that revealed American students' poor vision. A test of 1,000 Rhode Island schoolchildren, for example, found one-third had "defective vision" in one or both eyes; a similar study of nearly 5,000 Chicago students uncovered 35 percent with problems (Baker 1910, 5; Dresslar 1913, 228). Studies like these inspired a rapid evolution of lighting standards. These specifications affected school architecture by changing the typical classroom's size and shape and the school building's overall layout.

The earliest commentators on school architecture addressed the issue of adequate lighting in general terms. Henry Barnard's influential treatise *School Architecture* (1848), the first American book on school design, recommended abundant natural light that should enter the room from only one or two directions and be free of glare or reflection. Allowing light from only two sides of the classroom, through windows located three to four feet from the floor and not behind the teacher or facing the students, would accomplish this goal. Contemporary practice dictated that pupils were neither to face windows nor be attacked by "cross-lights" (light from windows on two sides of a room at right angles to each other). According to educator James Johonnot (1823–1888), these guidelines were not just commonsense observations—they were supported by science. He claimed, "In Germany, late scientific investigation has proved that a large proportion of the pupils of the intermediate and advanced schools have defective sight. In this country the same fact has been noticed" (Johonnot 1871, 34). This passage demonstrates two salient points: the case for proper lighting as a remedy for students' poor eyesight and the use of Germany (Prussia) as a model for American school architecture. Both of these practices began in earnest before the 1880s.

Educators and architects believed that the way light entered classrooms and corridors played a role in protecting students' eyesight. By the 1890s, the idea that pupils should receive light from a single source behind their left shoulder had been established as a rule (because all students were forced to write with their right hand). Writers in the leading chronicle of school architecture during this period, the *American School Board Journal*, cited this rule in countless articles and editorials emphasizing classroom lighting. This desire for unilateral lighting altered schoolhouse design, as schoolrooms were rotated in various directions in an effort to comply with the standard. The mandate that students should only receive light over their left shoulder remained virtually unchallenged until the widespread introduction of artificial illumination in the 1930s.

Such increased attention to light's effects on student eyesight also modified the individual schoolroom. Its proper dimensions were calculated in part by the amount and source of available light. At the turn of the 20th century, architects prescribed room dimensions with scientific accuracy. Edmund Wheelwright (1854–1912) was the first famous school architect in America, and in later years, he was universally recognized as a pioneer in the field. His solution to the lighting problem was highly regarded and very influential. The main drawback to proper schoolroom lighting, he thought, was the size of the room. Wheelwright argued that school boards needed to reduce class sizes to between 40 and 48 students; then classroom dimensions could be reduced to 24 by 32 feet for primary schools and 28 by 32 feet for grammar schools. This would allow light to properly penetrate all parts of the room from a bank of windows along the left-hand/exterior wall. Ideally, such windows would begin at a height three feet above the floor and extend to within six feet of the ceiling (Wheelwright 1897, 245). Wheelwright's lighting advice represented the culmination of 19th-century expertise. That body of knowledge also included formulas for the classroom's proper ratio of window-to-floor area. The commonly accepted rule by the turn of the 20th century called for a window area equal to one-fourth the amount of floor space, although this was often adjusted for school buildings in different regions of the country. This benchmark changed only slightly in the ensuing years; in the 1920s, for example, authorities suggested that a glazed area of 20 to 25 percent was acceptable.

By the end of World War I, rather than empirically derived formulas for the ratio of window-to-wall or window-to-floor space, scientists calculated precise light levels for the classroom. The new assessment of light intensity was the foot-candle, which measures the illumination of one candle at a distance of one foot. The first true specifications for school designers came from the Illuminating Engineering Society of North America, whose 1918 *Code of Lighting School Buildings* recommended schoolrooms include artificial lighting of at least 3.0 foot-candles, with 3.5 to 6.0 foot-candles considered ideal. Within a few years, the *Code* would be revised to advocate 5.0 foot-candles, and over time, that mark would be increased incrementally so that an architect designing a classroom in the early 1960s would be encouraged to provide 70.0 foot-candles of illumination for students. During the intervening period, artificial lighting became more popular, with the result that between daylight and artificial light, the schoolroom's illumination was no longer an architectural problem and had little ensuing impact on the room's shape or size.

With lighting issues largely solved by World War II, experts began to pay attention to glare from surfaces in the classroom and the world outside. The 1970s windowless-classroom movement, described below, arose in part as a means to control exterior glare. Proper planning could eliminate excessive glare and strong contrasts, both of which were considered damaging to students' eyesight. But glare was not a new dilemma. In the previous century, reformers believed the dark, cramped schoolhouse had evolved into an equally dangerous place where "the eye is dazzled, irritated, and often permanently injured by working on objects that are directly illuminated by the sun" (Burrage and Bailey 1899, 54). Architects, educators, and hygiene experts expounded on the proper color for blackboards (gray or green), classroom walls (buff, cream, or light green), ceilings (light but not white), dados (dull but harmonizing with the rest of the room), and window shades (light or cream), as well as acceptable materials for walls and floors. Above all else, white was to be avoided in the classroom: it was the most dangerous hue, liable to overstimulate sensitive children and damage students' eyesight. Some commentators even blamed teachers for the alleged epidemic of bad eyesight, decrying their ignorant manipulation of window shades and their failure to rectify the bad posture of young readers.

Heating and Ventilation

Educators' and architects' interest in adequate ventilation went hand in hand with proper lighting issues, and the two combined to significantly affect schoolroom design. Classrooms were created with not only natural lighting in mind but also an eye toward proper ventilation and heating. The room's form, height, and window size had consequences for the manner in which air could be circulated and the temperature controlled.

Heating and ventilation issues actually predated lighting concerns. Even the earliest urban-school buildings were simply too large to allow proper ventilation from open windows. Ventilation and heating thus became important considerations when designing schoolhouses; in fact, journal articles on school buildings from the late 19th century spent more time discussing heating and ventilating systems than any other aspect. But awareness of ventilation issues began much earlier. As far back as the 1830s, when public schooling was still in its nascent stages, Horace Mann complained about improper ventilation in urban schools (Mann 1838). By 1846, the quality of classroom air in Boston schools was so bad that the city's educators appointed a special Committee on Ventilation to investigate. The results were appalling. Dr. Henry Clark, a Boston physician, found that grammar-school classrooms received only 5 percent of the amount of fresh air necessary for a school day. The air the students did breathe was a "foetid poison" that hindered their health and ability to learn. Unfortunately, the study had little immediate impact on the design of the city's schoolhouses. Four decades later, the Massachusetts Board of Health found almost 90 percent of Boston schools to have inadequate ventilation. Another survey in 1895 again found serious defects in most ventilation systems. Unfortunately, Boston was not unique in this regard. Health investigators found extremely high levels of carbonic acid in the air in New York City classrooms during an 1873 examination; an 1888 article in the *Journal of the American Medical Association* described the American classroom as "a propaganda of contagion"; and in 1893, engineer John S. Billings complained, "Of all classes of municipal buildings in the United States, public or private, there are probably none which have until recently, been in such an unsatisfactory condition, as regards their ventilation, as the public schools" (Schultz 1994; Duffy 1979; Endemann 1873; Larrabee 1888; Billings 1893, 410).

The midcentury Boston schoolrooms investigated by the Committee on Ventilation were representative of urban rooms around the country—square or rectangular rooms, generally with no ventilation other than open windows, and overcrowded with students. Before the 1870s, there was little in the way of technical guidance for architects designing school buildings. Henry Barnard's treatise, for example, provided no advice about heating and ventilating the urban school; his discussion was limited to fireplaces and stoves, suitable for the problems of a single room but not an entire building. Pattern books—a popular format for the transmission of architectural ideas—favored homes and churches. In the rare event that a pattern book included the designs for one or two schools, only a facade drawing and floor plan would be presented.

Increasing concerns about student health led educators and architects to think about improving temperature and air quality. In particular, they tried to optimize the amount of cubic feet of airspace needed for each student, the amount of cubic feet of fresh air per minute per student, and the air temperature. A desire to avoid the debilitating effects of vitiated air in the classroom prompted the first two considerations. Architect Charles Dwyer had addressed this in an 1856 book, in which he exclaimed, "Want of pure air is the certain agent of destruction to our youth; and of all places its terrible effects are more potent and more certain in the school-room than in any other, because of the mass of exhalation from so many lungs, some already diseased and pouring forth their noxious vapors to be inhaled by the victims around" (Dwyer 1856, 57).

Ventilation standards seemed to be set fairly early, although they exhibited discrepancies among authorities. James Johonnot addressed the first major issue—the amount of airspace necessary for each pupil—as early as 1871, recommending 250 cubic feet of airspace for each pupil. He did not, however, relate how this would be worked out in designing the room or the ventilation system. Johonnot's advice was either amazingly prescient or represented an already-established norm—during the next 50 years, architects hardly deviated from his recommendations, with almost all authorities prescribing 200 to 300 cubic feet of airspace per pupil as a minimum.

The schoolroom's air-space-per-student requirement was linked to the second major issue in heating and ventilation: the amount of air provided to each student per minute. The *District of Columbia Schoolhouse Commission Report* of 1883 provided precise guidelines characteristic of the period. The report suggested ventilation equipment should be installed in district schools that could afford each student in a classroom 30 cubic feet of fresh air per minute (Stuart, Taylor, and Morrow 1908, 18). Like the norms for cubic feet of airspace, the cubic-feet-per-minute regulations varied; between the 1880s and 1920s, experts and amateurs recommended anywhere between 20 and 40 cubic feet of air per minute per pupil, with 30 being the most popular figure.

The third vexing issue in heating and ventilation was air temperature. Temperature regulation was linked to bad experiences in poorly heated and ventilated buildings. In the old one-room school, children seated near the stove were subject to extreme heat, while those in the room's remote corners were unlikely to receive any warmth at all. A similar problem occurred in rooms that relied on direct-radiation systems, which placed radiators near open windows in an attempt to heat the cooler outdoor air and make it rise through and out of the room. Students sitting by windows could either be overly warmed by the radiators or chilled by the incoming air. A 70-degree schoolroom was universally accepted by 1900, but the previous generation proved itself of heartier stock. In an 1877 article on schoolhouse ventilation and warming, for example, the author declared that 70 degrees was "uncomfortable," with the suggested ideal temperature range between 64 and 68 degrees. Even this rather chilly ideal was often hard to accomplish with inefficient heating equipment. Classrooms in New York City were measured between 47 and 70 degrees in an 1873 study (Winsor 1877; Endemann 1873).

School architects searched for ways to address the three considerations of airspace per pupil, fresh air per minute, and temperature. In general, two kinds of heating systems existed: direct and indirect. Direct radiation was the oldest form of heating the schoolroom. It consisted of a stove or a set of radiators in the room. The stove held a fire that radiated heat out into the room, and radiators accomplished the same result using hot water or steam. Direct heating was notoriously inadequate, and its failures led to the widespread installation of indirect systems in urban schools by the 1870s. Indirect systems blew air into the schoolroom that had been heated somewhere else, usually in the basement. Ventilation played a different role in these two heating systems. Direct radiation buildings tended to have little or no ventilation, prompting teachers to open windows for fresh air. Indirect heating included air-circulation mechanisms to provide fresh air as well as heating it.

Most school buildings prior to the 1890s contained heating and ventilating machinery that used heated flues to induce air flow and control temperature. The most common method was a basement furnace. Hot air, hot water, or steam from the furnace heated the ducts that traveled to individual rooms. Air circulated through the building because the air outside the building was colder and heavier than the air inside, and the temperature differential caused outside air to be drawn into the building and up into the vents. Hot-air systems, which forced heated air directly from the furnace to the classroom, were difficult to regulate and produced additional problems. They were at their best in cold weather, but rooms often were stiflingly hot or icily cold. The accumulation of discharged air from 50-odd bodies in a classroom was difficult to expel through temperature regulation. Windy days adversely affected the atmosphere inside the building by pushing cold outside air through the schoolhouse's many cracks and openings. And gasses and dust from the fuel (usually coal) used to heat the air managed to find its way through the flues and into the classrooms. As a result of these difficulties, some school architects and engineers began to experiment with circulating air through the school building by mechanical means. By the end of the 19th century, mechanical ventilation (using fans to circulate the air rather than temperature differentials) had become the method of choice. These "plenum systems" were an improvement over the complicated gravity systems of the prior generation. Plenum units used mechanical power (steam and then electricity) to drive large basement fans that circulated heated air through the building. A less-popular relative was the exhaust system, which placed the fans in the attic and pulled rather than pushed air through the ventilation circuit.

Plenums became popular in the 20th century. Electricity eventually allowed such systems to be centrally controlled. The advantage (or disadvantage, depending on one's position) was that the operation did not require the teacher to control room temperature. Unfortunately, the advanced systems often worked as poorly as their precursors. Despite improved ventilation technology, the schoolroom situation was not always ideal even in the 1920s. A study of New York City schools found that only 2 percent of the city's classrooms had functioning ventilation equipment (School Survey Committee 1924). These conditions often led to conflicts between teachers and administration when the teachers attempted to make their classrooms more comfortable. As in the case with classroom lighting, administrators habitually blamed teachers for causing ventilation troubles by unnecessarily opening windows.

Although the adjustments in heating and ventilation did not affect the schoolroom as visibly as the changes in lighting, there were nonetheless repercussions for the entire modern school building. New schools were intricate machines with huge mechanical instruments and many miles of hidden ducts, flues, and pipes. The complexities of the improved air-delivery systems forced school architects to gain useful knowledge about the mechanics of heating and ventilation or to associate themselves with experts in the field. Some cities employed full-time engineers to design and implement ventilation systems. The fact that all this attention was paid to the heating and ventilation of school buildings demonstrates a change in society's priorities. Children were becoming more valued as future societal resources whose health was worth protecting.

The industry standard of cubic feet per minute of fresh air remained at 30 until the adoption of air-conditioning began to make the classroom's interior atmosphere easier to control and the need for natural ventilation obsolete. Advanced scientific knowledge also led to revisions in the professional codes. By the early 1980s, experts recommended a mere five cubic feet per minute as acceptable, which has since been revised slightly upward. Also telling is the virtual elimination of anxiety about the air's content since World War II. Gone were the statements condemning the "foetid poison" and "noxious vapors" of schoolroom air; a popular postwar book on elementary-school design confidently declared, "Research has proven that the chemical composition of air does not change significantly even in crowded spaces. There need be no concern about oxygen or carbon dioxide content in schools" (Engelhardt, Engelhardt Jr., and Leggett 1953, 228). While the interior atmosphere of school buildings continues to be studied and adjusted in the 21st century, it no longer determines the size or shape of the classroom.

Hygiene

The educational discourse about proper lighting and ventilation related to another important consideration in the turn-of-the-century schoolroom design. Proper lighting was deemed necessary not only for safeguarding students' eyesight but also for maintaining their general health. A budding fascination with healthy living swept through American society in the late 19th century, and this movement was particularly pertinent for the school, where large collections of students in confined areas gave rise to a myriad of illnesses. Scientific schoolroom design was a weapon to combat these maladies. For example, in the early 20th century, "hygiene experts" promoted sunlight's health-giving aspects to educators and architects. One of the best-known hygiene experts was Fletcher B. Dresslar, a professor at Peabody College in Memphis, who stated a prevailing view in 1913: "Direct sunlight is the most economical and practical of all germicides. Schoolrooms that are kept thoroughly clean and receive a thorough sunning each day are not likely to need much further attention in the matter of disinfection. Cleanliness and sunshine are worth more than any artificial germicides that can be applied to schoolrooms" (Dresslar 1913, 359).

The germ theory of illness, which held that microscopic bacteria spread through casual contact caused illnesses, had gained recognition by this time in terms of the origin of disease, but knowledge of antibacterial techniques remained elusive. Many reformers, like Dresslar, still believed that direct sunlight could kill germs. School architects agreed with the disinfecting-light theory and emphasized the need to design school buildings so that direct sunlight could penetrate corridors, closets, and toilets.

All this attention to the schoolhouse's hygienic fitness was relatively new. In the mid-19th century, there had been no hygiene experts, few reports on schoolhouse conditions, and no real understanding of how illnesses were transmitted. With the new understanding brought by the widespread acceptance of germ theory, reformers led a full-scale assault on dust, dirt, and germs in the schoolhouse. They viewed schoolrooms as cesspools teeming with threats to students' health—like dust, dirt, soot, and the unseen germs that lurked in nooks and crannies.

Beliefs such as these arose out of the so-called dust theory of disease, which coupled germ theory to an escalating American obsession with cleanliness. The dust theory held that everyday dust was an insidious carrier of deadly bacteria. This belief arose in part from an earlier conception of disease transmission based on "fomites," a term applied to any object capable of carrying infectious material. The Massachusetts State Board of Health advanced the fomite theory in a publication on scarlet fever that warned about infectious transmission by "air, food, clothing, sheets, blankets, whiskers, hair, furniture, toys, library-books, wallpaper, curtains, cats, [and] dogs" (Massachusetts State Board of Health 1888, 61). The solution to the fomite problem was a clean schoolhouse, which could be achieved by eternal vigilance from the janitorial staff. Even in the 1910s, when germ theory was broadly acknowledged, Fletcher Dresslar and other experts blamed dust and dirt for causing illnesses.

Larger urban-school systems often created special hygiene departments to combat the health menace. The antigerm campaign could become obsessive, however, as seen in the rules promulgated by the Indiana State Board of Health that required all pencils, pens, desks, floors, windows, and woodwork be scrubbed and disinfected every day; refused entry to any student "with a dirty face or unclean clothing"; forbid open water buckets; and outlawed slate and slate pencils because they were "believed to be microbe hot-beds" ("Public School Hygiene" 1896, 8). It is doubtful that these rules were followed with any strict regularity, but their mere existence (along with similar laws in other states) demonstrates the seriousness with which school hygiene was taken. In addition to central vacuuming, the new hygienic mind-set inspired other adjustments, like bubbling-water drinking fountains, which replaced the water bucket and community cup; individual lockers in hallways, rather than wardrobes attached to classrooms; the increased use of marble and tile for toilet rooms; and, in some larger cities, baths. These modifications and many others were designed to reduce or eliminate the spread of tuberculosis, typhoid, diphtheria, and other prevalent illnesses. Sanitary improvements not only necessitated changes in the schoolroom; they also required a new way of thinking about the school building, and their inclusion in schools from this time period records a shift in American attitudes toward health in general and children's health in particular.

20TH-CENTURY REFORMS

Child Saving

These changing attitudes can be viewed in Americans' evolving conception of childhood. In the colonial era, adults tended to view childhood as an inconvenience—something to get through as quickly as possible on the road to maturity. Children often were dressed and treated like miniature adults and expected to participate in adult activities to supplement family incomes. Large numbers of children worked at part-time or full-time jobs, whether on farms, in shops, or in the increasingly common manufacturing plants. Financially stable families also encouraged (or required) their children to work, simply because many adults considered education a waste of time. In the early 19th century, however, a new attitude toward children began to develop. Manufacturers produced more child-specific goods—like infant clothes, toys, and small furniture—targeting middle- and upper-class parents, as adults took a greater interest in children's play and a more sentimental opinion of childhood formed. By the century's end, the public began to consider childhood a special stage of life, to be protected if possible to allow for proper moral and cognitive development. This emerging model has been described as "sheltered childhood."

Unfortunately, for many families, the sheltered childhood was an unrealistic middle-class dream. The harsh reality was that countless Americans were introduced to working life at a very young age. The U.S. Census Bureau reported 765,000 children ages 10 to 15 were "gainfully employed" in 1870 (13 percent of the population for that age group); 1,750,000 in 1900 (18 percent); 1,990,000 in 1910; and 1,061,000 in 1920, although these estimates are low. An Illinois Bureau of Labor Statistics investigation found over 5,000 children working 10- to 15-hour days in Chicago in 1880. A subsequent study two years later calculated that 5 percent of all Chicago children ages 8 to 15 had *never* attended school (Macleod 1998; Herrick 1971).

Such statistics appalled progressive reformers, whose beliefs were molded by the ideal of a sheltered childhood where children were unsophisticated and largely helpless beings who needed to be nurtured by adults in a sympathetic environment. Child labor was the antithesis of this ideal. Activists viewed the long hours and sometimes brutal conditions under which children often toiled as a source of mental and moral degeneration, which in turn resulted in higher levels of juvenile delinquency and antisocial behavior. Consequently, the reformers directed a sustained attack on child labor to get more children out of the workplace and into school. Focusing on crowded urban environments, the child-labor movement was another link in a lengthening chain of 19th century "child saving" initiatives promoted by social-reform groups.

Educators were keenly aware of child labor's dangers. As early as 1865, Chicago superintendent Josiah L. Pickard lamented that "many a child has been sacrificed mentally and morally as well as physically to the pecuniary interest of the parent" (Herrick 1971, 52). But the "evil" of child labor was not easily combated due to the combined effects of parental necessity or neglect and opposition from American business. Some parents saw no need to educate their children or simply could not afford to lose the child's income, while businesses objected to efforts to constrain their pool of inexpensive workers. The most common reform approach to dealing with these obstacles was to regulate, rather than eliminate, child labor. Beginning in the late 19th century, lawmakers restricted the hours children could work and the age when they could begin working. Advocates established the National Child Labor Committee in 1904 as a nonprofit organization dedicated to regulating child labor, and its efforts encouraged the proposal of a Child Labor Amendment to the U.S. Constitution. The amendment's sponsors sought to regulate the labor of children under 18. Most states ratified the amendment over the next 15 years, but with the passage of the Fair Labor Standards Act of 1938, interest in the amendment waned. The act helped the cause immensely and has led to a significant reduction in the number of children laboring in this country, but it excluded agriculture from its purview, with the result that even today hundreds of thousands of children are engaged in farm work.

Child-labor legislation often went hand in hand with compulsory attendance laws requiring children to spend a certain portion of each year in school. By 1918, every state had mandated school attendance to some degree. These laws generally obligated children between the ages of 5 and 14 to spend most of their days in school. Massachusetts had instituted the nation's first compulsory attendance law in 1852, but by 1886, only 15 states (or 39 percent of the country) had enacted similar laws (Tyack, James, and Benavot 1987). As the years passed, however, public support for compulsory attendance grew.

Although every state eventually passed some form of compulsory education legislation, these laws tended to be less successful for high-school-age youths, since most provisions either stopped at 14 or leniently granted excuses or work permits for those over that age. Yet there was an incredible rise in the number of high school students. Nationwide high-school enrollment increased from 202,963 in 1890 to 1,851,965 in 1920, representing an increase of over 900 percent in three decades, while the general population rose by 245 percent. Only 3.7 percent of the nation's 14- to 17-year-olds attended high school in 1880 compared to 31.2 percent in 1920. (By 1930, the number was 50.7 percent; in 1940, it reached 72.6 percent.) During that same period, the number of public high schools in America swelled from 2,526 to 14,326 (Tyack 1974; Angus and Mirel 1999; Schlereth 1991).

Compulsory attendance and child-labor laws cannot wholly explain the enrollment explosion, although those forms of legislation did act to rescue thousands of adolescents from the working world. Immigration was another major contributor. Over 23 million immigrants arrived in the United States between 1880 and 1920, many flooding the northern industrial cities. In Chicago, for example, some 30 to 40 percent of the population was comprised of foreign-born whites during that period; in 1880, that figure had been only 12 percent (Willrich 2003). In 1908, the U.S. Senate Immigration Committee studied nearly 40 cities across the country and found that 58 percent of all public-school students in those cities had fathers who were born abroad. These numbers are particularly compelling when considered in light of the decreasing population of native-born Americans during the same period.

In addition to compulsory-attendance laws, child-labor initiatives, and foreign immigration, rural-to-urban migration patterns also brought students into the nation's schoolrooms. America officially became an urban nation in this era. The percentage of the national population living in urban locations (defined as those with over 2,500 people) swelled from 35 percent in 1890 to 51 percent by 1920 (Tyack 1974, 2). The Great Migration of blacks from the rural South to the industrial North affected such statistics. Significantly, however, this exodus mainly influenced the lower grades in larger cities and had little impact on high-school enrollment. Across the country, black children accounted for less than 2 percent of all high school students by 1920, and their numbers in elementary schools were substantially lower than white students. Only in the 1950s did the percentages of black and other minority children ages 5 to 19 in public schools reach 50 percent, and only in the 1970s did these numbers approximate the percentages for white children (National Center for Education Statistics 1993).

Discipline and Order

The result of this massive enrollment surge was that many children who had no academic inclinations and would not have attended school in previous generations were there at the turn of the 20th century. Public-school administrators, particularly at the high-school level, faced the daunting task of determining how and what to teach these students. Their response was to exert more control over students' lives than ever before. As architects transformed the schoolhouse from a simple collection of boxlike rooms to a large, varied complex—a story that will be told in the next chapter—the building also became an instrument of control. Rising enrollments created unprecedented organizational and disciplinary problems. The modern school building was a partial solution, channeling students into architectural spaces where their behavior could be easily observed and directed.

Planning the school's physical environment with an eye toward regulatory measures was not a novel idea, having been an integral part of 19th-century monitorial schools. In monitorial schools, where children were given military-like orders and moved through their lessons in rigid sequences, the schoolroom's spatial orderliness complemented the personal regulation sought by society as a whole. The spirit, but not the method, of monitorial schools was imported into the nascent public-school system. School authorities tried to impose order on boisterous youngsters through a mixture of administrative and architectural means.

In the mid-19th century, educators had been aware of the connection between architecture and behavior. As schools grew beyond the one-room stage, there was an increasing need for physical environments to facilitate student control and impart order. St. Louis superintendent (and future U.S. commissioner of education) William Torrey Harris expressed the mind-set of many educators in 1871: "The first requisite of the school is *Order*: each pupil must be taught first and foremost to conform his behavior to the general standard" (Tyack 1974, 43). Educators considered discipline and self-control to be the foundations of both learning and participation in republican society, and schools, therefore, stressed deference to authority—and sanctioned corporal punishment. An example can be found in Dr. Joseph M. Rice's account of a St. Louis elementary-school classroom. "During several daily recitation periods, each of which is from twenty to twenty-five minutes in duration, the children are obliged to stand on the line, perfectly motionless, their bodies erect, their knees touching and feet together, the tips of their shoes touching the edge of a board in the floor," he wrote. "The slightest movement on the part of a child attracts the attention of the teacher . . . I heard one teacher ask a little boy: 'How can you learn anything with your knees and toes out of order?' The toes appear to play a more important part than the reasoning faculties" (Rice 1893, 98). The imposition of order was more prevalent in schoolroom behavior, as Dr. Rice found during his tour of American schools, than in architectural design.

Educators' interest in using the school building as an instrument of control intensified by the late 19th century. School officials found it easier to manage student behavior once architects began designing schools with broad, well-lighted hallways lined with lockers. When student lockers were added to hallways, replacing the closet-like wardrobes attached to schoolrooms in previous generations, the range of student behavior that took place under the authoritarian gaze expanded. Also, corridors were an essential tool in disciplinary design; they were best when long, straight, and brightly lit, providing teachers with excellent vantage points from which to thwart would-be troublemakers. Corridors coupled with transom windows in schoolroom doors allowed administrators to observe classes from the hall without being in the room. And the average classroom's physical arrangement, unmodified since the mid-19th century, likewise encouraged and imparted order.

Educational Reforms

Administrative and curricular changes in public education, prompted by secondary education's evolution, had a substantial impact on the schoolhouse's architectural transformation. Between 1880 and 1920, the framework of public education in major cities was largely restructured, and a fundamental shift occurred in the structure and operation of education. Citizens voted to reform school boards across the country in an effort to rid the educational system of political corruption. A centralized and bureaucratic organization, based on corporate models of efficiency, arose with new supervisory positions and stricter control over day-to-day operations. And, more important for architectural purposes, educators considerably altered students' studies. Expanded curricula and the addition of **manual training** and **vocational education** programs comprised the most visible changes.

These modifications affected the way architects approached school buildings. The evolving educational agenda forced school designers to find ways to accommodate unprecedented spaces in junior and senior high schools, like wood, metal, and print shops, model kitchens, sewing rooms, swimming pools, gymnasiums, and auditoriums. Architects also were confronted with a basic need to enlarge the schoolhouse simply because there were more students.

"Efficiency" was a particularly popular idea among early-20th-century educators. Efficiency pervaded every aspect of the educational world, from curriculum to organization, testing, and several other areas. In its many guises, efficiency—and its practical application through scientific management—influenced educational reform for decades. A very visible outcome of this obsession was the wholesale restructuring of urban education. Educational systems across the country were "centralized" by reformers who succeeded in altering the size and composition of school boards and changing the administration's organizational structure. The roles of superintendents, principals, and teachers were sharply defined for the first time, and all were encouraged to become experts in their field.

Reorganizing the nation's urban-school organizations along the lines of the "corporate-bureaucratic model" in the late 19th century was one of the most significant reforms in American education. Pivotal to this movement was a new idea of administrative control. The reformist model envisioned a small, centralized school board, a superintendent to oversee daily operations, and a professional staff to execute policies. It was intended to replace the ward-based boards of education found in most 19th-century cities. School boards in America's cities tended to be large, cumbersome bodies comprised of politicians and their cronies elected from local wards or districts. Under the traditional ward model, each political division in a city provided a member to the board of education—frequently a local politician drawn from among the class of small-business owners and professionals. These men were accustomed to wielding their power in the community. Once ensconced on the board, favoritism and influence peddling became standard operating procedures. School-board members rewarded friends and party members with teaching positions for their daughters and made lucrative side deals with dishonest building contractors and textbook manufacturers.

The middle- and upper-class reformers who advocated for changes in those urban systems' organizational structures sought to remove school administration as much as possible from the political arena and implement successful business or corporate principles in the educational realm. These reformers viewed centralized and consolidated school boards as more efficient school boards, just as professional superintendents and business managers—education "experts"—were considered necessary for the system's smooth operation. The project's widespread appeal was due in part to American society's willingness to embrace the doctrine of efficiency as a tool for social improvement.

The impetus for administrative reorganization had its roots in the 1880s. Massachusetts educator John D. Philbrick (1818–1886) promoted the idea that there was "one best way" of educating children—a uniform organization in which curriculum, **pedagogy**, and administration were standardized across the country—and that implementing this model was crucial to the nation's growth and survival. Philbrick was not alone in his beliefs. Across the country, educators and reformers fought to lessen political influence in educational decisions and argued for school systems modeled on American businesses, with a centralized decision-making authority (akin to the corporate board of directors), rigid hierarchies of control, and the delegation of duties to skilled managers. By the 1890s, these struggles began to produce results.

Between 1893 and 1913, the average number of school board members in the nation's largest cities dropped by over 50 percent; between 1893 and 1923, they contracted by two-thirds (Tyack 1974). The composition of these boards evolved as well; instead of the small businessmen and professionals of the ward system, new board members tended to be "large-scale capitalist businessmen, industrialists, and professionals who increasingly dominated the nation's political economy" (Reese 2002, 99). Along with this centralization of authority came an attendant increase in superintendents' powers. Developments like these arose out of progressive reformers' efforts to economize by reorganizing urban-school systems along the corporate model.

At the same time that educators implemented administrative reforms to revise the structure and functioning of their school organizations, they also began to alter the high-school curriculum. The public high school before 1880 was a unique creature whose role in the American educational system, as well as society as a whole, was ill defined. Educators were unable to agree on the scope and content of secondary education, and confusion lingered over the proper demarcation between elementary schools, high schools, and higher education. Despite widespread curricular diversity, high-school courses of study were united to some degree in reflecting the institution's rather select nature. In most cities, students were required to pass rigorous entrance examinations before being accepted for secondary study. Curricula were generally limited to two paths, neither oriented toward practical applications. Classical courses emphasized Latin and Greek while standard or general courses offered German or French (or sometimes English) as alternatives. Algebra, geometry, English literature, grammar, and history requirements were common to both paths. Minimal instruction was offered in basic sciences like chemistry and geology. Vocational training was almost nonexistent. The 19th-century high-school curriculum, like its counterpart in the primary schools, aimed at developing the mind rather than preparing students for any future profession. The efficacy of this mental-discipline approach would be challenged by educators interested in providing an alternative education for the great majority of children who would not be graduating into professional positions or enrolling in college. They argued instead for training in practical skills leading to stable employment and informed citizenship. In the face of rising immigration, stricter compulsory education and child-labor laws, and migrations from rural to urban areas, new options seemed necessary.

The result was a trend toward adding courses in manual training and vocational education to high schools. But the traditionalists stood firm against this challenge. At the end of the century, a strong contingent of humanists continued to champion the time-honored academically oriented curriculum even as reformers tried to expand the course of study to include more practical subjects for those students who were not college-bound. The traditionalists could point to the noteworthy "Committee of Ten" report of 1893 as support for their position. In the previous year, the National Education Association had appointed a Committee on Secondary School Studies to investigate college entrance requirements because diverse standards frustrated high-school administrators trying to prepare their students for higher education. In its final report, the Committee of Ten, as it was popularly known, circumvented its original purpose and focused on the high-school curriculum rather than collegiate requirements. The committee recommended curricular consistency at the high-school level. The report suggested four appropriate courses of study: classical, Latin-scientific, modern languages, and English. The courses were largely differentiated by the amount of foreign-language study involved, yet all four courses could equally prepare students for college. The final report also claimed the high school's "main function" was "to prepare for the duties of life that small proportion of all the children in the country— a proportion small in number, but very important to the welfare of the nation—who show themselves able to profit by an education prolonged to the eighteenth year, and whose parents are able to support them while they remain so long at school" (Willis et al. 1993, 92). Thus, the committee made no distinctions between college-bound and non-college-bound students: everyone had to choose one of the four tracks. So those youths preparing "for the duties of life" would be educated in the same manner as prospective college students.

Although the Committee of Ten had no binding authority over any school board, its suggestions would influence educators for decades. However, its supporters were fighting a losing battle. The differentiated curriculum, offering both academic and nonacademic programs for high school students, overtook American education. School administrators loosened their narrowly focused academic curriculums to include alternative courses of study. A team of educators examining 35 high schools found a 475 percent increase in the number of course offerings between 1906 and 1930, mostly in practical, nonacademic subjects (Angus and Mirel 1999). In Chicago, for example, the board of education engaged in a continuous pattern of curricular change. When the college-preparatory course was reestablished in 1891 after a seven-year absence, Superintendent George

Howland described the board's inclusive attitude: "The prime purpose of the high school is to prepare those who can go no farther, for the business of life, and to open up to those who would go farther the several avenues of scientific and literary culture which they may hereafter desire to follow" (*Thirty-Seventh Annual Report* 1892, 39). After just five years, however, the board of education retracted its support for dual courses of study and reinstated a uniform four-year curriculum for all of the city's high schools. This single course was considerably augmented by the addition of elective classes in 1900. Seeming to follow an accordion-like pattern, the Chicago board constricted the high-school course again in 1905, eliminating most electives, and loosened it in 1910 with the introduction of nine different vocationally oriented high-school curricula: English, general, science, foreign language, business, builders, manual-training, household arts, and architectural. By 1915, there were an astonishing 22 courses of study for Chicago high school students: 11 four-year and 11 two-year programs.

The curricular changes in Chicago reflected a national trend toward **comprehensive high schools**. High schools in this period broadened their focus beyond the traditional academic training and added general or unspecified courses of study as well as specialized areas. The differentiated, or comprehensive, high school would become common by the onset of the Great Depression. This tendency had been encapsulated in an important report that, like the Committee of Ten report 25 years earlier, both reflected and guided secondary education in America. The 1918 report of the National Education Association's Commission on the Reorganization of Secondary Education (popularly known as the Cardinal Principles report) announced the triumph of "social efficiency" as the guiding force in secondary education. Where the Committee of Ten report had accorded practical training a minor role in comparison to classical education, the Cardinal Principles took preparation for adult life as the high school's essential purpose. The Cardinal Principles report succinctly stated the principal objectives of secondary education: "1. Health. 2. Command of fundamental processes. 3. Worthy home-membership. 4. Vocation. 5. Citizenship. 6. Worthy use of leisure. 7. Ethical character" (Willis et al. 1993, 158). The committee proposed that classes dedicated to these objectives would help to create a well-rounded adult citizen; with the possible exception of "Command of fundamental processes," none could be learned through a traditional classical course of study, and none of the goals sought to enhance students' intellectual development. The mental-discipline approach was losing support.

Educators inserted the Cardinal Principles into curricula across the nation. The changes brought to the forefront the high school's evolving role in American society. Once considered an elite enclave for the privileged few, high schools were now charged with a new mission—to integrate the masses into adult society. According to the new philosophy, some students were to be trained for the subordinate roles they were sure to occupy. "If democracy means to try to make all children equal or all men equal, it means to fight nature, and in that fight democracy is sure to be defeated," wrote Harvard president Charles W. Eliot in 1908. "There is no such thing among men as equality of nature, of capacity for training, or of intellectual power." Sociologist Franklin Giddings was equally frank: "High school education should make citizens not learners" (Kliebard 1999, 43; Kliebard 2002, 33). The high school's job, in the minds of many, was to prepare adolescents for life rather than exercise their minds.

This nontraditional role for education found wide acceptance and resulted in the establishment of a differentiated curriculum with a nonacademic track for students with no inclination toward further schooling. High schools (and after their establishment in the 20th century, **junior high schools**) reoriented their curricula to provide more training in the skills students would need once they entered the adult workforce. Vocational education permanently altered the goals of American public education by offering alternative education for the nation's youth.

Vocational education was an outgrowth of a manual-training movement that began in the late 1870s. Manual training was originally intended to supplement the regular academic curriculum by encouraging students to utilize their hands as well as their minds to become well-rounded persons. Proponents stressed how the honest use of tools could serve as an antidote

A student in typesetting class, 1916. Vocational courses for high school students proliferated in the early 20th century, as secondary education expanded its original academic focus. (Library of Congress)

to the corruption of work by an increasingly industrialized society. Manual-training courses also proved particularly useful for teaching immigrant children a marketable set of skills. But what the early reformers clearly did not want was a program that replaced the traditional academic courses and instead taught specific skills to future factory workers.

Business leaders quickly sensed that these programs presented an opportunity to expand their labor pool and cut costs, since masses of workers could conceivably learn job skills on their own time without the entanglements of labor unions or apprenticeship programs. So manufacturers allied themselves with school administrators. The support of American businesses and their organizations soon tilted many generalized manual-education programs toward specific vocational training.

Vocational-education programs found increasing acceptance through the 1880s. Public manual- or vocational-training schools opened in places like Baltimore (1884), Philadelphia (1885), Toledo (1885), and Cleveland (1886), while other cities added new classes to their existing secondary curriculum to form comprehensive schools. Vocational-education programs, with their need for specialized facilities, made fresh demands on school architecture. Shop rooms required equipment and power sources that were unknown in the traditional schoolhouse. Domestic-science rooms called for cooking and ventilation equipment. Art and drafting rooms needed abundant natural light. To guide architects faced with designing such new kinds of spaces, educational journals began to offer articles on these topics. In many cases, shop equipment was kept in basements or separate buildings, but as vocationalism grew more popular in the late 1890s, some cities inaugurated separate manual-training or mechanical-arts high schools, with a majority of the rooms dedicated to vocational courses.

By the early 20th century, manual-training schools were better adapted to students' and educators' needs. An essay entitled "The Industrial Arts Department" from 1921 demonstrates how extensive and complicated the design of vocational/manual-training spaces could be by that time. The author describes materials and layouts needed for grinding rooms, foundries, and machine, pattern, forge, automobile, printing, electrical, sheet-metal, cabinet, and carpentry shops, in what was only a partial listing of the trades available to students. The elaborate requirements of such rooms included power sources, proper ventilation, special (and expensive) machines and tools, storerooms, washrooms, and demonstration areas (Donovan 1921).

Vocational education received a great stimulus in 1906 when the Massachusetts Commission on Industrial and Technical Education (known as the Douglas Commission) issued its report. The Commission criticized

Massachusetts's "old-fashioned" curriculum as out of touch with the practical demands of modern society. A declining apprenticeship tradition in the late 19th century had serious repercussions for American industry, and in a series of hearings held across the commonwealth, the Douglas Commission heard numerous complaints about the lack of skilled workers. Manufacturers looked to the public-school systems to remedy this problem. The commission chided existing manual-training programs, however, for being too narrowly focused on supplementing the academic course of study rather than providing an alternative. A new system should be created, wrote the commission, that would be more in tune with "callings in life . . . professional, commercial, productive and domestic" (Kliebard 1986, 87). Appended to the Douglas Commission report was a study of 25,000 14- to 16-year-old dropouts—none of whom had ever attended high school—which found that the main reason these children quit school was lack of interest, not economic hardship. Reformers used this evidence to support their call for broader curricula that could adequately prepare students for the future.

The National Society for the Promotion of Industrial Education (NSPIE) was founded in the same year the Douglas Commission report came out. The NSPIE proved instrumental in forming alliances with organizations like the National Education Association and backing state and federal legislation promoting industrial education, including the landmark Smith-Hughes Act of 1917. The Smith-Hughes Act provided states with federal matching funds for teacher salaries in agriculture, trade and industrial education, and home economics, as well as $1 million for teacher training in vocational education. This money was specifically meant for secondary schools. Such federal mandates helped change the face of American secondary education; by 1919, all 48 states had instituted vocational-education programs pursuant to the Smith-Hughes Act.

As part of the development of vocational education, there was a concurrent rise in programs for girls centered on domestic science and commercial studies. Girls made up the bulk of America's high-school population during this period. Nationally, almost 58 percent of all high-school pupils in 1890 and 1900 were female, and 56 percent in 1910 and 1920. After 1940, the balance of boys and girls enrolled in high school remained relatively equal. However, girls have always been likelier to graduate. The proportion of female high-school graduates was 65 percent in 1890, 63 percent in 1900, and 61 percent in 1910 and 1920. In fact, the total number of high-school graduates included more girls than boys for every year between 1869 (when the records were first kept) and 1990 (National Center for Education Statistics 1993).

Despite their majority, however, girls' status in the male-centered educational community was low. As late as 1925, a psychologist's startling description of the "average girl" demonstrates the mind-set that influenced girls' education: "What then can be expected of the average girl? There are certain things we know she cannot do; she cannot fill positions requiring the exercise of much initiative or executive ability; she has little capacity for leadership; she can think very little for herself; she follows her leaders blindly . . . she is more easily taught and trained, more apt to make an adjustment to her immediate social environment . . . by virtue of her very lack of intellectual ability she accepts things as she finds them and goes with the crowd" (Graves 1998, 170). Such beliefs formed the basis for the new vocational curricula. Domestic-science and commercial courses taught girls to be efficient homemakers or competent secretaries, maids, cooks, or seamstresses. This was partly a reaction to the increasing number of women in the workplace but also attributable to the growing importance put on the woman's role in managing domestic life. In preparation for this role, girls learned sewing, laundering, cooking, typing, stenography, and bookkeeping. Some of these courses required new types of architectural space. Early-20th-century high schools began to include fully operational kitchens, model dining rooms and bedrooms, and mock offices, as well as rooms for teaching bookkeeping, typewriting, stenography, and textile arts and sewing. Several cities even opened separate girls' vocational schools to rival industrial-arts education for boys.

Public high schools occupied a much different position in 1920 than their predecessors. They were now called upon to provide adolescents—a special group who were no longer children but not yet adults—with the means to make themselves into law-abiding, hardworking American citizens. Secondary education as a whole opened up to a wider range of students, for a number of reasons. These students found themselves attending classes more often in monumental, visually striking buildings that stood out in the physical landscape and spoke to society of the high school's new role in American life.

MODERN SCHOOLROOMS

The Healthy Classroom

Although school buildings enlarged in the 20th century, and the rooms inside them began to show more variety because of the curriculum's expanded range, the basic everyday schoolroom remained essentially unchanged from the latter 19th century until dual influences from modern architecture and **progressive education** infiltrated education in the **inter-war era**. Reformers offered new models for the schoolroom that used greater sophistication in lighting techniques, a more intimate connection between indoors and outdoors, and the subdivision of the interior space by activity to shape the American classroom into something different in the decades before World War II—a healthy, light-filled, indoor/outdoor space with the spatial flexibility to permit teacher-student interactions of all kinds.

One of the leaders of the new classroom ideal was Richard Neutra (1892–1970), an Austrian-born architect who came to the United States in 1923 and became famous for his elegant minimalist houses. Neutra's salient contribution to school design emerged from his emphasis on the close rela-tionship between indoor and outdoor classroom space, as visualized in a number of his seminal projects. The first was the unbuilt Ring Plan School (1927), a project that grew out of a larger scheme for a new urban envi-ronment ("Rush City Reformed"). The Ring Plan School was a one-story, elliptical building with classrooms ringing an open-air common area that could be used for play, school gatherings, or swimming. Neutra imagined the classrooms would be connected to the immediate landscape in two ways: first, students would enter the room from an outdoor covered walk-way rather than an interior hallway; and second, the classroom wall oppo-site the entry door was movable (and largely glass) so that it opened onto a patio with a grassy lawn beyond. Each outdoor space was demarcated by hedges or other greenery that extended the classroom's interior walls into the landscape.

Neutra's conception was motivated by Southern California's mild cli-mate and a regional history of school buildings that encouraged outdoor pursuits. As far back as the 1910s, some California schools had included outdoor corridors and verandas or terraces directly outside the classrooms, sometimes accessible through French doors, but these interior and exterior spaces remained separated by fixed walls. Even more significant to Neutra was his belief, shared by many modernist architects, in fresh air and activ-ity as crucial to maintaining health. In particular, the "open-air" school movement earlier in the century (explained in the next chapter) introduced a new relationship between the classroom and its surroundings.

Neutra's familiarity with these rather avant-garde California schools can be seen in his Corona Avenue School (1935) and unbuilt Lawton Avenue School (1936) in Los Angeles. Both buildings established a direct connec-tion with the outdoors through the sliding walls that Neutra had previously envisioned. And they both revealed his fascination with the possibilities of outdoor education. Neutra's schools relied on what he labeled "The In-Door

Out-Door Classroom," which placed a small paved patio and short spur walls beneath an overhanging roof to define the area immediately outside the classroom's glazed, sliding wall, adjacent to a grass yard circumscribed by hedges and containing a garden section. Never before in America had classrooms been so intimately related to nature.

Neutra's indoor-outdoor classrooms popularized an idea that was gaining momentum in the world of educational architecture. In just a few years, this trend would enter mainstream thinking. William W. Caudill (1914–1983), who would become one of the nation's preeminent postwar school designers, considered outdoor spaces a necessity, as articulated in his pamphlet *Space for Teaching* (1941), perhaps the first publication to approach educational design from a modernist point of view. According to Caudill, every elementary-school classroom should contain three components: the class area, the studio or shop, and the outdoor classroom area. The outdoor space was mandatory and expected to be at least twice the size of its indoor counterpart. Its stated purposes would be nature study and recreation, but a regard for children's health was another major impetus. Just a few decades earlier, outdoor areas were somewhat of a luxury, and school-design publications urged architects to incorporate pleasant landscape designs if only to enhance the students' aesthetic appreciation. Yet by the end of the 1940s, usable outdoor spaces had become integral to architects' and educators' impression of the healthy, progressive school. The notion that the healthiest classrooms incorporated outdoor space became commonplace by the early 1950s. Educators were advised to build new schools so that each classroom was on grade with the surrounding landscape and had a direct exit to an outdoor space—which was ideally at least as large as the indoor classroom.

Another student-health concern that affected the schoolroom was lighting. As described above, much of the discussion over proper classroom design in the late 19th century centered on proper lighting and ventilation. While the mounting interest in outdoor classrooms and activity spaces began to reshape classrooms, older trepidations about adequate light and air continued to play a significant role in educational design. Despite the specificity of lighting recommendations and the improved quality of artificial lighting, natural light remained enticing for school designers throughout the 20th century. When modernist ideas from Europe began to infiltrate American school architecture in the 1930s, one of their most attractive new solutions involved the introduction of daylight into the classroom. The work of pioneer American modernists like Neutra and Ernest J. Kump Jr. inspired school designers to adopt the one-story block (Neutra's "horizontal school") as the most efficient means to bring adequate light into classrooms. This model, with schoolrooms aligned along a single corridor, introduced light from two sides of the classroom—in direct contradiction with the 19th-century experts who decried "cross-lighting" and demanded light enter the room only from one wall. Neutra followed European modernist architects in arguing that such dual lighting enabled brighter schoolrooms and gave teachers flexibility in arranging the desks.

With a better understanding of light and its effects, other Depression-era architects found multiple ways to introduce daylight. The most common was to leave one long wall of a rectangular room almost entirely glazed and to perforate the corridor wall in some way, usually with a **clearstory window**. Other efforts utilized skylights or glass block partitions. This meant that the classroom's proper orientation was crucial. Authorities had long argued over the schoolroom's correct positioning: although eastern and western exposures seem to have been slightly favored by the early 20th century, followed by northern and then southern exposures, there were advocates for all. By the 1930s, it was generally agreed that rooms needing an exceptional level of light, such as art studios, should open to the north, while basic classrooms were best aligned so that their windowed walls were on the east and west.

After World War II, educators and architects shifted their focus away from the amount of light available in the classroom to the quality of that light. Instead of measuring foot-candles, the available informational materials—incorporating the latest scientific research—urged designers to consider light's intensity, glare, brightness, and color. Every possible surface or material in the classroom—including obvious reflective sources, like ceilings, walls, furniture, and floors, and also covering ink, paper, textbooks, mimeographed and duplicated materials, and chalkboards—was analyzed for its potential to cause distraction or fatigue in students.

The Active Classroom

In their seminal book, *The Child-Centered School* (1928), progressive educators Harold Rugg and Ann Shumaker described the emerging atmosphere in schoolhouses as notable for its "informality, flexibility, [and] freedom" (Rugg and Shumaker 1928, 15). Comments like this indicated the prevalence of a new attitude among educators—one that is visible in the schoolroom's evolution from a place of passive listening to one of active learning. Activity spaces began to appear in schoolrooms, or standard rooms were converted into areas for numerous pursuits, and again Neutra's ideas proved influential. Much of the impetus for activity spaces came from progressive educators inspired by the mounting evidence that the restrictions and limitations of traditional classroom practices had a deleterious effect on children's learning. This was part of a broader development that eventually led American culture to become "child-centered" over the course of the 20th century.

The interwar period saw an explosion of literature addressing issues of developmental and educational psychology. When translated to education, this resulted in curricula organized around such progressive principles as following the child's natural interests, recognizing individual differences, and using concrete projects to actively engage abstract subject matter. In 1915, John Dewey (1859–1952), America's most famous educator and philosopher, published a survey of progressive practices in various schools across the country entitled *Schools of To-Morrow*; similar studies, like *The Child-Centered School*, not only demonstrated the extent to which such practices were becoming accepted in kindergarten and elementary schools, but also gave a name to an evolving attitude toward children and education. "Child-centered" came to mean educating students according to their interests and allowing them agency in the process.

One of the distinguishing features of the new progressive education was activity. Children in 20th-century public schools participated in far more

A 1950s elementary school classroom. Informal groupings of movable furniture reflected the influence of active learning theories. (From the collection of the Schenectady County Historical Society)

and different endeavors than their counterparts from earlier times, especially in the lower grades. Educators began to emphasize individual and small-group activities to complement conventional large-group exercises. Expanding the universe of topics and techniques used to educate children meant adaptations would be necessary in the classroom. Changes to the schoolroom began with the youngest children in the lowest grades, involving smaller, movable furniture for different seating arrangements; alcove areas or some other portion of the room appended to the classroom in some manner that made it seem like an independent space; the incorporation of more storage compartments in the classroom; the installation of sinks for cleaning after messy activities; or any other adjustments to coincide with the increasing number of pursuits. For example, the most important book published on school architecture in the 1920s—John J. Donovan's *School Architecture* (1921)—included images of the architect's own Clawson Elementary School (1916) kindergarten room. Although Donovan did not comment on this, the Clawson School pointed toward a new direction for classroom design by altering the room's rectangular form into an L shape, with the short leg forming an alcove containing a sand table, a piano, and a toilet. Similarly, a photograph of San Diego's Francis W. Parker School (1912) in Donovan's book revealed a homelike kindergarten room, complete with domestic hearth, opening onto a screened porch through accordion walls. Other kindergarten-room designs indicate a separation of different areas dedicated to different activities but without physically altering the room. Such divisions made sense at the kindergarten level, where the informality of the program might lead one group of children to be listening to the teacher read a story while another worked on an art project. But in the higher grades, the pedagogic practices of teacher-centered instruction dictated a more formal atmosphere with desks oriented toward the teacher. Even Rugg and Shumaker admitted that "it appears to be impossible to find a school in America in which the child-centered philosophy is applied beyond the eighth grade" (Reese 2005, 172).

Over time, the notion of physically altering the classroom's rectangular box gained more adherents. Neutra and Swiss immigrant architect William Lescaze were early advocates of rethinking the classroom. The Corona Avenue School, designed so that one side of each schoolroom opened to an outdoor garden area, was strikingly different from the mainstream. So was the alteration to this scheme Neutra proposed for subsequent projects. In a 1935 article, Neutra presented his vision of the new school building as determined first and foremost by the classroom. His Lawton Avenue Elementary School project, depicted in the article, relied on schoolrooms with segregated areas—almost separate rooms—flanking the classroom entry for hands-on activities. This arrangement essentially gave teachers four distinct spaces for learning (counting the outdoor area) within or adjacent to the classroom proper. Such flexibility was becoming prized as the elementary-school curriculum, in particular, loosened itself from traditional restrictions.

Elementary-school classrooms evolved into multiuse spaces that might contain children engaged in numerous pursuits simultaneously. The 19th-century curriculum that taught children reading, writing, and discipline became almost unimaginably rich under the influence of progressive ideas. A review of popular literature aimed at educators demonstrates the wide range of schoolroom possibilities. For example, a book on school planning from 1953 attempted to give a sense of the breadth of contemporary elementary studies by listing the different things a student should be able to do in a good classroom. In addition to such expected topics as reading, writing, and making art, the authors conjured an impressive list of pursuits that children might undertake: growing plants, cooking, playing house, listening to records, dancing, singing, making models, caring for animals, giving speeches or acting in plays, and puppetry (Engelhardt, Engelhardt Jr., and Leggett 1953). This broad spectrum proved that the postwar schoolroom environment was much different than in preceding generations.

A major development occurred with the design and construction of the Crow Island Elementary School (1939). Built in Winnetka, Illinois, a suburb north of Chicago, Crow Island heralded a new era in American educational architecture, expertly meshing the architectural modernism and educational progressivism of its time. The school's architects extended the concept of multiple activity areas by reshaping the classroom altogether. The result was so successful that the Crow Island School would stand as a model for schools of all levels for decades. It was arguably the most influential school building ever constructed in the United States.

Crow Island's design was a group effort joining the young, unknown, local architectural firm of Perkins, Wheeler & Will with the famous architect Eliel Saarinen. Also involved in the building's development were Winnetka's superintendent, Carleton Washburne, who enjoyed a national reputation as a progressive reformer, along with the school's teachers, students, and janitors. With the support of a progressive school board, the designers tried to rethink the school building, integrating it with student activities in an unprecedented way. The process began with architect Lawrence B. Perkins (1907–1998), whose father, Dwight Perkins, had once been the architect for the Chicago Board of Education. The younger Perkins attended classes in the Winnetka elementary schools to learn teachers' practices and students' behaviors. He experienced Winnetka's progressive curriculum, which aimed to develop children's citizenship skills, personality, and emotional well-being through four main types of school behaviors: individual and group academic work, and individual and group nonacademic work. To these four activities, Perkins added two essential elements of school life from his observations: the handling of clothing (coats, boots, etc.) and use of bathrooms. Together these factors shaped the final classroom design.

Available evidence indicates that the Perkins, Wheeler & Will firm probably was responsible for Crow Island's formal planning, while Saarinen's team—consisting of Eliel; his wife, Loja, a weaver; his soon-to-be-famous architect son, Eero; and Eero's fiancée, Lillian Swann, a ceramicist—developed the building's aesthetic program. In plan, Crow Island formed a slightly straightened Z shape. The interior space was zoned into five separate areas for administration, communal activities (auditorium, library, art room, and playroom), kindergarten and nursery, lower grades (1–2), and upper grades (3–6). The designers gave each grading group its own wing, classrooms, and playground in an effort to minimize interaction between younger and older children. These wings contained spines of single- or **double-loaded corridors** lined with revolutionary L-shaped classrooms.

Classroom units at Crow Island School in Winnetka, Illinois, designed by Eliel Saarinen and Perkins, Wheeler & Will (1939). Crow Island energized the movement toward more informal school design, with its small scale and easy access to the outdoors. (Photo by Dale Gyure)

Crow Island's classrooms contained both traditional learning space and active work space, each occupying one arm of the L, and the two areas could be separated by sliding doors. The classrooms' main sections were intended for group and individual academic work and group nonacademic projects. Two walls made almost entirely of glass let in abundant natural light and visually connected the children with the outdoors. Movable furniture gave the teachers freedom to arrange desks and tables for different projects. One large wall opposite the windows was covered with pine and could be used as a bulletin board. Workspaces also contained toilets and closets. And Eliel and Eero Saarinen created a different decorative scheme, full of bright colors, for each room.

Beyond its innovative classroom design, Crow Island rejected most of the conventions of contemporary school buildings. It was one-story where they were multistoried; it was asymmetrical and nonaxial where they were formal and dominated by center and cross axes; its classrooms rejected traditional lighting practices and allowed light to enter through windows in more than one wall. Further advances included classroom ceilings only 9 feet high rather than 12 feet; toilets located within the classrooms rather than grouped in the hallway; workspaces integrated into the classrooms rather than being in separate rooms; and classroom and hallway walls covered with wood paneling. These improvements adapted the building to the school's progressive curriculum and pedagogy. Many of these features indicated the planners' desire to make the spaces less institutional and more homelike.

Within a year of opening, Crow Island had been celebrated in a 14-page spread in *Architectural Forum* and an article in the *American School Board Journal*. Within a decade, elementary schools across the country had been transformed, partly because of Crow Island. Architects and educators also began to consider how Crow Island's lessons might be adapted to the high school's more complex requirements.

By the 1940s, as the economic depression lingered and economics became an even greater factor in school design decisions, commentators touted the cost-saving benefits of placing activity areas within elementary-school classrooms. Caudill's *Space for Teaching* indicated the importance of activity rooms by listing studio/shop space as one of three necessary classroom components along with the class area and outdoor classroom. Lawrence Perkins, whose study of children in action in the Winnetka schools prompted the ground-breaking L-shaped configuration of Crow Island's classrooms, became an advocate of careful classroom planning. He continued to experiment with the relationship between class and activity areas. As the Crow Island School completed construction, the firm (from 1944 known as Perkins & Will) introduced a variation that returned the classroom to its traditional rectangular shape but segregated the "working space" from the desks and seats with a wall; it also allotted roughly one-third of the total classroom size to this workroom. The Rugen School (1942) in Glenview, Illinois, is an early example of this solution, and it can be seen in slightly altered form nearly 10 years later at the firm's Riverside, Illinois, Blythe Park School (1950).

POSTWAR VARIATIONS

In the postwar era, the active, healthy classroom developed by Neutra and others became the norm, facilitated by a revised approach to school design that incorporated lightweight steel frames and lightweight, glass-filled walls into everyday construction. The new schools were easier and quicker to build, which proved beneficial in part because a wave of student enrollments threatened to overwhelm the nation's public-school system. The baby boom between 1946 and 1964 increased the American population by 70 million babies. As a comparison, during the Great Depression, birth rates had averaged approximately 18 to 19 per 1,000 persons; by the peak of the baby boom, that rate rose to 26.5 births (Colby and Ortman 2014). Elevated fertility rates for 18 straight years produced an unprecedented number of children. Suddenly there were more students than ever before and not enough seats for them in the public schools. Overall, after holding relatively steady during the Depression and war years, public-school enrollments increased by roughly 10 million students in each decade between 1950 and 1970 (Weisser 2006, 298). Population growth was both a blessing and a curse for educators: increasing populations funded public educators' budgets through increased tax revenues and created unprecedented demand for trained teachers and educators but also strained their resources, including existing and sometimes aging school buildings whose maintenance had been deferred for years due to tight economic circumstances.

In addition to an expanding populace, the 1960s brought extensive social and cultural changes to the United States, and the educational and architectural worlds were not exempted from the spirit of radical questioning and experimentation that infused the decade. The *American School Board Journal*'s editor William C. Bruce alluded to this atmosphere: "The past five years have witnessed radical changes to the organization and teaching methods of the secondary schools." Among the educational variations Bruce mentioned were **"open classrooms**, free schools, open education, alternative schools, school-within-a-school, personalized education, humanistic schools, mini-schools," and others (Bruce 1963, 48). In such an environment, common ideas were reevaluated, often with repercussions for school design. For example, there was no longer a consensus on the school-room's proper size or shape. Some educators considered the 24-by-30-foot rectangular container, bounded by four immovable walls and a 12-foot ceiling, to be an ancient relic. Every aspect of that old classroom was reexamined and altered. Architects made rooms smaller or larger than the old standards, with lower ceilings and glass walls. Windowless schoolrooms were briefly popular. Other architects and educators experimented with unorthodox room shapes, like circles, hexagons, polygons, and ovals. These shapes, intended to evoke modern education's freedom, were mainly symbolic gestures meant to counter the old-fashioned boxlike classroom's constraints.

According to the Educational Facilities Laboratories (EFL), a non-profit corporation that researched the relationship between education and architecture and spearheaded advancements in school design, educators described older-generation schools with such words as "rigidity, isolation, sterility, formality, inaccessibility, uncommodiousness, starkness, immobility, permanence, constraint" (EFL 1968, 16). Traditional classrooms informed many of these perceptions. Reform-minded educators and architects viewed the destruction of the old schoolroom's boxy form as a step toward greater efficiency and a more perfect match between education and architecture. The EFL agreed. An organization dedicated to addressing the massive increase in new school construction fostered by the baby boom and to improving American education through collaborative school design, the EFL was a product of the Ford Foundation, working in collaboration with the American Institute of Architects (AIA) and the Columbia University Teachers College. Beginning in 1958, the EFL spent over a decade organizing symposia, conferences, and exhibits and publishing books and pamphlets on aspects of school design and case studies of successful school buildings, all promoting an integrated-design approach that brought architects, teachers, administrators, and educational researchers together to generate creative solutions to the nation's educational problems. When it came to experimental schoolroom shapes, the EFL claimed that "an even greater variety and freedom can be achieved if the right angle is deliberately set aside . . . the non-rectilinear shape begins to serve some of the advanced educational purposes of the coming American high school" (EFL 1961, 53).

No matter how difficult it was to arrange desks or store materials in multisided rooms, educators found themselves irresistibly attracted to them. Such rooms were believed to be "flexible," especially if they incorporated movable or demountable walls so administrators could reshape interior spaces according to their school's future requirements. Modern skeleton-frame construction made these movable walls or impermanent partitions possible, since it eliminated the necessity for interior walls to carry any of the building's weight. **Nonbearing walls** became so popular and varied that the EFL felt it necessary to categorize the different kinds of partitions available to designers (permanent partitions, "relocatable" partitions, "folding operable" partitions, and "skiddable-screen" walls). This multitude of options was unprecedented. Architects now conceived school buildings as a series of adjustable spaces wrapped with a thin skin. Flexibility was the ultimate goal. The EFL admitted that the term had become a catchword by the late 1960s, leading educators to rely on architects to solve educational problems; as a corrective, the EFL favored the use of descriptive terms like "expansible space," "convertible space," and "versatile space" (EFL 1968, 76).

In the era of flexibility, spaces limited to one specific pedagogical experience (e.g., lecture, laboratory) or subject were a luxury. Architects stretched their imaginations, and schools appeared with auditoriums that could be apportioned into classrooms, combination library/lunchrooms, and even library/gymnasiums. Within the modern school's new spaces, teachers used an equally inventive group of practices and materials to enhance their students' learning. The EFL effectively summarized the dichotomy between older and present-day education: "Time was when concepts like 'teacher,' 'class,' 'curriculum,' 'class period,' 'textbook,' 'classroom,' and 'school' each had an accepted definition," they wrote. "Now, suddenly, each of the old, standard building blocks of the educational program seems to be breaking up into parts, with the resulting release in energy that is the product of fission . . . In short, the standard components of the instructional program suddenly multiply and become diverse, flexible, variegated. Selection, design, utilization all become more complex—but also, there is reason to hope, more effective" (EFL 1968, 12). Educators viewed **team teaching** as a way to stimulate student interest and utilize teachers' strengths. Some schools hired teacher's aides to lessen classroom teachers' workloads and increase the opportunities for individualized instruction. Administrators occasionally altered the school schedule, sometimes creating shorter "time modules," while others eliminated class periods altogether. A few school officials even adopted the ungraded school, where students advanced along a sequence of courses at their own pace rather than moving en masse through four yearlong grades. All these developments revealed educators' desire to better address students' needs, abilities, and interests.

Traditional textbook, lecture, and recitation methods—though still dominant in the postwar era—yielded to more discussions and small-group or individual work. Independent study (often via programmed learning) also allowed students to proceed at their own natural pace and was thought to stimulate their interests. Films, filmstrips, overhead projectors, slides, phonograph and audiotape recordings, radios, televisions, and later computers supplemented the teacher's toolkit, as discussed below. Several of these innovations had architectural consequences. Junior and senior high schools now needed audiovisual centers; libraries increasingly became resource centers, with requirements beyond book stacks and reading tables; previously unknown rooms, like language laboratories, emerged; and many schools were built with a version of what one architectural journal labeled "Room A," an all-purpose room in a central location without a fixed use.

Flexibility as a concept was elastic; it could represent the ability to accommodate different pedagogical techniques within the same space, the building's capacity to adjust to significant expansions or reductions in student populations, the capability of configuring the same space in different ways to accommodate different uses, and many other things. Flexibility's emergence as a key idea was partly due to fluctuating school enrollments in the previous decades. After World War II, enrollments were *the* most influential factor affecting school design. High-school enrollments had fallen during the 1930s and 1940s because of the economic depression and war, but they rose by over 40 percent in the 1950s and 1960s (National Center for Education Statistics 1993, 16). Educators became keenly attentive to population growth patterns as a result of these surges and recessions, and the future began to play a greater role in their plans. Modern architecture was more successful at offering the kind of adaptable spaces needed to meet these varying enrollment demands.

Shifting populations were not the only motivation for educators to embrace flexibility. Progressive educational ideas from earlier in the century infiltrated the mainstream by the 1940s, prompting educators to make a greater effort to adapt curricula and pedagogical styles to students' individual interests and abilities. The school building was implicated in this effort because reformist educators increasingly viewed older buildings as obsolete. "Modern education seeks to adjust the school program to the child rather than the reverse," wrote Wilmington, Delaware superintendent. Ward I. Miller (1949) wrote, "Traditional building styles restrict if they do not altogether prohibit the implementation of good theory" (79, 85). Education was evolving, and the older generations of buildings, like conventional pedagogical techniques, were proving inadequate. Modern education required innovative forms, in part because interior spaces had become more complex. Spaces needed to be adaptable, reflecting the new curriculum's supposed freedom from outmoded constraints.

One of the foremost proponents of modernist school architecture was Chicago's Lawrence Perkins, who vaulted to national prominence after the Crow Island School's critical success. Perkins and coauthor Walter D. Cocking, in their 1949 book *Schools*, faulted earlier school buildings for being too big, too expensive, and not adapted to children's needs. They employed modernist rhetoric to emphasize how contemporary schools were planned with students in mind, unlike their precursors. But a new day was dawning, characterized by buildings that were flexible, efficient, and attractive, utilizing modern-age materials like steel, reinforced concrete, and large expanses of glass, and incorporating lessons from decades of educational experience. Echoing the language of prominent modern architects like Le Corbusier and Walter Gropius, Perkins and Cocking argued for a school building "planned by its activities," where the building "evolves from the classroom, or from a series of classrooms, each designed specifically for its specific jobs" (Perkins and Cocking 1949, 49). This next generation of school buildings would share common characteristics. They would have decentralized, campus-like plans, often consisting of multiple structures interconnected by covered walkways or breezeways, rather than an entire school in one building. These buildings would be single-story structures for greater safety, lower cost, and less formality. The schools would occupy larger sites to give children more room to congregate or play. Air-conditioning would be commonplace. Flexible spaces allowed by movable partitions and multifunction layouts would dominate floor plans.

By the mid-1950s, such ideas were becoming mainstream in the school-design community. Walter Cocking looked back—with obvious bias—on 10 years of school architecture and saw profound changes: "Prior to World War II, secondary school buildings were chiefly planned according to structural efficiency, compactness and capacity. Apparently little consideration was given to the characteristics of the youth who would use the buildings or to a program needed by youth. Since World War II there has been a slow but steady awareness of these two factors, and evidence indicates that there is now more emphasis given to them in planning new plants" (Cocking 1956, 185). Cocking listed a series of contemporary trends in high-school buildings, including one-story structures, campus plans, larger sites, and a greater connection with nature through the use of courtyards and larger windows. There was also greater interest in student and teacher social areas, decentralization of large spaces like lunchrooms, classrooms envisioned as "laboratories for learning or as work spaces," shops created for general rather than specific uses, and an overall suppleness that did not exist before the war (Cocking 1956, 188–190). A new approach to educational planning provoked the school building's evolution, according to Cocking. Prior to the late 1940s, school administrators usually helped architects plan buildings; thereafter, the process was enlarged when the school's entire staff, neighborhood citizens, and special consultants (such as psychologists, anthropologists, and sociologists), in addition to educators, became involved.

The Open Classroom

A polarizing development of the postwar era, in terms of the schoolroom, was the rise of open classrooms. First conceived as a physical corollary to the pedagogical and curricular progressivism of the 1960s, "schools without walls" proved extremely attractive to American educators and continue to resonate to this day as an appropriate means of accommodating the free-flowing quality of true progressive education. The dream of undivided but easily adaptable teaching space remains a powerful one, enticing 21st-century architects and educators to continue the quest for the open classroom. In many ways, open-classroom supporters sought a return to the old one-room schoolhouse but with a different pedagogy and disciplinary attitude.

The open classroom reached its peak of popularity in the 1970s, but its origins dated back to the early 20th century, when kindergarten educators, influenced by the child-centered educational theories of Johann Heinrich Pestalozzi and Maria Montessori, gradually integrated more free play into their daily routines. At the same time, they also increased the variety of activities available for these children. The combination of these two developments put a strain on the typical kindergarten classroom, which was often a regular classroom cleared of desks. At times the only physical difference between the spaces for kindergartners and their older counterparts was a faux-domestic fireplace, a popular feature of kindergarten rooms and libraries intended to make younger children feel more comfortable in public places by evoking their living rooms or library rooms at home. In an effort to make space for varied activities, kindergarten designers began to include small alcoves or garden rooms, altering the classroom's traditional rectangular box into more of an L shape, and including small stages or sink areas for washing. Lawrence Perkins adapted this notion to the elementary-school classroom in the famous Crow Island School.

Kindergartens thus provided a successful model for subdividing educational space to allow multiple activities simultaneously, and the model, in turn, relied on educators' widespread adoption of lightweight, movable, child-sized furniture in kindergarten rooms. This was an early instance of an educational revolution that would sweep through the century, leading to new theories of pedagogy and curriculum and new approaches to architectural and furniture design. The ultimate flexible schoolroom would be an enlarged version of these early kindergartens—a simple container, without internal barriers, to accommodate any potential educational use, from group lectures to small-group interactions to solitary reading.

This dream was translated into reality with the open classroom. Supporters of open classrooms began to promote the concept's applicability to primary and secondary education in the early 1950s, largely because of its success in kindergarten spaces but also inspired by the emphasis on **open plans** visible in increasing fashion in domestic design. Architects like Frank Lloyd Wright popularized home designs with flowing interior spaces enabled by removing barriers (like walls) between rooms and between the inside and outside of the house. In the postwar era, openness would become a hallmark of modernist architectural design, as well as an often-used metaphor for the United States—linking open architectural space with the free, democratic society that employed it in contrast to the backward and oppressive Soviet Union during the height of Cold War tensions. Consequently, sporadic examples of school buildings constructed without the walls that usually separated classrooms and hallways could be found in educational and architectural journals. William Caudill's well-known book, *Toward Better School Design* (1954), included a photograph of a schoolroom in one of Perkins & Will's suburban Chicago schools, along with a lengthy caption introducing "An Open Plan Classroom." Caudill described the open plan as "creeping into educational architecture" from domestic design but seemed nonplussed by the idea, although he admitted the important role sound and its control would play in creating such spaces (Caudill 1954, 87). More support for open plans came from an odd story related by Caudill in the same book. Caudill claimed that Wilfred F. Clapp, Michigan's assistant superintendent of schools, had sent him a letter describing a spontaneous experiment with open planning. A new elementary school in the Detroit suburb of Royal Oak was not quite finished at the beginning of the school year: large plate-glass panels for the upper portion of the walls separating classrooms from the corridor had not been installed. So the school "operated with little or no barriers between the classroom and the corridor" for a few weeks. "The corridor became really a part of the classroom," Clapp said (Caudill 1954, 86). Later several teachers opposed the installation of the glass partitions when they finally arrived, and the school's administrators partly heeded their advice so that when an addition to the school was constructed, it included a room open to the corridor. By the end of the decade, more designers and educators purposefully removed classroom walls. One of the earliest attempts to do so was at Michigan's Carson City Elementary School (1957).

From the outside, the Carson City school seemed unremarkable, even a bit regressive with its flat-roofed, cubic, **International Style** appearance, but the covered walkway, vast expanses of window, and obviously thin walls were quite contemporary. The floor plan hidden behind this mundane exterior, however, was radical. Louis C. Kingscott & Associates designed the school as a simple aggregation of three quadrilateral clusters, connected at the corners and approached by a covered walk. A large, two-story multipurpose room anchored the building's center. The two adjoined clusters were roughly square in shape; in the middle of each, a core of plumbing and toilets was surrounded by completely open, undivided space. In other words, Carson City's two classrooms were empty rooms, over 4,000 square feet inside, with a centralized plumbing core, and its third space was a multipurpose room of nearly equal size. This was the first noteworthy embodiment of the dream held by some progressive educators for decades: the totally unobstructed learning space. At Carson City, students moved around these spaces continually throughout the day with no permanent desk. They met each morning in their assigned home area to pick up their individual colored-plastic tote trays, which held supplies and books and were carried by the children from station to station. All furniture was movable, and classes were encouraged to utilize as much space as they liked.

The Carson City School was widely promoted by the EFL, the most significant educational trendsetter of the postwar era. It was prominently featured in an EFL publication entitled *Schools without Walls* (1965), a booklet extolling the virtues of the growing open-classroom movement and providing examples of recently constructed school buildings engaged with it in some way. A crucial point emphasized by the EFL regarding Carson City was that it was not just a uniquely designed building intended to serve a conventional curriculum. Instead, the school administrators sought a uniquely designed building to match their experimental curriculum. In addition to an evolving curriculum, course periods did not exist at Carson City. Lunch was served at a specified time, and certain groups were required to be present for a television broadcast at some point during the day, and every afternoon, a cluster meeting engaged a majority of the students in the closest approximation of a traditional classroom; beyond these three fixed points, however, the student's day was flexible, with lessons proceeding organically rather than fitting within prescribed time blocks. The teams of teachers responsible for each cluster of students organized their day as they wished, sometimes improvising, within a loose framework of spatial arrangements planned in three-week increments. In this environment, students flowed through the entire classroom cluster without barriers, and other groups or individuals were visible and audible to all. The openness was not total, unlike later experiments with circular or hexagonal school buildings; the three clusters remained physically distinct, as three square masses connected at their corners.

Team teaching would be integral to the open classroom's success. Drawing upon psychological studies suggesting that children more effectively learned when they were able to work at their own pace and in different places and that mixed grade levels actually enhanced such effects, educators devised new approaches that spread children around the classroom in small groups or individually. Unlike previous generations, students played a role in selecting their activities in many of these classrooms and had direct access to the materials they used in such activities. In these environs, the removal of dividing walls and the new organizational challenges emanating from this act, along with the number of activities that could now occur simultaneously, favored instruction by more than one person. And the teachers' roles required alteration to match the new scheme. Instead of the authoritative disciplinarian of the past, who transmitted knowledge and kept discipline, teachers were trained to act as coaches or facilitators who directed students' explorations in ways that allowed for self-discovery. Team teaching not only opened opportunities for innovation, its efficiency appealed to older conservative tendencies in American education.

Open-space classrooms eventually revealed other common characteristics besides team teaching. Experientially, they were places of much movement and noise. Teachers encouraged students to wander freely through their environment, with opportunities for standing, sitting casually, and even lying down at certain times. Such informality could also be seen in the way large, open structures were subdivided into smaller, secluded corners, pods, or learning centers for certain activities. Movable or demountable walls added flexibility, and carpeting helped to muffle sound. The symbolic gesture of removing walls did not pass unacknowledged; for many educators, the psychological benefit of open, undivided space necessarily complemented the removal of traditional barriers between teacher and student and between student and learning. Some schools, like Carson City, went even further, removing not just physical barriers but also more conventional constraints like time periods and warning bells, destructuring the school atmosphere as much as possible in a quest to maximize students' freedom in all respects.

Efforts such as these were enthusiastically backed (and reported) by the EFL. In a campaign against public schools' stern formality, the EFL called for educators to "de-juvenilize" the high school. It looked forward to a day when "the management of students will move toward a more adult relationship with the student." In these future schools, "the bells will cease to ring, the more mature and responsible students will be 'de-scheduled' from the close control and maximum security regulations in force for the more immature and irresponsible, and students will confront the prescribed bodies of knowledge . . . when they are ready to profit from such study and not just when the subjects are offered in the course of study" (EFL 1960, 134).

There is some confusion about the terminology applied to these postwar experiments, which came to be known by several related expressions. In general, when addressing the conceptual atmosphere and radical curriculum that utilized team teaching and integrated large-group, small-group, and individual activities within the same physical space, commentators tended to speak of the "open classroom." But when specifically focusing on the physical environment of learning spaces, "open-plan classroom" or "open-space school" was more common. The two were different manifestations of the same approach but not always interdependent. As Charles Silberman explained in *The Open Classroom Reader* (1973), "By itself, dividing a classroom into interest areas does not constitute open education; creating large open spaces does not constitute open education; individualizing instruction does not constitute open education . . . For the open classroom . . . is not a model or set of techniques, it is an approach to teaching and learning" (Cuban 2004, 70). That approach

Students work at various tasks in an open classroom, 1970s. In the postwar period some educators reacted against the traditional schoolroom's physical constraints, removing walls and encouraging informal behaviors that allowed students to pursue their individual interests. (Bill Peters/The Denver Post via Getty Images)

often—but not always—gave rise to physical alterations. Thus, open-space classrooms provided the places in which open education could occur.

Open-classroom ideas saw a dramatic increase in popularity in the late 1960s, spurred in large part by their perceived success in the United Kingdom. In a series of articles in the *New Republic*, Joseph Featherstone introduced American readers to the British "informal education" movement, an approach arising from the lower grades that emphasized cherished such progressive tenets as guided instruction based on play and experience, informal decorative schemes and student-teacher interactions, and following children's natural interests. These child-centered principles were applauded in the British Central Advisory Council for Education's 1967 report ("the Plowden Report"), a document widely circulated in the American educational community. Featherstone's laudatory articles directed attention to the British reforms; for example, in 1968 there were approximately 30 articles in American journals and magazines mentioning the British reforms, while three years later that number had surpassed 300 (Ravitch 1983).

Another potential influence on the development of open classrooms came from the business world. In fact, if school architects and educators sometimes looked to the single-family house for inspiration in the immediate postwar era, within a few decades, the corporate office would assume that role. A movement in the interior-design world in the late 1950s reconceptualized the office environment. Inspired by American offices' organization, which tended to feature a ring of executive offices around the perimeter of an open room filled with rows of secretaries' or clerks' desks (the secretarial pool), two German brothers imagined an office where the entire space was similar to the American office's core but without the orderly desks, walls, or partitions. Eberhard and Wolfgang Schnelle, working for the Quickborner Team, devised the *Bürolandschaft* (office landscape) as a more efficient way to make flexible space and also as a representation of a new power structure where office hierarchies would be less important. They first tested the idea in Germany, with the results well publicized thereafter. The office landscape's fundamental elements included open rooms without walls, free-form arrangements of movable furniture, carpeting, and plants. American architects would have been exposed to the office-landscape idea through the Action Office system (1964–1968) created by Robert Propst and George Nelson for the Herman Miller Company in response to the German advances. Thus, the modern office and the postwar classroom moved in a parallel direction in the late 1960s and early 1970s, as designers of both kinds of spaces experimented with less structured, more casual arrangements intended to enhance the office or learning experience by allow greater organizational flexibility and introducing the informality of everyday life.

Acceptance of open-classroom ideas was widespread. While many administrators balked at funding entire schools devoted to open education, some of its precepts became integrated into public schools, particularly at the elementary level. By the late 1970s, an article in *Architectural Record* opined that "nearly all [schools] use some form of the 'open' classroom, or at least offer the option" (Allen 1979, 127). When those words were written, however, interest in open classrooms had already peaked. Various external pressures and internal realizations were moving American education in a more conservative direction, meaning open classrooms became less attractive to educators, who grew increasingly interested in evaluative testing and standardized curricula. Historical studies indicate that while a great number of school systems experimented with open-classroom techniques in some form, very few of them fully implemented elements of informal education in their open-space classrooms. Because these rooms were intended to encourage team teaching and multiple activities with different groups, along with the diverse use of space, when used with conventional pedagogical methods there were inevitable problems. Noise was the biggest nuisance. Teachers quickly learned that while walled classrooms may have inadequately accommodated ambitious progressive practices, they actually were quite adept at controlling sounds. Without such walls, open rooms filled with excited young voices engaged in simultaneous tasks tended to raise a cacophony that could be extremely distracting. Throughout the 1960s, EFL publications made sure to address rumors about noise pollution in open classrooms, describing it as "background" sound that might be alarming to teachers and students at first but quickly receded from attention; the new soundscape would take some adjustment, but its problems could be overcome. "Noise and other distractions can be kept in reasonable bounds by proper physical planning (with special attention to acoustics), careful scheduling, and, above all, by not overcrowding the room," claimed an EFL pamphlet (EFL 1965, 54). Anecdotal evidence indicates that these suggestions did not always lead to success, and complaints about excessive noise by educators involved with these open classrooms were important determinants in the movement's eventual demise.

Beyond noise, other issues made open classrooms disappointing or objectionable. Selective attention proved to be another challenge. The continual movement, unorthodox sounds, and lack of defined physical boundaries often made it difficult for pupils to remain focused. Similar to the noise issue, experts advised educators to stay the course, predicting that students eventually would adapt to the visually and sonically stimulating atmosphere. The lack of privacy also proved difficult for some children, and the associated dearth of space for quiet reflection troubled educators who felt learning could not take place if students did not have places in the schoolroom environment to think (and be) by themselves.

School designers' attempts to rectify these hindrances resulted in comfortable nooks, window seats, breakout spaces, or other spatially defined areas that allowed children to temporarily separate from the group if necessary. An article on the evolution of open-plan classrooms in the 1970s admitted that classrooms needed "some restricted, closed-off areas where a child can go to be quiet and alone within a space that he can personalize as his own. The usual open-plan school, regardless of the degree of flexibility that has been designed into it, has not provided this" (Morton 1971, 69).

Alcoves or recessed spaces actually had a history in school design. Some California kindergartens had introduced auxiliary spaces decades before, and they had become pervasive in postwar kindergarten design. Another influence came from European modernist architects like Alfred Roth, who promoted alcoves and recesses for group activity and published examples of such practices in his international survey of school architecture, *The New School* (1950). Educators and architects turned to smaller, private spaces to counteract the openness of some postwar classrooms. Their efforts produced a range of solutions, from simple extensions of the boxy classroom to unorthodox rooms, like **kivas**. These specialized spaces—named after the partly subterranean, often circular rooms used by Pueblo Indians for religious and political purposes—provided a small, enclosed, quiet alternative to the rest of the classroom. The notion can be traced back as early as the mid-1950s, when *Life* magazine commissioned a hypothetical junior-high-school design from Perkins & Will, and the architects included a tiny circular theater-in-the-round they labeled a "kiva." Although they cited the kiva's origins in Native American culture as a separate, special space, the architects' use of the term for a theater room did not reflect historical usage. Nevertheless, a new term was about to enter the school-design lexicon, one which would be developed into a meaningful idea by admirers of American school design.

It took the work of a pair of British architects, David and Mary Crowley Medd, to demonstrate a more appropriate, educational use of the kiva. The Medds were seminal figures in the British educational world. During the 1940s and 1950s, they worked with a group of far-sighted individuals to develop a new kind of lower elementary school in Hertfordshire, outside of London, one that sought practical construction solutions in the context of wartime material shortages while also seeking spatial arrangements and physical environments that were better adapted to young children. The architects responded to the challenges of rapid design and construction and limited funds with a lightweight, modular, steel-frame system utilizing prefabricated parts from standardized drawings and derived from close collaboration with manufacturers. Hundreds of these schools were erected across England. Many of the new buildings were better scaled to their young occupants than previous schools and equipped with smaller, more mobile furniture and different kinds of spaces ("built-in variety") as a result of the Medds' conversations with teachers and students.

The Medds moved up from Hertfordshire to become members of the British Ministry of Education's Research and Development Team, where they attempted with mixed results to persuade local educational councils of the efficacy of the child-centered design approach. During this time, they continued to study children, consult with teachers, and analyze buildings in other cultures. This led the Medds to become curious about American school architecture. There were many similarities between the two countries: both were frantically trying to build (or rebuild) enough schools to keep up with demand, and both were engaging principles of modern architecture and mass production to do so. But the manner in which American educators and architects synthesized child-centered concepts and new architectural solutions seemed more prevalent. In an attempt to find out why, the Medds spent 1958–1959 traveling the United States, studying school architecture, and speaking with parties involved in educational design. They visited 200 schools and colleges in 40 states—including Crow Island—and made connections with people like Lawrence Perkins. The school buildings they most admired were designed by Caudill Rowlett Scott (CRS), and they held William Caudill's book *Toward Better School Design* in high esteem. In that text, Caudill discussed the importance of flexibility in the elementary-school classroom but recognized the need to control that flexibility lest the room get out of hand. His solution was to include small nooks or spatially removed areas for individual instruction.

Caudill never suggested the kiva as an appropriate model for a segregated space. And as mentioned above, Perkins & Will's *Life* magazine design—of the same year as Caudill's book—used "kiva" as a new name for a small theater area. But the two ideas became conflated at some point in the Medds' thinking, and the result featured prominently in their famous Eveline Lowe Primary School (1967) in London. That school, perhaps the best realization of the Medds' concept of "built-in variety" of teaching areas, combined interconnected spaces of different sizes and degrees of enclosure into an intimate whole. The school's linear plan contained a number of home bases that served as the main classrooms. To offer spatial variety, each home base included at least one bay, made possible by spur walls, and an enclosed room. The enclosed rooms allowed children the quiet or individual time that educators and the Medds felt was crucial to the learning experience. The couple designed one of these enclosed rooms at the Lowe School to be unique: a 12-foot-square carpeted room for up to 40 children with steps around three sides, bunk beds, and a low ceiling, labeled the "kiva." The Medds referred to the kiva as "a small snugly furnished enclosed space" where children could "sit on their haunches to hear a story told by their teacher, or read quietly" (Burke 2016, 202). The British educational press focused on the kiva as the symbol of the Lowe School's progressiveness.

The transatlantic exchange of information on school design increased during the 1960s, and in concert with attention from American architectural journals, it provided school architects with examples from the Medds and others working in England. The Plowden Report, widely known and often discussed, served to strengthen American interests in English education. So it is not surprising that shortly after the Lowe School opened, some school designs in this country began to include kivas. A 1972 survey of school architecture, *Design & Planning: The New Schools*, for example, printed floor plans of American schools of different levels, and two of these plans incorporated some kind of kiva. The first, an elementary school, used the concept but not the term, as its two square classroom pods (which could be left open or subdivided into six classrooms) each had one corner occupied by a small, octagonal, enclosed "special activity room" in the same manner of the Medd's kiva. The other example, a square room with four levels of circular steps, was labeled "kiva" and appeared in a high-school plan with no explanation of its use.

The notion of the kiva as a segregated space in an elementary classroom would no doubt be familiar to most American educators in the 1970s, even if their school did not include a literal kiva space. It became a shorthand for the kind of alternative spatial areas needed for education, particularly of younger children, and its promotors were among the most progressive advocates for change. The breakup of the open plan was under way, as teachers by this time had gained experience with open classrooms, and its strengths and weaknesses were now fully apparent.

As predicted by their supporters, the main strength of open classrooms was their flexibility. Once teachers became accustomed to team teaching or the unusual nature of the new spaces, they were able to devote more time to small groups or individuals. The weaknesses of the open classroom, however, were many. Observers of open-plan classrooms often commented on a greater tendency toward disorganization in these spaces, with a concomitant lack of discipline—particularly when compared to traditional classrooms. Such a tendency may have alarmed parents more than anyone else, many of whom viewed the general loosening of attitudes toward formality and authority under way in these years with suspicion. A Gallup public-opinion poll in 1969 revealed that Americans' leading concern about public education was a perceived lack of discipline. According to historian Diane Ravitch, "the loosening of adult authority [in open education] only exacerbated the public's perception that lack of discipline was the most important problem in the schools and contributed to the steady decline of public confidence in the schools during the 1970s" (Ravitch 1983, 251).

Despite supporters' efforts, continuing rumors and anecdotes of impossibly loud rooms, distracted students, and rampant permissiveness meant open classrooms became synonymous with the inadequacy of public education in many communities, and their numbers dwindled as their reputation plummeted. By 1975, a Gallup survey indicated that most American citizens admitted to not knowing what was meant by "the open school concept," and the minority that claimed to understand it were overwhelmingly opposed (Reese 2005, 280). In addition to loss of popular support, open classrooms were implicated as potentially counterproductive or even dangerous. Studies began to appear in the architectural and psychological literature detailing the noise and disruption of open offices and classrooms, with some hinting at potential discipline issues for children. Studies of open environments continue to be popular today, especially given the casual office atmosphere of the 21st century, but the research offers mixed results. A significant literature review performed in 2008 with applicability to educational contexts indicated that open-office environments may have deleterious health effects beyond noise and commotion issues. Examining articles and textbooks in online databases and search engines, the authors found evidence both for and against the open-office environment. The positive aspects included cost effectiveness, better communication and greater collaboration, and employee equality. But open workplaces were linked to loss of concentration, low productivity, privacy and status conflicts, feelings of insecurity, job dissatisfaction, high staff turnover, and several stress-related illnesses, including flu, exhaustion, high blood pressure, and musculoskeletal problems (Oommen, Knowles, and Zhao 2008).

The dream of unobstructed interior space facilitating a loosely controlled group of activities did not die in the mid-1970s, however. The open classroom's legacy lives on in American classrooms in the form of movable desks gathered together, free movement around the room, small-group lessons, and student choice of pursuits. Team teaching might be added to this list. In other words, open-classroom practices have become mainstream to such an extent as to become invisible, and they appear in primary and secondary schools alike. Even today, in the second decade of the 21st century, some educators and architects remain excited by the combination of these practices and the open-space environments originally spawned by them years ago. Schools in the planning and construction stages across the country demonstrate a recommitment to the school without walls, as architects and educators strive to find ways to solve its noise and commotion issues.

The Odd-Shaped Classroom

Some open-classroom spaces were quite different from the regimented rectangular boxes that had served as the foundation of public education for centuries. The liberal atmosphere of pedagogic experimentation seems to have inspired architects to search for expressive forms for enclosing classroom space (often without interior subdivisions) that might enhance the unusual activities taking place within. Creative classroom shapes often arose from decisions about the overall school footprint, but just as often, they were inspired solely by the room's potential uses. In the 1960s, architects introduced unconventional schoolroom configurations like hexagons, octagons, polygons, circles, wedges, trapezoids, and parallelograms. These were not new ideas; as far back as 1954, William Caudill predicted that classroom experimentation was just beginning with the L-shaped room popularized by the Crow Island School: "There are strong arguments for the circle, the pentagon, the octagon, the hexagon, and even the parallelogram . . . It has been said that the size and shape of the classroom cannot be determined until the number of pupils has been established and the kinds of activities have been set." While he recognized the interrelated nature of pedagogy, curriculum, and architecture, admitting that the function, equipment, furniture, and storage requirements of the classroom determined its exact form, Caudill also acknowledged the crucial role of modern architecture's "broadened concept of space." He aptly described the spirit of the new classroom in modernist imagery, exclaiming, "No longer are classrooms cages in which to work" (Caudill 1954, 28, 137).

Caudill may have been responding to the success of Perkins & Will's Heathcote Elementary School (1953) in Scarsdale, New York, the earliest renowned example of a **cluster plan** school. Heathcote assembled four classrooms in a pod at the end of a long corridor, removing the rooms from the main building to form their "own little school." The four classrooms allowed students from two consecutive grades to mingle but kept the youngest and oldest children far apart. While the cluster idea had been evolving for some time as a somewhat natural progression of the school building's decentralization, what made Heathcote unique was the cluster's reliance on hexagonal classrooms. Each classroom in the school had six sides, four of which were entirely transparent. Steeply pitched gable roofs led to tented ceilings above the rooms, which combined with the windows that rose from small bench seats all the way to the ceiling to create an unprecedented open experience. To enhance the feeling of openness, the architects minimized the roofs supports by resting them on thin brick piers flanking the main walls. Lawrence Perkins evocatively compared these classrooms and their open yet sheltered quality to the space beneath a tree.

Heathcote's hexagonal classrooms were unusual, but no one involved with the project viewed them as a gimmick; rather, progressive advocates considered them a great advance in the design of educational space. The EFL explained the reasons behind the hexagon: "one, that the typical rectangular or square classroom traps unusable space in the sharply angled corners, while the wider angles of the hexagon provide greater amounts of usable floor and wall area; two, the fact that children learn a great deal from their peers, perhaps, as much as from adults. A space shaped to direct youngsters toward each other has its own subtle educational value. There is no front or back to the classrooms at Heathcote" (EFL 1960, 11). In addition to these pedagogical and social advantages, the hexagons seemed more open spatially than the conventional classroom but at the same time sheltered and protected, all due to the architects' ability to manipulate the walls and roof.

The school was an architectural success and an educational inspiration. EFL literature published years after its opening praised Heathcote for earning the affection of all users. Children were so fond of the building they had to be kept off the premises before school and shooed away afterward, and the number of applications for teaching positions increased in number and quality. Furthermore, the EFL credited the classroom clusters with having a significant effect on the school's program by directly influencing teachers to spontaneously adopt team teaching techniques, sharing time and splitting duties, while also increasing teachers' freedom in grouping students. Because each four-classroom bundle spanned two grade levels, students could easily move between two or more of those rooms to make the best use of their individual abilities. Overall, then, the building's design enhanced educators' ability to explore team teaching and ungraded grouping options.

Other architects eagerly studied Caudill's suggestions, supported by educators and groups like the EFL, which urged designers to deliberately set aside right-angled walls and explore the variety and freedom possible in nonrectilinear rooms. Publications from the time indicate that conventional classrooms were highly regarded, however. Clearly, some architects and educators were dissatisfied by these unorthodox, "undirected" spaces. William Bruce probably spoke for many when he labeled the popularity of nontraditional, multisided classrooms "disturbing" and fretted that "these odd-shaped rooms have an element of inflexibility not found in the older type of quadrilateral rooms" (Bruce 1963, 48).

The Windowless Classroom

The 1960s spirit of pedagogical and architectural experimentation in schools gave rise to the windowless classroom, a trend that provoked some controversy during its brief run of popularity. Schoolrooms without windows were the triumph of technology to some, symbolic of design released from the vagaries of daylight and without the eternal distraction of the outdoors, while to others they signified an extreme indifference to children's psychological needs. They initially emerged, however, in an immediate postwar environment where cost effectiveness was crucial. In other words, windowless classrooms began as a way to save money and would always bear that stigma even when created for other reasons.

In 1949, on the eve of a nearly two-decade school-enrollment surge, the influential journal *Architectural Forum* commissioned architect Matthew Nowicki to design a school using the standard bay dimension (24 by 24 feet) used for American industrial buildings. The editors were curious about how close that bay was in size to a typical classroom. The clear need for mass-produced school-building components surely entered into their thinking as well. Nowicki responded with what would later be commonly known as a **loft plan**, where the building was left completely undivided inside except for support columns and, if desired, movable partitions. Frequently, loft plan buildings were illuminated from above, depending more on skylights than windows. These features replicated the most popular industrial buildings when spread horizontally and the office skyscraper when stacked vertically. Nowicki's proposal was no exception. Most of its interior light would come through plastic bubbles placed across the school's roof in a domino pattern. The sidewalls held only a few small windows shaped as vertical slots between masonry panels. While Nowicki's design did not include a windowless classroom per se, it offered an alternative to the typical school designs of the time with their obsession with daylight and windows.

The *Forum* praised Nowicki's school for its cost efficiency, singling out the reduced expense for glass and the shorter peripheral wall while overlooking the expense of custom-made, waterproof Plexiglas or plastic bubbles. Another article in the same issue captured a different aspect of Nowicki's economical proposal that proved equally significant. The article focused on multiuse corridors. After praising some early attempts to make corridors more efficient, the writer lamented that all of these efforts were hampered by the architects' dependence on windows. In the author's opinion, Nowicki's project offered a viable alternative "by assuming that minor use areas of schools need not have a view out, and can get their light from above, as interior areas of industrial plants do" ("Toward Better Schools" 1949, 101).

Within a few years, this had become a full-fledged design concept. School buildings with windowless classrooms captured the attention of administrators in cash-strapped local school districts. By the mid-1960s, the windowless classroom's economic advantages began to be supplemented with explanations of its potential pedagogical advantages—and psychological detriments. Teachers seemed to enjoy the lack of glare, the easily controlled temperature, and the apparent increase in children's attention levels, and they even recognized the cost effectiveness of a windowless school, but some questioned whether something valuable had been lost in the transition. Educators who tested students in windowless classrooms to investigate this possibility, however, indicated that windows had little impact on the child's ability to learn.

Although the windowless school building seemed to have no effect on students' learning, it certainly offended the aesthetic sensibilities of parents and other citizens. The windowless school's image became that of a place of incarceration, especially those urban schools that sprouted in cities across the country during the flurry of postwar school construction. A debate arose as architects and educators lauded windowless schools' ability to save money while sparing children the constant visual reminder of the deteriorating environments that often surrounded these schools, and opponents attacked the schools as ugly, poorly designed fortresses or prisons for children.

One windowless school in particular highlighted the complex interplay among educators' goals, architects' desires, and local community perceptions. Intermediate School 201, or the Arthur A. Schomburg School (IS 201), opened in 1966 in Harlem as a showcase junior high school intended to symbolize the future of New York City's public-school system. The architects were Curtis & Davis of New Orleans, who had been recognized in the past for their school designs in that city. They found the urban site, next to elevated train tracks in a deteriorating neighborhood, to be a much different challenge than the spacious lots afforded schools in New Orleans.

Arthur Schomburg School in the Harlem neighborhood of New York City, designed by Curtis & Davis (1966). Also known as I.S. 201, this became the most publicized example of the windowless school—an urban phenomenon that polarized educators, parents, and school designers. (Corbis/Bettmann Archive/Getty Images)

In response, Curtis & Davis designed a self-contained building with no traditional windows. It appeared as a stark, two-story brick box with a concrete frame raised off the ground by 14-foot-tall tapered concrete piers. The brick walls were textured to provide visual interest but largely lacked openings except for a few vertical strips where small perforations in the wall marked the ends of internal corridors; in those spots, a glass wall behind the brick screen illuminated the hallways. The cafeteria, gymnasium, and other rooms were placed partly underground, and the space beneath the elevated building was intended to serve as a playground for the surrounding neighborhood, an important concern since the area lacked a community center or other recreational amenities for its children. A central air-conditioning system—one of the first in a New York school—compensated for the lack of windows.

The educators and architects involved with the project were proud of their practical approach: the windowless walls reduced construction and maintenance costs, and the insulated building blocked the noise and distraction of the adjacent train tracks. The building's open plan and movable walls were additional points of pride. Curtis & Davis's design was well received by the architectural community, collecting the top prize in the annual New York City School Awards Program sponsored by New York's AIA chapter. IS 201 gained a reputation as *the* windowless school due to the publicity surrounding its opening, but it was by no means alone. Windowless classrooms' brief popularity during the 1970s energy crisis and aftermath was widespread, as were entire buildings like IS 201 with no visible windows.

In itself, the windowless classroom failed to alter the classroom as much as seal it off from contact with the outside; this required no particular shape or arrangement of walls or desks. But anecdotal evidence seems to have been powerful enough that even ardent supporters of architectural innovation, like the EFL, withheld their enthusiasm when addressing windowless classrooms. An EFL publication reporting on a symposium of architects, teachers, and administrators cosponsored by the Institute for the Development of Educational Activities (IDEA), for example, displayed none of the confidence of typical accounts: "The conferees admitted that one architectural problem has not yet been solved—schools with or without windows. While having no windows in a school minimizes the problems involved in climate control and cross lighting, a number of conferees pointed out that elementary children object to not being able to look outside" (EFL 1970, 29).

Since the 1970s, decades of research has revealed the positive effects of natural views on people inside buildings, but other research continues to find advantages to windowless classrooms, including more wall space, better lighting, reduced noise and maintenance, greater temperature control, and no overall differences in academic achievement. So the windowless classroom continues on into the 21st century, with fewer proponents than in the past but still a legitimate option in some situations. Recent tragic events at schools, however, have made security more of a priority than ever, with the result that transparent or semitransparent interior rooms are becoming more common in the design of new schools, as explained in the next chapter.

The Technological Classroom

A strong argument can be made that the open-space-classroom model was the last major change to the physical space of the classroom. Since the mid-1970s, as outlined above, many of the model's constituent parts have become standard in contemporary schools, like movable furniture, activity areas, and an overall environment that can accommodate multiple endeavors simultaneously. But such elements now take place almost exclusively within a rectangular space bounded by four walls. The traditional-classroom model—which envisions the classroom as the building block for the school (both conceptually and architecturally), with classroom activities circumscribed by some kind of limitation (subject matter, grade level, etc.)—still dominates American public-school systems.

The particular expression of education, however, continues to change, and the most powerful agent of the past two decades has been the increasing impact of technological developments. Many of the recent advances have had a substantial influence on teaching practices, but in almost all cases, the new technology has simply replaced an earlier tool used for a similar purpose: for example, an interactive whiteboard (such as the SMART Board) is an updated, high-tech blackboard. But computers are something altogether different. Fulfilling a dream first manifested in the 1920s, computers have seemingly infinite possibilities for presenting material in an interesting and effective manner, especially through interconnectivity and specialized software, and teachers at all grade levels are relying on them more and more. This has introduced a new problem to classroom design. While many colleges now require students to purchase and use portable laptop computers, our nation's public schools, always under financial constraints, tend to rely on desktop versions, which occupy more space. Designers are investigating ways to accommodate them. The physical size of computers themselves, the wiring necessary to connect terminals or even laptops if wireless access is not available, the space needed for server equipment, airflow requirements to dissipate the heat emanating from the system—all of these require new solutions.

It is difficult to predict what future classrooms will look like given the extraordinarily rapid pace of technological development and the expanding marketplace of educational software. However, barring unforeseen circumstances, the essence of schoolrooms will probably remain much the same as always: segregated spaces where a group of students and their teacher(s) can interact in intimate or group settings, using the techniques of the day.

Chapter 2

SCHOOLHOUSES

School architecture is subject to fads and trends like any other field of endeavor, but over the course of American history, at least three themes recur in regard to the design of the schoolhouse as a whole: the decentralization of the building into differentiated spaces to adapt to curricular adjustments (beginning in the 19th century); the influence of health and safety considerations; and the impact of external pressures like population shifts and economic fluctuations.

The first school buildings in North America opened in the English colonies over 300 years ago. For more than half of that time, most schools consisted of either a single room or a small grouping of identical or nearly identical rooms. Schoolhouses, as they became known rather early, were not asked to do much by educators, and as a result, even the largest urban schools tended to be rather simple stacks of classrooms. But then, a multitude of forces converged in the latter part of the 19th century to alter the schoolhouse, including rising student enrollments, curricular changes, and mass migration and immigration to America's cities. In response, school architects—working with educators, as the field of school design became a recognized specialty—initiated a campaign that dispersed the blocky buildings of previous generations into distinct units and differentiated interior spaces according to their use. Specialized rooms for nontraditional activities—like shop classes, home economics, cooking, and even physical education—appeared for the first time. School buildings with alphabet-shaped footprints (e.g., U, E, and T shapes) arose as school experts strove to separate spaces by their use and make the building as healthy and safe as possible. As public education assumed a greater role in American society, the buildings began to reflect this new status by embracing the architectural language of civic architecture, which included a more monumental appearance and the adoption of appropriate historical styles.

Decentralization began in the late 19th century when high schools expanded their curricula to accommodate nonacademic courses of study. Studies show a dramatic increase in course offerings in the first three decades of the new century and reveal that most of this growth was in nonacademic subjects. These classes were practical in nature, usually requiring machinery or special equipment and manual work of some kind, which meant educators needed to find alternatives to the standard schoolroom space. The initial response by school designers was to simply enlarge the existing schoolhouse prototype to add these rooms and judiciously place them according to their use. For example, a successful design did not situate the music room next to a classroom or library. Specialized rooms caused the buildings to expand horizontally as well as vertically, taking up more space and necessitating larger lots. At the turn of the 20th century, the first truly modern schoolhouses were designed and constructed—large, fireproof school buildings containing an auditorium, gymnasium, and specialized rooms, like science laboratories and manual training shops. By the 1910s, urban-school buildings had assumed their modern form.

High schools led the way in this development out of necessity. The demands of new nonacademic subjects in the nation's high schools compelled a reshaping of the building. A 1919 study documented the high school's rapid transformation over the previous decade. The author's analysis of over 150 high-school floor plans printed in the *American School Board Journal* between 1908 and 1917 revealed an amazing 109 different types of rooms. The majority of the school buildings depicted, independent of the size of the community in which they were built, contained *at least* the following rooms: "class- or recitation-rooms, a chemical and physical laboratory, with a lecture or demonstration room for these sciences, an assembly room or auditorium with a stage for same, a library room, a gymnasium, an office for the principal, a room for general storage, and boys' and girls' toilets . . . to this meager list may be added some provision for manual training and domestic science . . . for the larger communities we may also add a laboratory for biology, a mechanical-drawing room, boys' and girls' locker-rooms, and a reception- or waiting-room to the principal's office" (Koos 1919, 593–594).

This remarkable diversity and complexity truly distinguished the modern high school from its predecessors. It also initiated a decentralization process whereby the blocky, cubic school building began to grow and spread across the urban and rural landscape, with rectangular or square footprints giving way to E-, U-, T-, and H-shaped configurations that permitted educators to efficiently "zone" school interiors, keeping noisier or more disruptive activities away from rooms where quieter environments were required or optimizing natural light for art studios. Safety considerations also favored the move away from the old-time schoolhouse; the newer-generation buildings tended to have fewer floors and more stairways and access points to facilitate evacuation in case of fire (a very widespread problem at the time), and their shapes allowed more fresh air and sunlight to penetrate school interiors. As described below, many architects and educators—especially those attuned to the development of modernist architectural ideas—advocated greater exposure to nature for reasons of physical and psychological health, and the decentralized schoolhouse enabled greater continuity between indoors and outdoors.

The 1920s and 1930s saw the introduction of modern architecture, with its emphases on function, economy, and health, leading to extensive innovations in interwar school buildings like lower profiles, more windows, informal planning, and emphasis on outdoor classrooms. Many of these advances originated with European modernist immigrants like Richard Neutra and William Lescaze. With the economic depression, World War II, and postwar baby boom occurring in sequence, educators and architects spent 20 years reconceiving the schoolhouse in an atmosphere of constraint, where small budgets and simple construction were the norm. These hard years were followed by an age of abundance and a postwar suburban explosion that prompted a golden age of school architecture. Architects created new floor plans that spread the school's parts across suburban landscapes while educators began to experiment with innovative, sometimes radical methods that often required architectural responses, like the open classroom. But then shrinking enrollments and an energy crisis in the 1970s forced educators and architects to reassess the postwar school; the result was a compact, sometimes fortresslike mass, especially in urban areas. School buildings in the 1980s and 1990s reflected the popularity of postmodern architecture. Many were designed as single structures intentionally made to look like a compilation of disparate parts, and unique facade configurations with contrasting materials emerged. Behind the walls, however, a back-to-basics movement led educators to redirect curricula toward traditional academic subjects, and at the same time, architects revisited qualities first introduced in the monumental-school era, including alphabet-shaped floor plans, grand public entrances, and a more imposing aesthetic image incorporating historical architectural elements. In the first decades of the new century, school buildings continue to display a variety of shapes and sizes, flavored by new concerns like security and sustainability, but the basic components of their composition and the relationship of those components to each other remain relatively unaltered.

The schoolhouse's physical decentralization culminated in the post–World War II suburban school. Americans flocked to the suburbs in record numbers after the war while the birth rate soared. The resulting baby boom challenged educators' ability to rapidly develop inexpensive buildings capable of easy alteration and expansion. In many communities, it was impossible to accurately predict enrollment growth for even one year; administrators were trained to assume that their building eventually would need to expand. Designers took advantage of larger suburban lots to elongate school facilities. Their ideal school was a one-story structure surrounded by playgrounds and athletic fields, often with individual classrooms acting as independent structures loosely attached to indoor or outdoor corridors. In terms of their physical environment, many larger suburban schools had more in common with college campuses than old-fashioned cubic buildings. Toward the end of the century, external pressures like the energy crisis and the sustainability movement and internal changes in curriculums and standardized testing influenced architects to contract school buildings into compact forms and to question the usefulness of the campus model (except in suburban or rural locations, where land was plentiful); inside the school, however, the decentralization that characterized the evolution of the modern school remained firmly in place. Today, school buildings come in all shapes and sizes, but all remain connected to the first modern schoolhouses of the 20th century—sometimes through their forms, materials, and layouts but always in terms of the ongoing impact of decentralization and health concerns.

Early School Buildings

Education in the colonies and first few years of the republic tended to be a small-scale affair. For generations, communities managed their needs with existing buildings—any space large enough to hold the children and master would suffice. In many cases, classes were offered by individuals in their own homes. When parental interest and population growth combined to increase the demand for schools, some cities and towns responded with the kind of primitive one-room structure described in Chapter 1. One of the most prevalent criticisms of schoolhouses, made by educational reformers and former students alike, concerned their location. Community participation may have reflected citizens' high regard for education, but their investment was not always visible in the schoolhouse itself. In those places where children were fortunate to have a dedicated building for their studies, the school often occupied land that nobody else wanted or that could be purchased cheaply, such as at the bottom of a hill, on swampy soil, or adjacent to busy roads or railroad tracks. A document written by Horace Mann introduced the problem. In his first annual report as the secretary of the Massachusetts Board of Education in 1838, Mann appended a statement of over 60 pages devoted to the state's schools. His account was remarkable for its solitary focus on the design and furnishing of schoolhouses. Prior to this time, educators published few comments on school architecture in any venue.

Mann's opinions sprung from personal experience. He claimed to have inspected nearly 800 school buildings across the commonwealth, which, if true, provided him with far more experience in evaluating schools than any other individual in the country. His complaints regarding the schoolhouse's physical environment ranged from its siting to its construction. Mann argued that school buildings were commonly built too close to an existing public road and too often forced to the geographical center of a school district without regard for the quality of the land. Other examples of inappropriate locations for schools included those placed in a "bleak and unsheltered situation," buildings on a "sandy plain without shade or shelter" or on "low marshy grounds," and schools constructed on "a little remnant or delta of land, where roads encircle it on all sides." Mann urged educators to select, instead of these poor choices, natural sites with woods and hills to help mitigate inclement weather, far from roads and other buildings where distracting activities might interfere with the educational process, as a way to contribute to students' development of "a sensibility to beauty" (Mann 1838, 6, 29).

A decade later, when Henry Barnard published a second edition of his book *School Architecture*, little had changed, prompting Barnard to repeat Mann's litany of unsatisfactory schoolhouse sites. Such criticisms applied more to rural situations, however, since urban schools on crowded city blocks faced their own challenges. While rural educators struggled to erect decent quality buildings in healthy or less-dangerous locations, their urban colleagues often had difficulty finding enough space to house their students. Commentators like Mann and Barnard forcefully argued for school buildings in parklike settings surrounded by nature and removed from danger and distraction. Barnard wanted as much nature as possible around the school or, at the very least, a rear lot behind city schools for a decent and protected playground. Similarly, those few publications addressing school design before the Civil War tended to illustrate schoolhouses as Elysian visions with extensive landscaped grounds. In reality, however, urban-school buildings joined their neighbors in being constructed along busy streets, pushed out to property boundaries in an effort to gain as much interior space as possible.

Urban schoolhouses in the early to mid-19th century were small and unsophisticated because low enrollments and narrow curricular and pedagogical requirements reduced the need for specialized spaces. As outlined in the previous chapter, students were taught all subjects in the same classroom, where they sat on benches or at desks bolted to the floor in neat, orderly rows facing the teacher's desk, which was often on a raised platform. The buildings that held these schoolrooms tended to be square or rectangular and compact in form: most rural schools were a single story, while city buildings could reach up to four stories in height. Basements held heating equipment, storage, wardrobes, and washrooms. Each floor above the first was subdivided into equal-sized, identical classrooms. If the building had an assembly hall for gathering the students, it was almost always on the top floor. From one building to the next, however, schoolrooms inside these schoolhouses varied widely in size and slightly in shape. Most were rectangular or square, like the buildings themselves, with windows in all exterior walls. The floor plans of these buildings tended to fall into one of a handful of types. One group of smaller schools (which might be thought of as the "stuffed box" plan) had no internal corridors; individual rooms on the upper floors were accessible through staircases. The second group had a single corridor running across the building, usually lengthwise if the building was rectangular. The third group had cross-shaped or T-plan corridors. All of these colonial and early republican buildings shared common characteristics: they were not designed with circulation, ventilation, or lighting as important considerations as later schools would be, and they generally held only classrooms, an assembly room, and an office for the headmaster. Occasionally a classroom was altered by introducing scientific equipment or removing walls to increase its size, and some schools included small recitation rooms for intimate instruction, but as a whole there were no specially designed rooms in the schoolhouse.

The earliest school structures were constructed with wooden frames and walls. As more students became involved in the educational system, safety concerns compelled educators to utilize brick or even stone wall construction if they were affordable. On the exterior, school buildings of all kinds were utilitarian in appearance, although some architects attempted to mimic the popular period styles in muted forms. For example, architects could intimate Greek Revival style, considered appropriate for educational buildings, with simple elements like pilasters or a pediment over a doorway. Small-scale grandeur could also be achieved through the judicious use of arches, moldings, corner quoins, and cupolas or bell towers. Religious buildings and large private homes were attractive models for school designers. In New England in particular, the early generations of school buildings derived their forms from religious meetinghouses, thereby serving to visually connect the nascent education system with the region's religious traditions.

In cities and larger villages with enough students to support primary, grammar, and secondary schools, single buildings combined them all. Primary classes, for the youngest children just learning to read, often occupied the basement of a grammar-school building; parings of grammar- and high-school classes in the same structure also were common. The search for space in the largest cities could lead to multifunctioning buildings. In Boston, for example, administrators regularly included engine houses (fire stations) and/or watch houses (police stations) in grammar-school buildings until the 1840s.

19TH-CENTURY DEVELOPMENTS

The Quincy School

The first architecturally significant school building in the United States was the Josiah Quincy Grammar School. As introduced in Chapter 1, the Quincy School transformed American education with its division into individual classrooms. The building's appearance, as a rather stark four-story structure of brick construction with a gable-and-valley roof, was typical of Boston's schools, even if its internal organization was unique. The Quincy School had a rectangular footprint that was subdivided inside by a corridor along the shorter axis on the first through third floors. On each side of the corridor, two schoolrooms were placed back to back; each could hold up to 60 students. The building's fourth floor closely approximated other Boston schoolrooms, containing an open space with no dividing walls and a 16-foot-high ceiling. It was used for large gatherings and could hold all of the school's students at once.

The graded classroom (or the "Quincy plan"), like common schools, remained more of a dream than a reality for much of the 19th century. Although the entire American public-school system would eventually be divided into age-grade levels, initial progress was slow and limited to larger cities with enough students to attempt the experiment. Within a few years, Boston had opened three more grammar schools on the Quincy plan, for example. Prominent educators like Henry Barnard and Horace Mann championed its effectiveness, and Barnard described the Quincy School at length in subsequent editions of *School Architecture*, but in rural areas outside of New England (and especially in the Southern states), graded schools took decades to become established. When they did, they began

Second Josiah Quincy Grammar School, Boston, original design by Gridley J. F. Bryant (1848). This rebuilt structure copied the first Quincy School (destroyed by fire in 1858), which introduced the graded school concept to American education. (Boston Athenaeum)

to fundamentally change elementary-school buildings at the same time as the first generation of high-school houses appeared.

Boston Latin and English High School

The newly opened Boston Latin and English High School was described in an 1881 letter to the *American Journal of Education* as "by far the best specimen of school architecture in the country, – the first conspicuous example of a *new type*" (Philbrick 1881, 401). The letter's author was John D. Philbrick, former superintendent of the Boston schools, who had intimate knowledge of the building and its design. Philbrick partially based his opinion on the fact that the building exhibited architectural aspects previously unknown in American schools, such as interior light courts, a military drill hall, and toilets on every floor, as well as rarely used features like a gymnasium. The Boston Latin and English High School marked the beginning of a major transformation in American school architecture.

Philbrick had been involved in the development of the landmark Quincy School as its headmaster and may have had input into that school's design. His curiosity about the physical environment of education continued during his two terms as superintendent of the Boston schools. In that position, Philbrick toured Europe and took particular interest in European school architecture. In a letter to Henry Barnard, he admitted to being deeply impressed by the Akademische Gymnasium in Vienna. The Akademische Gymnasium building was a four-story hollow square with classrooms arranged around the outside of the building and corridors ringing the interior court. Like other Austrian and Prussian schools, it

Boston Latin and English High School, designed by George A. Clough (1877). This was the first school in the United States to include influences from Prussian school design, including internal courtyards, and a significant number of specialized rooms to supplement the standard classrooms. (City of Boston Archives)

included a gymnasium space for physical activities and an examination hall for large-group instruction in addition to regular classrooms. In terms of size, efficient layout, and number of special rooms, no school building in America could compare.

The Akademische Gymnasium probably influenced the Latin and English High School's design. City architect George A. Clough created the school in 1877, probably with Philbrick's input. The building proved exceptional in many ways. Its wide variety of specialized rooms for the time—science lecture rooms, a chemistry laboratory, and administrative offices—was unique. Other contemporary schools had some of these rooms but rarely all of them. But the Boston Latin and English's salient features, adapted from the Akademische Gymnasium, were the interior courtyards. This may have been the first instance of such a courtyard plan in an American school. Rooms were placed around these courts on the outside of a **single-loaded corridor**, just as in the Prussian schools Philbrick admired. Arranging schoolrooms around these courtyards increased the amount of air available to them. The plan also improved students' circulation within the building. In addition to these innovative features, other factors shaped the building's design. Health concerns inspired administrators to include the gymnasium. Safety concerns were evident in the state-of-the-art fireproof construction and in the location of the two-story chemistry laboratory in a corner of the building separated from the rest of the school by fireproof walls. And care was taken to adorn the corridors with statuary for the students' aesthetic appreciation. Some aspects of the design, however, were firmly within 19th-century tradition. Room sizes were standardized at 32 by 24 feet, with no spatial differentiation for the subjects taught within them. The auditorium was located on the top floor, indicating that it was for student use only and generally inaccessible to the public. And the building's exterior reflected common stylistic tastes, appearing somewhat as an enlarged version of an upper-class Boston house with its large, sloping roofs and conspicuous chimneys.

High Schools

The Boston Latin and English High School was an important early milestone in American school architecture. Two decades after opening, it was still being praised by educators and architects as the first well-designed American school building. Just as the Quincy School determined the basic format for 19th-century grammar schools, the Boston Latin and English High School provided a model for the modern high school. It was appropriate that such a significant design came from the secondary level of education. The invention of the high school was a crucial achievement of the 19th century. From rough beginnings as a finishing school for small groups of students, high schools evolved into a dominant institution that prepared teenagers for adult life.

Secondary education developed much later in this country than primary schools. The first American high school that can truly be called "public" (in the sense that it was supported by tax revenues) was the Boston English Classical School, which opened in 1821 as an alternative to the city's venerable Latin Grammar School. The latter offered a classical curriculum, with Latin and Greek as the main subjects. As a contrast, the educators who created the English Classical School intended it to be more practically oriented. Boys over 12 years of age who passed a rigorous entrance examination were eligible to undertake a 3-year course offering advanced work in English literature, ancient and American history, mathematics, and science. Boston's educators hoped this broader curriculum might appeal to a wider population base. The English Classical School's lead was not quickly followed, however, as others larger cities formed public high schools at a rather leisurely pace, including Philadelphia (1838), Cleveland (1846), New York (1847), Cincinnati (1847), St. Louis (1856), and Chicago (1856). Despite a slow start, approximately 80 cities had opened public high schools by 1851 (Herbst 1996, 42).

The earliest buildings housing these high schools—for those few not located in existing grammar-school buildings—were modest, as the pedagogical techniques and curricular requirements of the day placed few demands on designers. High schools across the country, like their elementary-school counterparts, tended to be square or rectangular one- to four-story blocks with minimal ornamentation or architectural embellishment. Since almost all subjects were taught in the same way, from English grammar to the sciences, there was little need for specifically tailored spaces. In a related manner, curricula across the country demonstrated a high degree of similarity. High schoolers in the 19th-century took academically oriented classes that leaned heavily toward such classical fields of study as Latin and Greek, algebra and geometry, history, and sciences like geography and botany.

From these simple origins, the high school spread throughout the States, becoming particularly popular in larger cities. However, despite Americans' general enthusiasm for education, some tended to view secondary education with skepticism. Wary of big government, they believed public, state-sponsored education to be the death knell for local political control and could lead to higher taxes and infringe upon individual freedom. This led to contentious battles in many cities. Even after municipalities created public high schools, they were by no means unanimously accepted. Detroit educators faced a bitter battle over the necessity of a public high school in the early 1880s, more than 20 years after the city's school opened, while opponents persuaded Cleveland's public-school superintendent to investigate "the so-called High school question" in 1885 after charges of elitism were raised against an institution that had existed in that city for nearly four decades (Akers 1901, 212).

Among the considerations that fueled resistance to public high schools, three were most significant. The first involved the very legitimacy of secondary education. Many citizens felt the purpose of public education should be limited to moral character building and the three R's, all of which were addressed at the elementary and primary levels. They could see no benefit to extending formal schooling beyond that point. The *Chicago Tribune* argued for a greater investment in the lower grades rather than the high school by querying "whether it is more important that a large number of persons should learn to read, write, and cipher, or that a smaller number should learn the differential calculus and the catalogue of the ships" ("Reducing the School Expenses" 1878, 4). This position was stronger before the 1880s, when high schools had not yet begun to teach manual skills and offer vocational training. Before and just after the Civil War, these schools offered little if any "practical" education for America's youth.

A second and often more compelling factor giving rise to public-high-school opposition involved the necessity of child labor. Despite reform efforts beginning in the 1830s, vast numbers of high-school-aged children—in both urban and rural settings—worked rather than attending school. Many American families could not afford the luxury of unemployed children, relying on their meager earnings for survival or to make modest economic progress. A child in school was a child not working. High-school enrollment statistics confirm child labor's impact. Throughout the 19th century, high schools were populated by youths whose parents could afford to let them spend the better part of three or four years preparing for the future, which meant only a small percentage of all teenagers.

A third reason some contested public high schools, although it may be difficult for us to understand today, was that throughout the 19th century much of the public considered high schools to be undemocratic and therefore contrary to our national ethos. Many Americans perceived the high school not as a "people's college" but as an elitist enclave. Criticisms ranged from the legal (using public tax revenues to fund a "palace of privilege" for a minority of "wealthy" children while ignoring the majority violated state constitutions) to the absurd (the word "high" was too exclusive and signaled elite status). In response, educators worked tirelessly to expand the socioeconomic range of their students and to persuade naysayers that the public high school was the very antithesis of an undemocratic institution. However, there was an element of truth to the critics' claims. Although enrollment of students with blue-collar fathers increased slightly during the second half of the century, the majority of high school students were somewhat privileged. High school students in St. Louis with fathers who were clerks, managers, businessmen, or professionals, as measured by the board of education, remained steady at around 60 percent of the total enrollment (Graves 1998). In the late 19th century, 80 percent of the 13- to 16-year-old sons of professional fathers attended St. Louis's public schools, compared to only 32 percent of the children of unskilled workers (Troen 1975). To deflect elitist criticism, educators repeatedly underscored the high school's egalitarian nature.

Public high schools remained ill-defined institutions with multiple problems throughout most of the 19th century. High-school enrollments continued to comprise only a small portion of the nation's total student population. A mere 4 percent of America's public-school students in 1873 were in high schools. In 1880, only 3.7 percent of children ages 14 to 17 were enrolled in secondary education nationwide. A survey conducted in 1890 found that the average high school student attended just 86 days, and the graduation rate was a paltry 10.7 percent (Tyack and Hansot 1992; Angus and Mirel 1999; Cuban 1993). High-school teachers, including many recent graduates, were barely competent, and facilities were inadequate. But the most pressing problem concerned the curriculum. Urban educators in the late 19th century were not prepared for the types of students the high schools now were responsible for educating. A mass exodus from country to city, rising foreign immigration, and increasing child-labor and compulsory-attendance legislation brought more students to America's high schools, but these schools were not constituted to accommodate the newcomers' wide-ranging interests and abilities.

By midcentury, educators recognized that an attractive and expensive schoolhouse could advertise the high school to the middle-class parents of potential students; this was a crucial development, since secondary schooling as a whole was still viewed with skepticism by a substantial portion of society. The impressive appearance of these new high-school buildings hid relatively simple interiors. Classrooms were the building blocks and main components of these schools. Their standardized and interchangeable character echoed the rigid nature of pedagogy and curricula at this time. Some buildings had an assembly hall for such public events as graduations or awards ceremonies. These spaces were almost always on the top floor, because construction techniques were not sufficiently advanced to allow a large open space anywhere other than immediately below the roof. Such buildings might also include, tucked in among the classrooms, a principal's office, a small recitation room, or a "special" science room, which was often a normal classroom with a few pieces of scientific equipment. Overall, however, there remained few unique rooms in these schoolhouses.

Evolving public attitudes toward childhood and a concern for working youngsters were not the only new influences on American secondary education. In the early 20th century, the stage of life that we now know as adolescence was first recognized in psychological studies of the differences between younger and older children. The "invention" of adolescence had a permanent effect on American society. Historian Joseph Kett has pointed out that in the decades after 1900, "a biological process of maturation became the basis of the social definition of an entire age group," which resulted in "the massive reclassification of young people as adolescents and the creation of institutions to segregate them from casual contacts with adults" (Kett 1977, 215–216).

Educators, psychologists, journalists, jurists, and social workers were largely responsible for distinguishing this age group. A major catalyst for such interest was the seminal book *Adolescence* (1907), by psychologist G. Stanley Hall, leader of the "child study movement" in the late 19th century. Like much work in developmental studies at this time, Hall's approach was informed by evolutionary theory and its emphasis on change over time. He described the teenage years as "a stormy period of great agitation, when the very worst and best impulses in the human soul struggle against each other for its possession," and recommended that young adults be provided opportunities to participate in athletics, group activities, and other organizations to shelter them from the pressures of the adult world while they negotiated their way through this often-confusing stage of life (Hall 1907, 135).

A salient characteristic of the adolescent stage was a powerful desire to form peer associations. Hall therefore suggested that, rather than lose boys to wanton street gangs, their natural impulse to congregate could be accommodated through boys' clubs and playground organizations, which would provide them with productive outlets for their energies. Progressive Era playgrounds were not simply urban parks with teeter-totters and sandboxes; they also provided the opportunity for adults to properly direct children's behavior in ways that would promote moral and cognitive development. Reformers considered urban playgrounds so crucial that they persuaded city governments to spend over $100 million on playgrounds during this period (Reese 2002).

Other factors, in addition to shifting conceptions of childhood and adolescence, have been advanced to explain the prolonging of childhood dependency in the 19th century, including the shrinking ratio of children to adults (making children scarcer and more precious) and the increasing complexity of a production-oriented society. And there was a Darwinian argument as well; according to a Chicago public-school superintendent, evolution favored extended childhood. "We are realizing and striving to obey the biologic law," wrote E. Benjamin Andrews, "that the species, race or nation that longest protects and trains its young is the most powerful in the struggle for life" (Andrews 1900, 269). Whatever the sources, the consequence of this revised perception of America's youth as adolescents was that it set them apart from—and considered them not quite ready for—the adult world. If teenagers were not to be treated like small children but were not yet prepared for work, what were they to do with their time, and how were they supposed to channel all the powerful impulses described by Hall into constructive behavior? The logical answer was to keep them in school. Public education became the nation's leading adolescent-raising institution. Educators would have to remodel their curricula and facilities accordingly. But the mental-discipline and moral-virtue traditions still reigned, and few urban high schools were in a position to fulfill their new responsibility to broaden the educational mission.

Population statistics reveal that American cities contained more teenagers in the late 19th century than at any previous time. But that fact did not necessarily correlate with higher secondary-school enrollments. Something beyond poorly enforced legal decrees had to entice adolescents into the schools. Evidence suggests that a new attitude toward secondary education was a major influence on the rising high-school enrollment. The public began to realize the virtues of expanded education for its young adults. The idea that school could lead one to a successful life and that education was a good thing in itself became more common. Working-class people started to look to education as a means to alleviate their economic anxieties and prepare their children to function in a new industrial world that was rapidly changing. In particular, the public's stance toward high schools improved during the Progressive Era. No longer considered elite "culture factories" for children of privilege, by the early 20th century, common people increasingly perceived the high school to be "the citizen's college"—a vehicle of social improvement that could benefit adolescents of all ethnic backgrounds and social classes.

The high school's elevated status was part of an emerging public trend toward recognizing education's role in maintaining social order and perpetuating cherished ideas like freedom and democracy—a partial resurgence of the native Protestant ideology so influential decades earlier. John Dewey, the nation's foremost progressive educator, asserted, "Education is the fundamental method of social progress and reform" (Dewey 1897, 30). Likewise, in *The Promise of American Life* (1909), the quintessential statement of American Progressivism, Herbert Croly preached education as the salvation of American democracy and the true path to individual self-improvement. "The real vehicle of improvement is education," wrote Croly. "It is by education that the American is trained for such democracy as he possesses; and it is by better education that he proposes to better his democracy" (Croly 1909, 400). However, although many agreed that education stood as a pillar of American society, problems arose when trying to determine just what education should be offered to the nation's adolescents.

As proponents worked to standardize a multitiered system of public education, they also tried to delineate the functions of each level. The primary grades were clearly for imparting basic skills and information, but neither the high school's mission nor its relation to higher education were so sharply distinguished. Some school officials clung to the 19th-century ideal of the high school as a place to train the elite, although "elite" came to mean intellectual more than social. They advanced the position that the nation had a selfish interest in nurturing generations of future leaders rather than leaving that obligation to chance. An alternate viewpoint focused on secondary education as a means for developing individual talents and personal values rather than as a breeding ground for future leaders. A third group of educators called upon the high school to specialize in vocational education to prepare teenagers for their adult jobs. This approach was aimed particularly at working-class youths. Under such a program, wrote an educator in 1882, "the poorest and most neglected child is led to feel that there is something in the world for him to do which shall be well worth doing" (Hancock 1882, 164). These positions often conflicted, and their tensions were never satisfactorily resolved. But all three perspectives attached a social significance to the high school that did not exist in previous generations.

Educators' growing concern over the unique characteristics of adolescence eventually led to the creation of junior high schools or middle schools. The initial junior high schools opened in the first decade of the 1900s. During the 1920s and 1930s, they became a national fad, their popularity driven by both educational and economic motives. On a practical level, the insertion of a new step on the educational ladder could alleviate high-school overcrowding by separating the seventh and eighth graders from the older students. In addition, educators and psychologists had identified early adolescents as a group with special needs; they believed that placing these youngsters together in their own school without the interference of younger or older classmates would stimulate their development. The junior high could also help to prepare those children for the types of subjects and classes they would encounter in high school. And junior-high-school systems could allow educators to begin the process of vocational channeling or tracking students into different courses of study, based on their interests and abilities, at a much earlier age. Their intention was to encourage those large numbers of children who dropped out after the eighth grade to remain in school. American manufacturers supported junior high schools because they promised an inexpensive way to train the growing non-college-bound workforce.

The creation of junior high schools (or middle schools) had no visible effect on school architecture. Architects around the country designed junior high schools in the same manner as high schools—albeit often at a reduced scale, given the smaller number of students in these grades—with manual and vocational facilities, gymnasiums, and auditoriums. Like their senior counterparts, junior high schools before World War II often made a symbolic statement with their monumental size and historical ornamentation.

The Image of the Schoolhouse

One of the more significant developments in school architecture involved a symbolic transition from the 19th-century "schoolhouse" to the 20th-century "school plant." While metaphors of the school as "temple" and "citadel" spanned the entire period, there is an undeniable shift in urban areas from a school architecture that largely imitated contemporary domestic models to an aesthetic that tried to evoke monumentality and importance on a limited budget. This evolution arose from the physically larger school buildings needed to meet expanded enrollments and the high school's new role in American society.

School buildings began as utilitarian objects and maintained that status for some time. The earliest writers on school architecture, like Horace Mann, focused on the sorry state of the ventilation, construction, and location of America's schools and tended to disregard the way they looked. When published articles commented on school design, starting in the 1830s, they privileged convenience over inspirational or didactic value. Even Henry Barnard, one of the first popular advocates of improved school architecture and the author of the earliest comprehensive American book on the subject, favored floor plans over facade designs in his publications. But he also advised that schoolhouses should "be calculated to inspire children and the community generally with respect for the object to which it is devoted" and be comparable in "attractiveness, convenience and durability with other public edifices." Barnard viewed the schoolhouse as "a temple, consecrated in prayer to the physical, intellectual, and moral culture of every child in the community," and thought it should be "associated in every heart with the earliest and strongest impressions of truth, justice, patriotism, and religion" (Barnard 1848, 55).

Despite such advice, the school building's aesthetic image did not change very much until after the Civil War. Urban-school systems used taxpayer funding to erect more and larger buildings, but their muted domestic or historic appearance paled in comparison to the architecture of other civic institutions, like government buildings or the ever-growing number of commercial structures. In rural areas, school buildings' sheer mass (frequently they were the largest structure in town) made them focal points without need for artistic embellishment. This situation changed when an increased awareness of two aspects of the schoolhouse began to take shape in the late 1800s: its didactic value and its place in the urban landscape. An editorial in the *American School Board Journal* addressed the first issue, exclaiming that "a ramshackle building is a discouragement to educational interests. A plain structure, even, is not stimulating. The outward appearance of a [school] building has its influences which cannot be overestimated" ("Costly High Schools" 1896, 10). School architects agreed with such assessments, and educators became particularly adamant about warning the public of bad architecture's ill effects on the nation's youth. William George Bruce, editor of the journal, spoke for many when he wrote: "The education of the community is affected by its architecture—hence, an edifice dedicated to the cause of education, above all other public buildings, ought to set the pace for taste, simplicity and dignity in the matter of form and design. If we inculcate the rising generation, by worthy example, with a correct taste in architectural expression, the future will bring forth higher achievements in that direction" (Bruce 1906, 4).

These kinds of pronouncements were absent from architectural and educational journals before 1890. Their proliferation after that date suggests education's growing importance in American society. As a gauge of that increased status, numerous writers advocated a schoolhouse that not only had didactic value, but also symbolized public regard for education or even reflected the virtue of its citizens. "Local pride in an educational system finds its gratification in a handsome structure," the *American School Board Journal* stated. "It is something that can be seen, and is regarded as an index to what the rest might be—in fact, serves as a sort of advertisement for many towns" ("Costly High Schools" 1896, 10).

Beyond its local significance, educational architecture was now linked to broader social ideals. Even observers outside of architecture or education believed beautiful school buildings could instill a sense of refinement in students, which was considered a foundation of good citizenship. University of Chicago sociologist Charles Zueblin related the schoolhouse to the success of the urban environment: a well-designed schoolhouse could teach children about beauty, and in turn they would demand it in their city's parks and buildings (Zueblin 1902). And other commentators described public schoolhouses as embodying society's higher ideals, such as democracy, free education, and charity. These opinions and many others promoted a school architecture that materially embodied the unique and multifarious mission of public education in a democratic society.

Another factor that may have influenced the school's enhanced architectural image was the challenge faced by the public schools from Catholic education. America's growing Irish and Eastern European populations were particularly partial to parochial schools, and with many new immigrants having no educational background (and thus no experience with a government-supported educational system), the Church may have seemed a logical and safe source for teaching their children. The more elaborate fin-de-siècle architecture of the public schools, then, might well have been aimed in part at the working-class immigrant ranks, to present a persona of tradition, stability, and dignity and therefore to help persuade the masses of the public school system's worth.

As education became more important to American life, the public-school building became more visible on the landscape, and the discourse on its proper image grew. There was a great deal of agreement in the educational world of the early 20th century that older school buildings were aesthetically deficient and that better architecture was needed to express the significance of what went on in the schools. In 1907, one commentator rejoiced that "all turrets and towers, as well as the high slant roofs, have been abolished. It has been found that dignified and graceful exterior effects can be achieved without resorting to steeples and towers" ("High School Architecture" 1907, 8). Architects across the country tried to enhance the visual presentation of their buildings by designing high schools that employed the same architectural language of civic authority as city halls and courthouses. But there were few recommendations regarding what style should be used. Some architects, however, did venture stylistic advice. Architect Edmund Wheelwright, a widely respected authority on school architecture and Boston's city architect, suggested that architects design the schoolhouse according to practical requirements (lighting, economy, etc.) and not by style. Since the building's internal arrangements influenced its external appearance and the main consideration in arranging the interior was light, Wheelwright believed that the windows' size, distribution, and form would have the greatest effect on the exterior. The regularity demanded by lighting concerns precluded picturesque effects and suggested instead the regularity and orderliness found in Italian Renaissance and colonial Georgian architecture. Wheelwright also felt that these styles, which required little external decoration, would help to keep school buildings economical.

Other architects recognized the same practical limitations but reached different conclusions from Wheelwright regarding their effect on the building's appearance. William B. Ittner (1864–1936), the most famous school designer of the early 20th century, admitted that "the necessities of a schoolhouse interior do not permit much expression of the artistic in exterior design . . . The demand for the adequate lighting of each classroom calls for a liberal number of windows of certain sizes. These have a tendency to cut up the design, and for a certain treatment of the exterior, which does not cultivate the highest ideals in architectural expression" ("St. Louis School Architecture" 1904, 8). Unlike Wheelwright, however, Ittner believed that these limitations did not preclude the use of nonclassical styles. Ittner personally found school buildings with an Old English or Flemish flavor to be the most suitable. The Colonial Revival style also had its adherents, especially in New England. Ernest Sibley advocated the colonial in a 1923 article entitled, "Why I Prefer the Colonial Style." The main reason, the author admitted, was personal taste, but he also felt that the colonial references linked the country's great educational institution with the spirit and traditions of the past. This type of nationalism was common during the 1920s when patriots promoted the Colonial Revival as not only a true American style, but also an Anglo-Saxon style, which was a bulwark to white New Englanders in an era of mass immigration from southern and eastern Europe. Sibley's comments on the colonial, regarding this point, echoed those of Alfred Busselle, who wrote the following in praise of the Colonial Revival: "Special emphasis is laid upon the traditions of the early building along the Atlantic seaboard, because it is the principles of the Fathers of the Republic *which we are endeavoring to instill into our alien races*" (Busselle 1921, 129, emphasis mine).

Notwithstanding the dearth of specific stylistic advice, a review of contemporary examples reveals that most American school architects designed school buildings with classical, Gothic, or colonial motifs. Some cities even seemed to carry on stylistic traditions. In St. Louis, Ittner's schools were usually castellated Gothic or English Renaissance; there were no classical designs. On the other hand, Chicago board architects favored classicism. Despite the widespread agreement on acceptable styles, a few architects experimented with alternatives. For example, Charles B. J. Snyder, school-board architect of New York City from 1890 to 1918, favored a Flemish style for his major works, like the Dewitt Clinton High School (1906).

One factor that undoubtedly influenced architects' aesthetic decisions was the tight budget allotted for school construction in most urban-school systems. The general public during this time period justly recognized schools as social investments and sources of civic pride, but the investment was tempered because school systems perennially were hampered by insufficient funds. This situation often forced school architects to create muted versions of classical or Gothic buildings: a portico on an otherwise plain brick facade or a curved or crenellated roofline and a few pointed arches. Even the most elaborately classical- or Gothic-styled school buildings had very little in the way of decoration. Only a handful of schools around the

United States had any form of architectural sculpture during this period. Restricted budgets limited school decorations to abstract terra-cotta patterns on the outside and perhaps a mural in the auditorium. The themes evoked in these decorations tended to be rather historical or related to the general idea of education.

The Monumental Era

No matter what style was selected for a school building at the turn of the 20th century or whether or not it was conceptualized as a house or a factory, it was likely to be larger and more prominent than its predecessors. In many instances, massive urban schoolhouses containing thousands of children loomed over their surrounding neighborhoods like no other building, sometimes more visible than church steeples and bell towers. Even at a smaller scale, in rural communities across the country, the schoolhouse was instantly noticeable, and in most cases, its size and architectural embellishment, however elaborate, spoke of the community's commitment to educating its children. Accordingly, the era beginning in the late 1880s and continuing into the 1940s was characterized by the monumental school.

Monumental schools departed from their immediate predecessors in two meaningful ways. The first involved the evolution of the school building's size and appearance, as described in the previous section, into a recognizable type with symbolic significance. The second momentous development of the monumental era saw the school building reshaped from its boxy origins into various other forms. Architects generally had two choices when it came to creating the basic footprint of a school building: a closed floor plan or an open one. **Closed plans** were rectangular buildings with (or occasionally without) a large open-air courtyard occupying the center, although a common adaptation placed the auditorium in the middle flanked by smaller courtyards. The Quincy School and Boston Latin and English High School had closed plans. Alternatively, open plans broke apart the box-style building and reformed it into alphabet footprints in an effort to open every room to air and light. These included buildings shaped like a T, a U, or an E. The H plan proved particularly useful for schools wedged into tight city lots, as architect Charles B. J. Snyder demonstrated in New York City. Evidence indicates a definite trend away from closed plans and toward open plans as the 19th century gave way to the 20th. By the 1920s, closed plans were almost nonexistent in the larger urban areas. The open plan triumphed because of its superior ability to provide light and air to the schoolhouse.

Louis Agassiz Grammar School in Boston, a monumental school designed by Edmund M. Wheelwright (1894). School architecture in the early 20th century was dominated by monumental schools—large, impressive buildings that were meant to convey the importance of public education. (City of Boston Archives)

Near the end of his career, William B. Ittner aptly summarized the revolution in school design he had helped initiate: "The fundamental change in schoolhouse planning was initiated about 1899 when the so-called 'closed' plan gave way to the open and semi open plans," he wrote. "The significance of this change will be appreciated when consideration is given to the fact that practically all important subsequent improvements in planning and construction, in lighting and ventilation, to say nothing of the improvements in design, may be traced directly or indirectly to this change" (Ittner 1931, 49). The new schoolhouses designed by Ittner and his colleagues not only were more efficiently planned, safer, and healthier than their predecessors. They also acted as conspicuous landmarks on the American urban landscape, employing historical architectural styles to imply civic importance. At the same time, these schools were products of their culture, and their symmetry and controlled spaces signified a desire for order and control that many felt was lacking in a society in the early stages of industrialization. The 19th-century schoolhouse had been transformed into a civic icon, a community center, and a symbol of America's unshakeable faith in public education.

Minority Schools

The monumental schools sprouting in American cities promised a new era of education for the nation's children. But that promise was largely limited to white students. The history of schooling for minorities, though, is a story with few highlights. Black Americans in particular have struggled for educational equality since the first slaves were imported to the colonies. Before the Civil War, most Southern states passed laws prohibiting slaves from being educated. Free blacks in the North likewise faced discrimination—their children were often segregated from white students or refused admission to public (tax-supported) schools. In these circumstances, slaves were forced to educate their children in secret, and northern blacks had to form their own educational institutions. The abolition of slavery following the Civil War did little to improve the situation. Although some states began to fund black schools as part of Reconstruction, not all did, and segregation—both in law and in fact—remained the norm. A combination of northern philanthropy and black self-determination provided the foundation for black education as the 20th century dawned, but the quality of that education remained in question. A debate raged over the nature of that educational experience, with one faction supporting Booker T. Washington's focus on vocational and industrial education to help blacks gain employment skills and lift their standard of living, while opponents sought equality with white schools by adapting their academic curriculum. Both sides, however, agreed that great improvements needed to be made in the quality and number of black schools for either approach to succeed.

Minority-school facilities varied, although in general, schools serving minority populations tended to be either older buildings formerly used for white students or hastily (and cheaply) built new structures. Like their white counterparts, minority schools incorporated Progressive Era characteristics like (muted) historical styles, specialized rooms separated according to use, and floor plans adapted to maximize air and light. Because school boards often failed to earmark adequate funds for minority schools or diverted their funds to white schools, maintenance was lacking in these buildings, and equipment was sparse and frequently outdated. In some rural areas of the Deep South, schools for black children were barely an improvement over the one-room schoolhouses of previous centuries.

One of the few bright spots in minority education occurred during the Progressive Era with the implementation of the Rosenwald school program, which produced 5,000 new schools for black children in 15 states between the years 1920 and 1932 at a cost of over $28 million. Established by philanthropist Julius Rosenwald (president of the Sears, Roebuck and Company) and his charitable foundation, the program reshaped the landscape of black education in the South, providing educational opportunities to many poor rural blacks for the first time. A historian who studied the program, commenting on its significance, claimed that by the early 1930s one out of every five black schools in the American South was a Rosenwald school (Hoffschwelle 1998).

The Rosenwald Fund aimed to provide modern school design to communities where it had been lacking. In order to qualify, participants needed to select an approved plan by a professional designer, thus guaranteeing that the buildings would be up-to-date. To help in this process, the fund published a book of model school designs, *Community School Plans* (1921), by Samuel L. Smith, who had trained with Fletcher B. Dresslar. These designs reflected the contemporary discourse on the importance of lighting and ventilation for preserving children's eyesight and maintaining their health. Because the focus was on inexpensive and easily buildable schools in small communities, Smith's proposals eschewed high styles or decorative adornment. Most were simple rectangular buildings with few classrooms. Larger buildings adopted H- or T-shaped floor plans to accommodate more varied interior spaces. Models ranged from simple wooden-framed, one-teacher buildings to fully equipped, multistory brick urban high schools. Some of the biggest Rosenwald schools actually mimicked the historical styles of white urban buildings, but the majority followed Smith's suggestions. A second edition of *Community School Plans*, revised by Cleveland school architect Walter McCornack a decade later, expanded the range of available options. The Rosenwald schools program was so prominent that even famed architect Frank Lloyd Wright attempted to participate. In 1928, he proposed an idiosyncratic Rosenwald building based on triangular motifs as a teacher-training school for the education department at the Hampton Institute in Virginia, but it proved too expensive to construct, and the project was left on the drafting-room table.

The Rosenwald Fund project was the most publicized black-school program in America, but it was not alone. Other northern philanthropists added support to the cause in various ways. Simultaneous with Rosenwald's efforts, for example, industrialist and General Motors executive Pierre S. du Pont, of the famous du Pont family, engaged in his own attempt to improve the quality of Delaware's public schools, particularly those serving black neighborhoods. Du Pont donated millions of dollars to the effort. In 1919 he incorporated the Delaware School Auxiliary Association (DSAA) to supervise a statewide building campaign and enlisted George D. Strayer and Nicholas L. Engelhardt, two prominent educators associated with the movement to improve school facilities, and James O. Betelle, a noted school architect from Newark, New Jersey, to write a set of standards for school-building design and construction that were officially adopted by the Delaware legislature. Like *Community School Plans*, these designs featured simple materials, construction, and floor plans, easy expandability, and an emphasis on providing well-lighted, healthy environments. This sweeping program was one of the most beneficial of the Progressive Era: according to Robert J. Taggart, the DSAA "provided funds and supervision to construct almost all of the public schools built in Delaware between 1919 and 1927," including more than 80 school buildings specifically for black students (Taggart 1988, 122).

Standardization

The Rosenwald school buildings were disseminated to the rest of the country through school administrators' conferences, architectural and educational journal articles, and architects' books. This network had the effect of largely standardizing American school architecture by the 1920s. A natural outgrowth of the popular efficiency/economy mind-set, architectural standardization was attractive for its cost-saving features and for its ability to make solutions to architectural problems available to the smallest communities. By the 1920s, it was manifested in three distinct areas: a movement to standardize construction, a narrowing of "appropriate" schoolhouse plans and elevations, and an increasing number of public and private interstate projects to provide standardized school buildings to rural communities.

Educational standardization found increasing acceptance in the early 1900s. When Boston educator John Philbrick advocated for "one best system" to be used across the country in the 1880s, based on the idea that "Modern civilization is rapidly tending to uniformity and unity . . . The best is the best everywhere," he reflected the views of educators seeking to standardize curriculum and instruction (Tyack 1974, 40). Their primary goal was to unify the educational process for all American children; a secondary concern was the economic advantages (in terms of both time and money) of implementing and operating a predetermined system. To help further these goals, educators turned to the relatively new tools of testing and measurement. For example, the comprehensive high-school curriculum's promise of tailoring students' studies to their interests and abilities required extensive knowledge of those traits. Scientific testing was viewed as a means of acquiring the necessary information. At the same time, educators desired a way of evaluating student progress to see if their programs worked. These needs influenced the development of standardized testing. Historian David Macleod has described educators' mood at the time: "Drawing on business models of measured efficiency, the quest to regularize student advancement triggered an 'orgy of tabulation' as educational researchers sought to quantify current achievement levels and embody them in standardized tests" (Macleod 1998, 82). It was only natural then that architectural standardization was seen as a perfect complement to these educational trends.

Writers like Henry Barnard and James Johonnot had promoted a type of standardization when they outlined architectural norms in their mid-19th-century books. The first outright calls for architectural standardization came in response to the dangerous conditions of the average schoolhouse. The *American School Board Journal* was a strident voice in seeking nationwide construction laws to combat the ever-present fire danger. Several widely publicized school fires in the early 1900s shocked the educational community into action. Preceding this panic, however, was the long process of developing informal architectural norms described in Chapter 1. The educational network had succeeded in spreading standards for lighting and building orientation to such a degree that, even in the 1880s, educators with no architectural background felt comfortable writing about how schoolhouses *should* be built.

Partly as a response to the fire menace, and at the request of Dr. Luther H. Gulick of the Russell Sage Foundation, Boston architect Frank Irving Cooper undertook a review of the laws and regulations pertaining to the planning, construction, fire protection, sanitation, and furnishings of American school buildings in 1910. The results were appalling, and Cooper was indignant: legislated standardization lagged behind informal customs. He found that only 8 of the 48 states had "passed laws worthy of the name bearing on schoolhouse construction," and 22 states had "no laws or regulations whatever to prevent school buildings from being built as crematories" (Cooper 1911, 2). Perhaps motivated by this experience, Cooper thereafter became the most visible architect in the standardization movement.

When the National Education Association created the Committee on Standardization of Schoolhouse Planning and Construction in 1916, it named Cooper as chairman. The committee was interested in both regularizing construction and safety codes and devising standards of space and usage. As part of that project, the committee examined 150 school buildings from 26 states, measuring floor space and evaluating construction. Six main categories of floor space were recorded: administration, instruction, accessories, stairs and corridors, flues, and walls and partitions. The percentage of each category in an individual building was expressed relative to the building's total floor space. The results were used to create an informative diagram entitled "The Candle of Efficiency in Schoolhouse Planning." According to the committee's research, greater efficiency and less waste would be achieved if the school building had the following divisions of space: Walls and Partitions, less than 10 percent; Flues, less than 5 percent; Stairs and Corridors, less than 20 percent; Accessories, less than 3 percent; Instruction, over 50 percent; and Administration, over 12 percent. The committee expanded on these recommendations in a book-length report (National Education Association Committee on School House Planning and Construction 1925).

In that report, the committee proposed a scientific approach to school planning. Floor plans were to be subjected to tests, for example, to determine their suitability in eight key categories: Adaptation to Educational Needs, Safety, Healthfulness, Convenience, Expansiveness, Flexibility, Aesthetic Fitness, and Economy. The last category formed the heart of the evaluation. Architects could conform to the requirements depicted in the "Candle of Efficiency" if they accurately determined the size needed for each room, created rooms with more than one use, and eliminated waste areas pursuant to the committee's division of space recommendations. Plans that passed all of these tests would be acceptable—and, as one might imagine, very similar.

George D. Strayer and Nicholas L. Engelhardt, two Columbia University professors, devised a system in the late 1910s for designing school buildings that epitomized architectural standardization. Their technique was designed to guide both the planning of new schools and the assessment and refurbishing of existing school buildings. The key to the system was the "Strayer-Engelhardt Score Card," which assigned points to a proposed plan or existing building according to a detailed set of standards. These standards were based on experience gathered from Strayer and Engelhardt's surveys of schools for cities and states around the country.

The follow-the-numbers approach to school design advocated by educators like Strayer and Engelhardt reflected the ongoing influence of the efficiency movement in education, as well as the source for such efficiency ideas, the business model. Standardization was a way to use acknowledged architectural solutions to minimize costs and accelerate the design process. Architectural standardization also fit nicely with the educational standardization that was taking place in curriculum and instruction. The *American Architect* aptly summarized the argument for standardization: "The education of children in public schools is quite generally standardized and a pupil in a certain grade of the elementary schools on the Atlantic Coast will find practically the same educative methods in the same grade in Pacific Coast schools . . . As the teaching of pupils in a certain grade is practically uniform throughout this country, it follows that certain physical surroundings and accessories should be uniform" ("Standardized School House Design" 1918, 559–560). Not everyone, however, was sold on the virtues of architectural standardization. Some educators condemned architectural standardization as the physical embodiment of overly mechanical educational procedures. "The standardization of the classroom and the obsolete lock-step promotion system go hand in hand," wrote educator E. Morris Cox (Donovan 1921, 88). Despite such warnings, American secondary school architecture was highly regularized by 1920. A review of any issue of the *American School Board Journal* from that time or compilation books like William C. Bruce's *High School Buildings* demonstrates the similarities in plan and elevation of most of the buildings depicted.

Further evidence of architectural standardization's importance can be found in the numerous interstate building programs that arose in the early century. The earliest example of a statewide standardization program may date back to 1899, when Minnesota offered limited funds to schools meeting certain standards. By 1920, the U.S. Bureau of Education reported that 27 states were in the process of standardizing rural schools. In Tennessee, for example, the state legislature authorized the superintendent of public instruction to issue model schoolhouse plans in 1907. The superintendent was given no authority to enforce compliance, but the plans proved popular throughout the state. The model plans for small schoolhouses were based on accepted norms for window-to-floor ratios and cubic feet of air per pupil. Strong Progressive agents in the state succeed in creating the Interstate School Building Service (ISBS) and the Tennessee Department of Schoolhouse Planning by 1928. The ISBS was a private organization supported by private funds, although most members were educators from state departments of education. The organization promoted a standardized architecture for rural Tennessee through regular meetings and the dissemination of model plans and specifications.

In contrast to Tennessee, Virginia operated a school construction program in the 1920s that was not founded on private contributions. In 1920, the commonwealth formed the School Buildings Service (SBS) under control of the Department of Education. This made official a service that had previously been carried out by the commonwealth superintendent of public instruction. As early as 1911, for example, the superintendent reported that 16 different sets of plans and specifications were available for two-, three-, four-, six- and eight-room schoolhouses without cost. The SBS similarly created a variety of standardized plans for rural, suburban, and urban schools. The program's goal was to introduce architectural reform into the commonwealth's rural school systems. The Division of School Buildings was in charge of designing or reviewing school plans to make sure they complied with the most recent developments in lighting, heating and ventilation, and fire safety. The division's basic model was then tailored to the individual circumstances of each locality. As a result, there is a great uniformity in schools designed throughout Virginia (and similar states) during this period.

Considerations of economy influenced secondary-school architecture in important ways. The formidable presence of business values in the educational world and its accompanying emphasis on efficiency led educators and architects to seek a more efficient alternative to the traditional schoolhouse; as a result, they created a building that was better adapted to the curriculum and healthier for the pupils. And for the first time, in the late 19th century, school architects were recognized for their special knowledge. The development of a class of school architects helped to spread that knowledge across the country, which in turn provided the basis for a nationwide standardization of school architecture.

DEPRESSION AND WORLD WAR II

In many ways, the modern school building achieved completeness in the 1920s. Schools were safer, better designed, larger, and more attractive than ever before, and their internal arrangements fit the pedagogies and curricula used in the nation's primary and secondary levels. Other than improvements in electric lighting and the introduction of air-conditioning later in the century, the schoolhouse's constituent parts were all in place. Educators and architects faced new challenges, however, when the stock market crashed in October 1929, setting in motion a series of events that caused the Great Depression—the worst economic crisis ever seen in the industrialized Western world.

During the depths of this worldwide depression in the 1930s, the U.S. government established numerous public-works programs to build infrastructure and stimulate the economy. The Public Works Administration (PWA) was the most relevant of those programs from an architectural and educational standpoint. Between 1933 and 1941, the PWA spent billions of dollars on public projects, including over 100 schools. These buildings were designed around recent advances in lighting and ventilation, but their appearance revealed a continuing preference among educators, architects, and the public for historical styles. Almost half of the PWA schools at all levels presented a colonial or classical face to the world; in the elementary schools, the rate was above 60 percent. Equally as popular, however, were buildings whose style might be variously described as Art Deco, Deco Moderne, or even "PWA style"— structures with minimal but implied classical ornamentation that sought a middle ground between traditional academic classicism and avant-garde modernism (Short and Stanley-Brown 1939).

Even more than the PWA schools' appearance, their floor plans revealed the conservative nature of America's school designers. Only about 15 percent of the PWA schools at any level had L-shaped floor plans, which was a marker of modernity in the 1930s. Not surprisingly, elementary schools were most likely to utilize an L plan, given the limited room diversity required at that level. Many architects found it easy to design elementary schools as a straight row of classrooms connected to a perpendicular kindergarten room at one end, with the principal's office in the elbow—in the manner of Neutra's Corona Avenue School. But more architects continued to rely on the same kinds of room arrangements that had dominated the first two decades of the century: closed box-type plans with every function of the school held within a square or rectangular container; alphabet plans like the letters U, E, T, H, or some variation; and in-line floor plans that elongated the entire building along a single, continuous corridor.

Interwar Modernism

The first inklings of a new approach to school design had begun to emerge in the late 1920s as the country entered the era of financial depression. It was during this time that European modern architecture, developing since the early years of the century, gained more of a foothold in the United States. School architecture, along with single-family residences, proved to be one of modernism's initial entry points into the American architectural world. The modernist emphasis on function over style meshed nicely with the efficiency orientation that dominated education in this country for years, and the modernists' use of contemporary materials while shunning mere decorative effects established a trend toward cost-effective school construction just when it was most needed. The unusual appearance of modernist buildings, however, would engender a debate over the school's symbolic value and aesthetic propriety.

On one side of the dispute were those who were open to an expanded visual language for school buildings that included more than the ubiquitous classical and Tudor Gothic styles. But these proponents for "loosening up" American school design were opposed by historicists, such as William B. Ittner, who relentlessly advocated the historical styles. The traditionalists and modernists clashed in conferences and in print. Ittner and William Lescaze (1896–1969), a Swiss-born architect and internationally renowned modernist leader, debated each other at the National Educational Association's annual conference. Ittner defended the propriety of historical styles for the education of children. Lescaze spoke in favor a functional approach to school planning and considered any historically derived design as "a lie" and a "fake" (Weisser 1995, 147).

A similar exchange took place between architect Guy Study and the Museum of Modern Art's Philip Johnson in the pages of *American School and University*. Both writers built their arguments around the concept of functionality. Study, supportive of period styles, adopted the established École des Beaux-Arts notion of the importance of a building's "character" and then proceeded to explain how character is a functional aspect of school design because it can help develop the student's character. Study's essay concluded by naming Tudor Gothic and colonial styles as America's "true heritage" and arguing that their utilization would acquaint students with the great cultures of the past.

Philip Johnson's retort, entitled "Modern Architecture for Efficiency," lashed out at the type of architecture Study prescribed: "Architects have been more concerned with the system of design which they learned by heart in architectural school than with the functional needs of the building which they were planning. The results were bad lighting, bad planning and high costs." The paradox of period styles, wrote Johnson, is that copying a historical style correctly makes for an "uneconomic and functionally inefficient modern school," while adapting historical styles to accommodate the functions of contemporary schools leaves "no resemblance in letter or spirit to the original style." While the short essay put much emphasis on economics, Johnson also argued that modern schools could be judged beautiful according to the same criteria as historic styles—proportioning, detail, and materials. However, "in contrast to the imitative monumentality of structures built with an eye to the past, modern buildings have a cleanness, lightness and simplicity which accord well with our machine civilization. To surround the growing generation with bad parodies of dead architecture is a foolish anachronism" (Johnson 1933, 31–33).

The functionalism-versus-style debate was not merely an argument over degrees, with traditionalists advocating efficient floor plans wrapped in historical garb versus modernists seeking to extend the plan's efficiency to the building's exteriors. Rather, it was a disagreement over what efficiency really meant. Supporters of contemporary architecture believed the early-20th-century school model developed by architects like Ittner to be perfectly adapted to educational needs, while modernists advocated a total rethinking of the school building inside and out without the emphasis on external appearance. Pioneer school designers like Wheelwright and Ittner had been among the first generation of architects to actively collaborate with educators (administrators and even sometimes teachers) when designing schoolhouses. The modernists supplemented this approach with an openness to scientific and psychological research on children's health and behavior. The buildings and methods of both groups were efficient in their own way and equally affected by cultural changes, from the professionalization of architecture and education to the increasing role of science in everyday life and the rise of psychology as an academic discipline.

School buildings influenced by modernist ideas materialized sporadically throughout the 1930s and 1940s along with those structures reflecting the continuing authority of historical traditions. Institutions, such as the Museum of Modern Art (MoMA), helped introduce new European architectural ideas to America's culturally oriented citizens, while architects and educators who recognized modernism's potential to improve school architecture advanced their cause through symposia and publications. One of the first instances where modernists sought to extol the benefits of new architectural thinking for schools was in the MoMA's 1932 exhibition *The International Style: Architecture Since 1922*—an exhibition conceived and executed by Philip Johnson with Henry-Russell Hitchcock, an architectural historian. On display among the now-iconic buildings of European modernist pioneers like Ludwig Mies van der Rohe, Walter Gropius, and Le Corbusier were a handful of schools, including two in the United States from the Philadelphia firm Howe & Lescaze. Press releases touting the exhibit stressed the advantages these new schools had over their traditional counterparts, including "freedom of planning"—individual rooms created to fit the needs of students and not packed into preconceived forms like the alphabet-shaped floor plans that dominated American school design. This freedom, the curators claimed, allowed more variety (and larger sizes) for windows and hence more opportunities to provide sunlight and fresh air; when combined with outdoor terraces connected to the classroom, a new, healthier school building could be devised.

A decade later, the MoMA presented its first exhibition devoted entirely to schools, entitled *Modern Architecture for the Modern School*. The accompanying materials emphasized the positive psychological benefits of the new generation of schools while reiterating the increased openness, fresh air, and sunlight provided by such designs. "The really modern school should be a rambling, child-scaled, one-story building, gay and friendly, direct and unpretentious," wrote curator Elizabeth Bauer Mock, "that welcomes the outdoors as enthusiastically as the old-fashioned school sought to exclude it" (Museum of Modern Art 1942). The exhibition was praised by the educational community, and its relevance led to a four-year tour of venues throughout the country.

Both of these MoMA shows highlighted Richard Neutra's unbuilt but influential Ring Plan School (1927). Neutra had envisioned a school building in the form of a one-story elliptical ring surrounding an open playing field. Single-story structures were less expensive to build and easier to evacuate in case of fire but took up more room on the ground; Neutra's oval school was intended to counteract that problem. He also removed interior corridors, placing 30 classrooms side by side and connecting them with a covered walkway along the ring's inner edge. Every classroom opened to its own private outdoor space bounded by hedges and trees. The Ring Plan School's low, horizontal profile, abundant natural light, direct access to the outdoors, and casual atmosphere anticipated the most popular new developments of school architecture in the 1930s.

Neutra continued to explore these components in a pair of schools constructed in the Los Angeles area, where external circumstances made them even more attractive. First of all, some school architects in the region, seeking to take advantage of the mild climate, had begun to experiment with French doors in classrooms by the 1920s. Local educators extolled the virtues of fresh air and outdoor experiences for children, and informal school buildings that linked inside and out caught their attention. Also, in the spring of 1933, an earthquake off the California coast rocked the areas south of Los Angeles, particularly Long Beach. Over 200 school buildings were destroyed or damaged beyond repair. In the aftermath, the state legislature passed a law mandating changes to school construction: unreinforced masonry buildings were banned, and all new construction required seismic considerations.

Neutra's emphasis on one-story height and lightweight construction meshed perfectly with the new regulations. His first opportunity to put the Ring School scheme into practice came with the Corona Avenue School (1935) in Bell, California. Neutra straightened the Ring Plan's oval shape into a single, one-story row, terminated at one end by a perpendicularly placed kindergarten room. The classrooms were linked with an outdoor corridor and, like the Ring Plan, opened out on the opposite side to an outdoor room flanked by greenery. The walls on this garden side were almost entirely glazed and movable so that the demarcation between interior and exterior disappeared. Corona Avenue's five classrooms were full of natural light and fresh air. Neutra expanded these concepts for a more complicated design at Emerson Junior High School (1937) in Los Angeles.

Corona Avenue School in Bell, California, designed by Richard Neutra (1935). Inspired by developments in 1920s German educational architecture, Neutra pioneered the indoor-outdoor schoolroom in the United States, creating classrooms that extended outside to take advantage of Southern California's mild climate and abundant sunshine. (Los Angeles Public Library)

Neutra's schools were included in the MoMA's *Modern Architecture for the Modern School* exhibition, alongside the work of another European immigrant, William Lescaze. Like Neutra, Lescaze considered educational architecture vitally important, and he sought to improve American school design through the application of modernist principles. His educational work actually predated that of Neutra by a few years, and it is fair to say Lescaze designed the first modernist schools in the United States. Although he worked in partnership with George Howe, Lescaze was the driving force in the firm's school designs. Their first endeavor along these lines was a nursery-school building for the Oak Lane Country Day School (1929) outside Philadelphia. This tiny building would have an outsized impact on American school architecture. The structure was intended to have two classrooms side by side with a connecting area containing a kitchenette, restrooms, and a teacher's office, but only one of the classrooms was built. The building's arrangement of interior space was not particularly innovative, but its large window wrapped around the classroom's southeast corner, flat roof, streamlined entrance canopy, and overall "white box" aesthetic of the International Style made the school visually unique for its time.

Howe and Lescaze followed the Oak Lane nursery school with the Hessian Hills School (1932) in Croton-on-Hudson, New York, and a few years later, Lescaze designed the Ansonia High School (1937, Vernon F. Sears co-architect) in Connecticut, one of the earliest uses of modernist aesthetic and planning ideas at the secondary-school level. Ansonia High School's asymmetrical floor plan resembled a U with unequal arms: a short one terminated by the gymnasium, and a longer arm comprised of a covered porch (below a second story of classrooms) attached to an auditorium. Anchoring the scheme was a two-story, double-loaded corridor of classrooms. Lescaze anticipated the postwar obsession with flexibility by including undesignated spaces inside, and he argued that the school's steel-frame structure and open arrangement allowed for easy expansion in the future. The facade of Lescaze's brick-faced building was starkly plain, featuring the flat roof, unembellished white walls, and large expanses of windows indicative of the burgeoning International Style.

POSTWAR EXPERIMENTATION

The Great Depression and World War II forced educators to view the economics of school buildings in sharper focus than ever before. Nearly two decades of continuous hardship and sacrifice trained them—and their architects—to think about costs before any other factors. The practice would serve both groups well in the immediate postwar period. Even with the American economy soaring to unprecedented heights during the 1950s and 1960s, educators still faced extreme challenges. Now, however, they were caused by abundance, as a record number of births dating back to the war years gave rise to the baby boom, the greatest period of sustained population growth in the nation's history. Simultaneous with this population explosion was a suburban migration that drained residents from cities and relocated them among the proliferating suburbs that came to dominate the landscape. This mass redistribution of students caused problems for urban and suburban administrators alike, particularly the latter, who often were unable to build schools quickly enough to keep pace with rising enrollments. Architects focused on creating schools that could be altered and expanded as necessary. Many of these new buildings took advantage of spacious suburban sites to accelerate the school building's decentralization, stretching schools into low-rise, campus-like facilities in ways that matched the increasing emphasis on casualness and informality that infiltrated American education during this time.

Opening the School

A particular type of school building came to dominate most regions of America from the 1940s through the 1970s, with the basic model being exported to other countries as well. These schools were low to the ground (ideally one story) and horizontally oriented, with flat or **shed roofs**; they were organized by corridors connecting the classrooms and provided much visual or actual access to the outdoors, either through covered walkways or arcades, classrooms opening to an outdoor area, or large sections of windows. This format thrived in suburban and rural places with plentiful land, although attempts were made to adapt the model for cities. In many ways, it continues to serve as the foundation for today's school designs.

The school building just described evolved from a combination of sources, all of which were intended to promote healthy educational environments for children. Three influences in particular shaped the development of this characteristically American school form: (a) "California" type schools of the early 20th century; (b) the international open-air school movement for tubercular children that began in Europe and spread rapidly through the Western world; and (c) a tendency toward extending classrooms outdoors, originating in the modernist schools and publicized through the work of Richard Neutra.

In the first decade of the 20th century, some school designers began to adapt school buildings to the mild and sunny Southern California climate. They rejected the monumentality expected in schoolhouses in favor of a friendlier, less formal aesthetic and smaller size; most of their schools were one-story structures at a time before this design alternative became widely popular. Classrooms were arranged side by side, with one wall opening to a covered walkway or arcade and its opposite full of windows for abundant light and air. Architects often formed two of these classroom rows into arms parallel to each other, with the corridors facing inward; the arms were connected to a perpendicular section containing an assembly room or auditorium. The ground in the middle of such an arrangement could be left open as a playground or patio. Overall, then, the floor plans resembled a U (sometimes closed off at the open end). Educators and architects endorsed their ease of access to patios and gardens and the free circulation of fresh air in these schools.

Designs such as these offered numerous advantages. They were safer, in the sense that students could simply walk out of their classroom to safety in case of fire without encountering hazardous stairways. These buildings were healthier, since lighting and natural ventilation were easier to control in one-story structures. They could be extended by adding another arm, "finger," or row of rooms, and instruction could continue in one part of the building while construction or extension occurred in another. And the buildings were deemed "friendlier" by their supporters due to their lowered profile and smaller scale. At a time when educators tried to craft environments for students that were less intimidating and more like their homes, this was an important consideration, especially for the youngest children.

Perhaps the first such California school, as they became known, was constructed in Pasadena in 1907. The Polytechnic Elementary School, designed by Myron C. Hunt and Elmer Grey, displayed all of the traits listed above: an H-shaped floor plan anchored by an assembly hall in the center connected to two parallel classroom wings; covered walkways lining the interior courts for circulation; rooms opening directly onto the corridors, with large banks of windows on the opposite wall; and a low, one-story profile. Hunt and Grey based their school on the formal characteristics and informal atmosphere of historical California ranches. The building was simply designed in an almost residential manner, with rafters exposed in the corridor roof, whitewashed wood siding, and plasterboard interior walls.

The Polytechnic Elementary School featured prominently in a 1917 *Architectural Forum* article highlighting schools of this type, "One-Story and Open-Air Schoolhouses in California" (Hays 1917). Its design revealed some of the tendencies appearing in the work of several Southern California school designers of the period. Another significant example came from San Diego, where William Templeton Johnson's Francis Parker School (1912) displayed analogous qualities. Johnson represented an important link between the California design community and the international open-air school movement. He explained his unusual school design as an attempt to extend the proven health benefits of open-air schoolrooms to *all* children: "The first open-air schoolrooms were designed particularly for anemic and tubercular children, but the results obtained were so remarkable that authorities have come to realize that all children do better both physically and mentally in open-air environment [sic]," he wrote. "The problem of the open-air school in America is a comparatively new one, but its successful solution will be of incalculable benefit to thousands and thousands of school-children" (Johnson 1916, 161).

Johnson was referencing a generation of foreign schools that had attracted attention with their unorthodox approach to school design. In Europe in the early 1900s, educators began erecting schools with few or no walls to house children suffering from tuberculosis or related respiratory ailments (Châtelet 2008). At the time, the preferred treatment for the disease involved rest, plenty of sunlight, and constant exposure to fresh air. Images of children bundled in winter clothing and sitting at their desks outdoors are startling to us today, but there was evidence that such conditions helped children. The first open-air school materialized in a Berlin suburb in 1904, and similar institutions quickly spread through Western Europe and across to the United States before World War I. Officials for the Providence, Rhode Island, public schools made the first effort in this country to adopt the approach, opening a classroom in early 1908. An unoccupied two-story brick schoolhouse was selected for the experiment. Educators removed one of the exterior walls from a second-floor classroom, replacing it with a floor-to-ceiling bank of windows that could be opened with a pulley system so that no barrier remained between the interior and the outdoors on that side of the room. Student desks were turned so that their back was to the open wall to avoid drafts in their faces and approximate the correct angle of light falling on their desks. Boston followed Providence's lead later that year, teaching tubercular students in tents until architects designed a new structure on the roof of an existing refectory building. An outdoor classroom 30 feet long and 20 feet wide, with a wooden frame and canvas walls on all four sides, allowed students to receive their lessons in sunlight and fresh air. Chicago's educators created a comparable room shortly after, while in New York the initial open-air schools took place on ferryboats. By 1910, over a dozen cities operated open-air schools, resulting in hundreds of rooms by the time Johnson wrote about his Parker School in 1916. Many of them were no longer makeshift or temporary structures, but real classrooms or even small buildings. To Johnson's credit, he attempted to unite mainstream education with open-air school practices so that all students might reap the benefits of fresh air, sunshine, and immersion in nature.

The international development of open-air schools was associated with a transformation in the design of European sanatoriums or hospitals for tuberculosis patients. These larger-scale buildings, some of which were well publicized, displayed the promise of the new International Style-modernism with its emphases on function and hygiene. Architects working in northern Europe and Scandinavia, in particular, applied modern design concepts to health-care facilities of all kinds, to improved open-air schools, and eventually to public-school buildings as early as the 1920s. One of early modernism's most iconic buildings, for instance, was Jan Duiker's Cliostraat Open-Air School (Amsterdam 1927–1930), one of two European schools featured in the 1932 *International Style* exhibition at MoMA. It was a crystalline cube-like building sheathed in glass with one completely unenclosed corner on each floor set aside for use as an outdoor classroom. Duiker's school was not for tubercular children but, rather, emerged as part of a campaign for healthier public schools. Other architects soon followed. In 1936, French architects Eugène Beaudouin and Marcel Lods' Open-Air School at Surèsnes, outside of Paris, included individual classroom pavilions that far surpassed the minimal and sometimes improvised quality of some open-air schools of the time. At Surèsnes, eight individual pavilions each held a classroom, cloakroom, and toilet room within a rectangular form; they were attached to a main outdoor corridor by a short covered walk, and the pavilions all faced south for maximum solar exposure. These classroom boxes used unorthodox floor-to-ceiling folding windows on three sides, which could open accordion-style to eliminate the barrier between inside and out. Each pavilion also had a roof deck for even greater exposure.

The move to extend classrooms outdoors received greater support after the open-air schools proved successful. In England, for example, educators, architects, and doctors recognized the beneficial effects of fresh air and cross ventilation on tubercular students and sought to apply them to public elementary schools, which led to the veranda-type school building. Most pre–World War I English schools were clustered around a central hall, but architects started deviating from this plan and lining classrooms in rows. These structures used folding doors opening out to verandas and clearstory windows to guarantee continuous air flow and proper light levels. By the 1920s, the verandas were sometimes replaced by grassy courtyards, further strengthening the indoor/outdoor connection. At roughly the same time, in Frankfurt, Germany, architect Ernst May and his team developed so-called pavilion schools as a part of their reformist social agenda. These school buildings featured lower, horizontal profiles, glass-walled classrooms opening onto student gardens, and small, lightweight, movable furniture. The Friedrich Ebert School (1931) included an enclosed courtyard for each terraced group of four classrooms to facilitate outdoor class activities. Here, as in the other Frankfurt schools, integration with nature was seen as a vital aspect of the curriculum.

American educators' acceptance of such concepts was slower. After the California-plan schools appeared in the 1910s, the moniker became well known, but the ideas were not particularly influential until the 1940s. After that, educators and architects involved with the first generation of postwar schools began to accept the one-story schoolhouse for reasons of efficiency and flexibility. One-story schools could be cheaper to build, light, and ventilate and easier to modify, and they were safer in terms of fire and less intimidating to younger children. The notion of easy access to the outdoors, however, took longer to become popular.

Although such design moves arose logically from the ideology of modernist architecture, the architects were not alone in recognizing the importance of outdoor activities. They were joined by psychologists and progressive educators, like America's John Dewey and Italy's Maria Montessori, both of whom considered children's development to be stunted if they were not allowed regular outdoor activities. These kinds of views became more popular in the 1920s. In *The Child-Centered School*, Harold Rugg and Ann Shumaker asserted that nature was valuable not only as a subject of study, but also as a physical addition to the school. They argued that "the whole child" must be educated if the pupil is to develop into an individual, and to accomplish that, "the materials of education" must be "as broad and interrelated as life itself" (Rugg and Shumaker 1928, 5). Similar sentiments were expressed by British educators in the Hadow Report (1931), an analysis of England's primary schools that dealt in part with children's physical environment. Progressive-minded educators on both sides of the Atlantic found opportunities to broaden educational space by extending classrooms into the areas outside the school walls.

Richard Neutra followed architectural developments in Europe closely and was aware of experiments like Duiker's Amsterdam Open-Air School—which he visited. His indoor-outdoor classrooms and Corona Avenue School were kindred spirits to these European counterparts. Neutra's designs in turn were extensively publicized in American architectural journals and known among educators. His work inspired many school designers to create buildings with long one-story rows of classrooms side by side and connected by a single-loaded corridor. The corridor tended to be an outdoor covered walkway in milder climates or an interior hallway in cooler regions. Often these buildings formed an L, like the Corona Avenue School, with the addition of a larger space for a gymnasium or auditorium attached perpendicular to the classroom arm. This arrangement formed a pocket that could be used to shield student play or recreation areas from surrounding streets; it also reflected emerging formal tendencies in domestic architecture as popularized by Neutra and Frank Lloyd Wright. As school enrollments increased, these classroom arms were extended, but in some cases, architects, responding to educators' concerns about the disciplinary and physical challenges of extremely long corridors, began to multiply the arms. The resulting **finger plan** was one of the first widely accepted variations of the rectangular box or the L plan and, like the latter, demonstrated a growing tendency for school buildings of reduced height and broader width. Schools were spreading out, decentralizing, and opening up to nature, and finger plans were the vanguard of educational architecture.

A typical finger-plan school involved the conceptual slicing of the traditional school building into component parts, placing each part on the ground, and connecting those parts. In its simplest form, seen in designs like Franklin & Kump's Acalanes High School (1939) near Oakland, the finger plan stretched across the landscape with classroom groups, administrative offices, cafeteria, library, shops, and gymnasium each in its own building, linked by long, straight covered walkways and surrounded by courtyards and playfields. The classroom fingers were in parallel rows with outdoor space in between. They were oriented on the site so that the largest windows faced north and avoided direct sunlight. Along the south side of each finger was a continuous porch for lockers and circulation, and above it, a row of clearstory windows added extra light. There were no interior hallways. Schools like Acalanes High School extended the ideas that had originated in Southern California decades earlier into the modern age of electric light and steel framing.

Acalanes High School was one of the most highly regarded of the new generation of school buildings in the late 1930s, along with Neutra's Corona Avenue School and the Crow Island School. The latter—the most famous school building of its time—uniquely combined the L plan and the finger plan to make the most of each. Crow Island resembled a straightened Z shape. Perkins, Wheeler & Will extended classroom wings from opposite ends of a central block containing the main lobby, library, offices, auditorium, and playroom. Each wing lined Perkins's revolutionary classrooms along a corridor, one for primary-school students and the other for intermediate-school classrooms. Small spaces for a nursery and kindergarten connected to the elbow of the main block next to the lobby. This arrangement gave each classroom its own courtyard. The orientation of the building allowed sunlight to stream through the two transparent walls of each classroom, and one of these walls always faced south, guaranteeing continuous illumination.

The school buildings of both Neutra and Ernest Kump Jr. received extensive publicity in architectural journals, and the building form that each utilized introduced a kind of vernacular school that became very popular in the immediate postwar era. Both architects favored a horizontally oriented, one-story school with a corridor or walkway along one side and the other with an extensively glazed wall that gazed out at or opened up to nature. This building type evolved because it was simple to design, easy to construct, and inexpensive. While it often embodied some of the advances to classroom design described above and certainly represented improvements over the previous generation of school buildings in terms of lighting and ventilation, the driving force for both educators and architects was cost. Educators taxed by the economic constraints of the depression and war years must have felt absolutely overwhelmed by what happened next. As a leading architectural journal joked in a special issue on school architecture, "children, not tanks, planes or bombs—were the greatest output of the U.S. during World War II." In a more serious vein, the editors sketched a dire scenario for American education in the foreseeable future: experts calculated that the nation's schools needed 400,000 new classrooms over the subsequent 11 years to meet the extraordinary mass of young children headed for the public schools—at a cost of $10 billion ("The Need" 1949, 82).

The 1950s brought America an invigorated economy, a soaring birth rate, and record public-school enrollments. In the race to construct schools quickly and cheaply, alternatives to the finger and L plans sprouted in suburbs and small towns across the country. School buildings increasingly sprawled across the landscape. Architects introduced complex versions of finger plans and explored variations like cluster plans or campus plans—while an equally numerous group built loft plans, inspired by the simplistic steel-framed and glass-sheathed structures that were beginning to symbolize corporate and industrial America. So while one group of school designs continued the decentralization process begun before the war, emphasizing centrifugal layouts and physical distinctions among the school's individual parts, another group worked with circumscribed boxlike forms. In both cases, the interior openness and spatial flexibility resulting from steel-frame construction worked simultaneously with educators' desire to make schools into pleasant, even happy environments for children.

The Casual School

A new type of school building emerged in the United States after World War II during the suburban migration and the baby boom. These schools were much different from the grand, multistory brick monuments dressed in historical styles that preceded them. Instead, the postwar-generation schools were intentionally unimposing. While the formal development of these school buildings flowed in part from such precedents as the open-air schools of the early 1900s and the climate-adapted California schools of the same time, there were two important cultural factors that affected the American school building's evolution from monumentality to casualness: an extraordinary cultural focus on children and parenting and a shift in the secondary-school curriculum to emphasize individual fulfillment and societal roles over mental training or mastery of subject matter.

Casual schools were intended to encourage students to feel good about themselves and enjoy learning. This sense of informality in the school was new and unique, engendered by a changing conception of children and their development. American society became much more child-centered after World War II. A growing preoccupation with the needs and interests of children—fueled by psychologists, physicians, and educators—pointed toward a different school environment for students. From scientific research on developmental psychology to the popularity of psychoanalysis to the proliferation of child-rearing advice from experts like Dr. Benjamin Spock, newspapers and popular magazines assailed parents with messages about how to raise their children. The underlying messages were consistent: children were much different from adults, and parents needed to pay more attention to their children's wants, needs, and interests than in the past.

In response, educators sought to maximize students' learning experiences by making school interesting and fun, an approach that affected curricula, pedagogy, and architecture at all levels of the public-school systems. Architects designed schools to be less intimidating and more homelike, with lower ceilings, larger windows, curtains, bright colors, carpeting, and direct access to outdoors. Simultaneously, the evolving child-centered culture demanded that education become appealing and

A postwar casual school. In contrast to the previous monumental generation of schools, educators, and architects in the 1950s and 1960s tried to create relaxed, "fun" learning environments tailored to children. This resulted in one- or two-story structures, open to the outdoors, with smaller-scale rooms and furniture. (Charles L. Franck/Franck-Bertacci Photographers/The Historic New Orleans Collection)

accessible to the "average" student. In American high schools, a **life adjustment** curriculum that became popular in the 1950s was intended to address "real-life problems" rather provide an academic foundation. It shifted the emphasis from learning basic fundamentals, core concepts, and cultural milestones to readying students for everyday life as an adult in a democratic society.

Casual schools emerged in a culture where social norms were changing, and some of the schools' defining attributes paralleled those of contemporary suburban homes. At the same time that the public schools were moving toward informality, family, social relations, manners, and fashion were becoming noticeably less constrained. The relaxed postwar atmosphere was especially visible in the design of the American home, where the increasing popularity of family rooms and recreation rooms in middle-class houses signaled a casual, more easygoing lifestyle. Most of these houses were constructed in the suburbs, where residents were devising novel forms of popular entertainment centered on patios, backyards, televisions, and recreation rooms. One advocate for casual-school design in the mid-1950s challenged traditionalist opponents by referencing this lifestyle: "But is our way of life today based on formality? Isn't the present pattern of living (outdoor barbeques, do-it-yourself projects, the flight to the suburbs) quite the opposite?" he asked. "If our present living pattern expresses itself through informality, do we really wish to surround our children with a physical school environment that appears to oppose their pattern of living?" (Rogers 1956, 83).

The new generation of postwar schools, which were touted by supporters as healthier, safer, and better adapted to modern pedagogies and curricula, did not, however, guarantee a better educational experience for students. This may have been best demonstrated by the events surrounding the famous desegregation of Arkansas's Little Rock Central High School in 1957. The story began with the U.S. Supreme Court decision of *Plessy v. Ferguson* (1896), wherein the court decided that a Louisiana law requiring racial segregation on railroad cars did not violate the Constitution. The court held that as long as black citizens were provided with "separate but equal" accommodations, there was no discrimination and no violation of their civil rights. In the aftermath of the *Plessy* decision, numerous Southern states enacted laws requiring racial segregation in public schools, claiming they were following the law by offering black students equal facilities and opportunities. This legalized discrimination was bitterly opposed by parents, educators, and political groups across the country, but it was not until the 1954 Supreme Court case of *Brown v. Board of Education of Topeka, Kansas* that the decision was recognized as unconstitutional. In *Brown*, the court superseded *Plessy*, ruling that racial segregation in public education was a violation of the Fourteenth Amendment to the Constitution and held that "separate educational facilities are inherently unequal." The decision established the basis for an end to legal discrimination in public education, although de facto discrimination continued as Southern states resisted in various ways.

Parents of black students throughout the South, who had been forced to send their children to underfunded, dilapidated, and inferior schools, rejoiced at the decision. But change would prove slow and difficult. In Little Rock, for example, the school board took steps to begin desegregation after the *Brown* decision. As part of the plan, nine students volunteered to transfer from the city's two black high schools to the all-white Little Rock Central High School. Six of those students came from Horace Mann High School, a new facility designed as a suburban casual school, which included all of the features made popular in those schools, like a one-story height, outdoor walkways, courtyards, and vast expanses of windows. Horace Mann won an award from the Arkansas branch of the American Institute of Architects and received a six-page write-up in *Architectural Record*.

The fact that six of the "Little Rock Nine" ventured to risk their safety and well-being by transferring from the new, modern facility to the racially hostile environment of Little Rock Central is meaningful, given that the latter structure was a monumental, Collegiate Gothic-style building from 1927—exactly the kind of building that Horace Mann and others of its type were intended to replace. This was a very visible demonstration of the lack of a correlation between the newness of a school building and the quality of the education provided therein.

Curricular Changes

Educators' desire to make schools pleasant reflected the evolving content and methods of American education. This was particularly true at the high-school level, where efforts to offer a more practical education for teenagers had already given rise to vocational courses of study. By the mid-20th century, the long-established academic high-school curriculum was largely replaced by a differentiated curriculum aimed at preparing adolescents for adult life.

The 1918 Cardinal Principles report and its seven educational objectives had codified the direction that American high-school curricula were beginning to take at the time. In 1933, the governing body overseeing secondary education reduced the desirable high-school goals from seven to four, none of which were academic in nature. Students would be expected to achieve health and physical fitness, explore vocations and vocational efficiency, develop successful social relationships, and learn proper uses for their leisure time. Such nonacademic pursuits reflected a different set of priorities now that larger numbers of students attended high school. Only 10.2 percent of all adolescents between the ages of 14 and 17 were enrolled in high schools across the country in 1900. By 1930, that figure had reached 50.7 percent, and by the end of World War II, it was over 70 percent (National Center for Education Statistics 1993, 16). Much of this increase was attributable to the Great Depression, which significantly weakened the market for child labor, but the enrollment surge also indicated the public's mounting respect for secondary education. High schools began in the 19th century as a privilege for a small percentage of America's youth, but by the interwar period, they had turned into a valuable institution and a dominant presence in the lives of teenagers.

Educators formulated a new kind of postwar high-school curriculum to comply with the Cardinal Principles report and make high school more meaningful for those students uninterested in college or lacking the means to attend. According to the U.S. Office of Education, "Most boys and girls are headed for jobs that require little training. These youth need and want an invigorated general education that relates to their everyday lives" (Rummel 1950, 5). Educator A. J. Foy Cross described the life-adjustment curriculum's goals: "a) Personal, individual growth in health, happiness, and well-being; b) Growth among individuals of an active interest in the health and well-being of all other people; c) Continuous growth within individuals of a confidence in their ability to recognize and solve the little and big problems of living in a satisfying and socially acceptable manner" (Cross 1956, 28). Courses in family life, civic responsibilities, interpersonal relations, and other life skills replaced foreign languages, art, and higher mathematics. "If the products of our schools turn out to be healthy and patriotic citizens who are good husbands, good wives, good fathers, good mothers, good neighbors, good workers, good employers, wise spenders of income, wholesome users of leisure time and so forth," wrote one educator, "we know that our schools are good" (Nickell 1949, 154).

A major presumption behind the life-adjustment curriculum was that most students were neither talented enough to complete a college preparatory course of study nor interested in the specificity of vocational education. In order for these students to avoid wasting their time in school, educators sought a general education that was not too demanding. Noted educator Charles M. Prosser famously claimed—without proof—that 60 percent of all high school students fit this description. His speculation would be adopted as fact by supporters. Thereafter, life-adjustment education caught on quickly. By 1947, just two years after Prosser made this statement at a conference (it would be known as the Prosser Resolution), the first life-adjustment conference was held. In December of that year, *Time* magazine published an article on the movement, reporting that schools in 35 states were involved with life-adjustment education.

However, life-adjustment education's moment in the spotlight was relatively short. It never gained the support of traditionally oriented educators, and soon some very public critiques turned enthusiasm for life adjustment into wariness. A major blow came in 1953 when University of Illinois professor Arthur E. Bestor Jr. published *Educational Wastelands*, a book that caused a national sensation with its virulent attack on the alleged class-solidifying, undemocratic tendencies of life-adjustment education. Bestor argued that life adjustment taught students to accept their place in the economic order by directing most of them toward vocational or general education, which was not the school system's purpose. He favored intellectual training in the 19th-century tradition and emphasized the need for core subjects like mathematics, sciences, English, history, and foreign languages. Numerous educators agreed with Bestor's assessment. For example, a survey of over 1,000 high-school principals revealed that the majority believed high schools demanded "far too little work of students," contained too many easy classes, and overemphasized extracurricular activities over such fundamentals as reading (Angus and Mirel 1999, 107).

In October 1957, the Soviet Union launched the Sputnik satellite, inaugurating the space race and inciting critics across the country to blame public-school systems for devaluing academics and permitting the United States to slip behind its enemy in the sciences. Education became a matter of national security as school curricula entered into the Cold War. Anxious administrators scrapped life-adjustment courses and altered curricula to emphasize basic subjects like math and science again. By decade's end, however, countless fears had been assuaged by the publication of James B. Conant's book *The American High School Today*. Conant, a scientist, diplomat, and former president of Harvard University, was a public figure who commanded educators' respect. His survey of comprehensive public high schools found nothing fundamentally wrong with them. Instead, Conant suggested minor improvements to the existing system while continuing to require different courses of study for college-bound and non-college-bound students. According to Conant, this format exemplified democracy at its best—contrary to the Soviet system—because it allowed students to achieve to the best of their ability. The Conant report was widely publicized in mass-circulation magazines and newspapers, as well as debated in educational journals. It seemed to settle debates about the direction of the high-school curriculum in favor of the comprehensive school and curricular differentiation. After withstanding the challenge of life adjustment, curricular differentiation was entrenched as the standard high-school model.

Life-adjustment curricula, tailored to students' interests and real-life situations, meshed perfectly with the notion of the casual school. However, this shift toward student-centered curricula was not accompanied by a corresponding change in the pedagogical methods used to teach high school students. Evidence suggests that high-school instructors used the same teacher-centered tactics as their predecessors, including recitations of memorized material, daily assignments from textbooks, and disciplinary control. While some inventive educators employed such alternatives as audiovisual technology, individualized instruction, group discussions, and active learning, the truth was that secondary-school teaching showed little influence from a half-century of progressive innovations. "Basic teaching procedures reflect to a large degree the prescientific era when learning was regarded as a passive process and education was directed toward disciplining the 'mind,'" admitted the authors of a 1962 textbook on the high-school curriculum (Alberty and Alberty 1962, 13). Many teachers even rejected the fresh possibilities offered by casual schools. For example, educational and architectural journals of the period are filled with photographs of students sitting in movable desks that have been arranged into orderly ranks, mimicking the old-fashioned classroom with its seats bolted to the floor—defeating the purpose of portable furniture.

Thus the freedom implied by casual schools' informal ambiance often was contradicted by the austere reality of their formal pedagogies. But this was not the only contradiction visible in casual high schools. The entire educational system was entangled in a conflict between child-centered concepts and student-centered environments, on the one hand, and age-old paternalist practices, on the other. The social construction of adolescence, begun early in the century, was fully developed by the 1950s. For the first time, teenagers, being a mere step away from adulthood, were widely recognized as having unique interests, needs, and pressures. Statistics concerning Americans' average age of marriage and childbirth confirmed these impressions: most men married by age 23 and women by 21, and they began having children shortly thereafter, with many starting their new families soon after high-school graduation (May 2008). Despite this sprint into adulthood, teenagers were not treated as young adults in the public schools. The strict schedules, social rules, and rigid pedagogical techniques of previous generations continued even as school architects strove to make buildings more casual. Although their high-school curricula became increasingly oriented toward courses emphasizing their imminent roles as parents and workers in a free, democratic society, high school students remained relatively infantilized, with their movements, clothing, and behaviors tightly controlled by adults. A book for American high-school educators reminded readers that "rigid, regimented, routinized programs, coupled with dreary and obsolete buildings," did not "personify the American dream of education for all youth" (Taylor, McMahill, and Taylor 1960, 395).

Despite the best intentions of their designers, postwar school buildings facilitated administrators' ability to control students as much as the monumental generation of schoolhouses. As the buildings became increasingly transparent with the popularity of glass walls and larger windows, they also became more open to surveillance. Architects designed the schools without spaces the students could consider their own or places to congregate outside the watchful eyes of their teachers. In reality, these casual schools could be deceptive; often their relaxed architectural appearance disguised the institution's strict formal nature.

Suburban Schools

The decentralizing process of separating school spaces according to their use and diminishing the solid block building, which was over half a century old when World War II erupted, reached its culmination in the decades following the war, stimulated by the development of suburbs, where land was plentiful and inexpensive and school architects and educators could finally craft the parklike setting advocated by pioneers like Henry Barnard. Some suburban high schools grew as large as college campuses. Smaller neighborhood schools sprouted in tiny pocket parks surrounded by single-family homes. Educators touted the reduced scale of these schoolhouses, their abundant play areas, and their proximity. In an era before public-school systems extensively bussed students, children's ability to walk to and from school without crossing outside the residential enclave was a powerful selling point among prospective homebuyers. Neighborhood schools became embedded in American suburban life, not just as places of education and recreation, but also as community gathering spaces where adults voted, held meetings, and retreated to shelters in case of natural (or nuclear) disasters. In almost every case, the schools of this new generation were less imposing than their predecessors, opting for casual friendliness instead of monumental dignity. The suburban-school building surpassed the urban school as the nation's educational ideal—to the benefit of suburban-school districts and their administrators but the detriment of urban schoolchildren, who more likely than not had to suffer in old, deteriorating buildings. Postwar architectural journals practically ignored city schools until the EFL focused attention on them in the early 1960s, probably because few urban schools were constructed during the 1950s and those examples were constrained by forces that limited the options for interesting design solutions.

Unfortunately, a majority of those urban schools were used by black inner-city students. Their neglect was directly attributable to some of the reasons that gave rise to the neighborhood schools in the first place. A shift in the American population was occurring at the time, with whites moving to the suburbs in record numbers while blacks remained locked into deteriorating urban neighborhoods and dilapidated older school buildings, victims of mass discrimination techniques, such as redlining, where real-estate companies, banks, and mortgage lenders teamed to prohibit blacks from obtaining suburban properties. Simultaneously, the Great Migration of blacks from the rural South to the northern industrial cities continued, pouring millions into poor urban neighborhoods. As a result, the proportion of white people living in America's cities dropped while the number of blacks rose. Despite these changing demographics, educators and activists who proposed integration of existing schools or improvements in black facilities were met with stiff opposition.

The neighborhood-school policy that was so attractive to white families was viewed differently by the black victims of discrimination. School boards used tactics similar to the banks to exclude blacks from white schools by implementing rules that forced children to attend schools located within precisely drawn districts that helped keep the races separated. When combined with school-board decisions that funneled money into white schools and away from their black counterparts, this created extreme disparities in some areas: black students were often overcrowded into substandard older buildings because they were the closest schools to their homes, while just a few miles away white students studied in new facilities with empty seats and rooms to spare. This was not a new phenomenon: evidence indicates that as early as 1849, a free black parent sued the Boston public schools because his daughter had to walk past white schools to get to her black-only school. The Massachusetts state court ruled against the man, saying that separate schools were allowable as long as they were equal, thus prefiguring the "separate but equal" doctrine memorialized at the end of the century in the infamous *Plessy v. Ferguson* case. A few years later, the Massachusetts legislature passed a law mandating integrated classes in common schools, but no other states followed. Even after the U.S. Supreme Court invalidated legal segregation and the notion of "separate but equal" accommodations in the *Brown v. Board of Education of Topeka, Kansas* (1954) decision, neighborhood schools created de facto segregation in school districts across the nation.

Quite a few fortunate suburban schools in white neighborhoods, though, faced virtually no constraints in terms of finances, property size, quality of teachers, or numbers of students. In this atmosphere, architects explored the possibilities of extending the decentralized school even beyond the finger plan. One interesting result of these investigations was called the cluster plan. The October 1953 issue of *Architectural Forum* evaluated school designs and included case studies displaying the latest trends, like cluster planning, loft planning, zone planning, and multiuse corridors. The issue's highlight was its feature on the cluster plan, which the *Forum* called "1953's biggest news in schoolhouse planning" ("Case Study Schools" 1953, 127). Proclaiming the cluster plan's educational, economic, and even biological advantages, the journal could muster only one weak criticism—that some cluster-plan buildings were losing their unity of design as architects broke them into too many parts.

The cluster plan was a recent phenomenon on the American educational scene—so recent, in fact, that its prototype and "Patriarch," according to the *Forum*, was still under construction as the issue was published. The Heathcote Elementary School (1953) in Scarsdale, New York, demonstrated Perkins & Will's continuing innovativeness. Although many of the firm's educational buildings in the previous decade had explored variations of their Crow Island School, the Heathcote School extended its predecessor's best qualities into a new, attractive, soon-to-be popular form.

Similar to Crow Island, the Heathcote School's design derived from a new kind of classroom. Perkins's transformed the L-shaped room into a hexagon, gathered it with three other hexagons around a lozenge-like common area in a cluster, and detached the clusters from the building's core but connected them by a ramp inside a long corridor so that each cluster resembled a pinwheel at the end of a stick. The clusters' occupants were purposefully grouped by grade so that each assemblage (except for the kindergartners) held students from two consecutive grades in its four classrooms. The school's administrators hoped the cluster feature, in addition to providing the distinctive schoolrooms, would increase both pedagogical and curricular flexibility. Much stock was put in the commons areas in that respect. As a multipurpose space, each commons area—or foyer—contained movable coat-storage units, a piano, and a film projector. It was to be used for large-group activities, watching films, or playing indoors during inclement weather. The foyer also allowed children of different grades to mingle informally or attend classes together and seemed to inspire the teachers share projects and support each other.

The EFL felt Heathcote's architectural design inspired a movement toward team teaching and ungraded organization—two approaches that would become prevalent during the 1960s. It might also have added Heathcote's nascent house-plan organization: physically separating students into clusters gave the students a sense of belonging to a distinct unit, which educators were beginning to realize had a significant effect on morale and achievement. This notion would evolve into the so-called school-within-a-school concept over the next decades and continues to be an essential aspect of schools around the country. Although clustered classrooms and team teaching anticipated the future of American education, at least one commentator recognized something old-fashioned in both. One of the first commentators to review the Heathcote School discerned that the clusters actually resembled the old 18th-century schoolhouse: four classrooms in one building, one to each corner. "And the scheme wins back the intimacy of the 'school family' which those small, tightly knit schools often had," claimed the author ("Schools: Fresh Ideas and Long Range Criticism" 1952, 115).

Another new kind of school-building arrangement, called the loft plan, debuted in the late 1940s and became just as popular as cluster or finger plans. Its roots were in a hypothetical project sponsored by the *Architectural Forum*, which challenged architect Matthew Nowicki to speculate on the future of school design. Specifically, the journal's editors asked Nowicki to design a school building using the standard bay size of 24 by 24 feet from American industrial architecture and to replicate the factory's compact form rather than spreading out into long, thin fingers; both requests were inspired by an attempt to build as economically as possible. "*Forum*'s School for 1950" was the result: a rectangular one-story building for an elementary school containing nine classrooms, offices, a kitchen, and a combined gymnasium/auditorium. The bay system divided the building into a grid, with each classroom one bay wide and one-and-a-half bays long. The classrooms faced each other on either side of an open area that allowed circulation but was more than a traditional corridor; on the drawings, Nowicki labeled the space alternatively as "lunch-recreation-exhibition" or "general purpose area." In either case, it was a pioneering move in the development of multipurpose corridors. The school's appearance, as sketched in a few quick drawings, was odd from the outside, partly due to its unusual lighting scheme. The low-profiled box had few visible openings (the architect described them as "view-slots" rather than windows) and relied on top lighting, in the form of a domino-like pattern of plastic bubbles across the roof. In a concluding statement, the *Forum* felt the unique combination of industrial-bay sizes, compact floor plan, top lighting, and the multipurpose corridor was visionary and demonstrated a new, economical trend for school buildings.

Within a few years, the loft plan, as it became known, became a common feature of the school designer's repertoire. Loft plans returned school buildings to the closed-plan forms so popular in the 19th century. They had square or rectangular footprints, with all rooms in a single building organized around a courtyard or atrium. In effect, loft plans opposed the suburban model by "recentralizing" the schoolhouse. Educators responded positively. Loft-plan schools appeared in suburban and rural locations around the country. Their popularity arose from their economic benefits. Loft-plan schools required less wall surface than the decentralized finger- or cluster-plan buildings and fewer windows, which in itself was a considerable savings. But even more attractive was the flexibility of a one-story, steel-framed building with no interior partitions. Repetitive-bay structures were easier and faster to build. In many cases, the steel framing was left visible as part of the design.

Perhaps the most prominent early example of a loft-plan school was John Lyon Reid's Hillsdale High School (1956) in San Mateo, California. A massive structure enclosing five acres and holding over 1,000 students, the Hillsdale High School turned Nowicki's proposal idea into a reality. Hillsdale held all of its important parts within the confines of its walls, as Reid rejected the decentralization of finger or cluster plans; although large, the building was compact in that sense. The loft plan created an inward facing, self-contained structure. Its focal point was a parklike open-air courtyard encircled by covered walkways, with outdoor swimming and diving pools located at its center.

Reid's plan also rationally segregated interior space in the modern school tradition. The building's rectangular structure aligned to the cardinal points: the western section formed the academic wing, and the eastern area contained an auditorium, music rooms, and boys' and girls' gymnasiums. In between, the cafeteria, small theater, and shop rooms flanked the courtyard. Beyond the academic wing, the entire complex was further organized according to topography. Reid and his architects took advantage of a sloping site to form three terraces, each corresponding to a different aspect of the school's program. The academic area was on grade with the main parking lot. Then the building stepped down to the middle terrace, which contained the courtyard and surrounding rooms. The lowest level was for gymnasiums and the auditorium. In keeping with the school's noticeably casual atmosphere, the Hillsdale school included no staircases in the design. Students traversed between levels by ramps at each end of the courtyard.

Another point of similarity between Reid's and Nowicki's designs concerned the industrial basis of both. Nowicki had responded to the *Forum*'s request for a school building based on the standard bay size for industrial architecture. Reid followed suit, using a slightly larger bay (28 by 28 feet) but following the industrial format with a steel-grid framework and regularly spaced columns, a flat roof, and few fixed interior walls. This severe architectural language, associated with Ludwig Mies van der Rohe and seen in his most famous works, like Crown Hall at the Illinois Institute of Technology, connected school design with broader currents in the architectural world. To maximize the loft plan's potential, many of Hillsdale's classrooms included movable walls.

Hillsdale's academic wing belied its simple appearance. Also forming a rectangle—within the larger rectangle of the building proper—it was bisected along the short axis by an atrium for circulation and socializing. The atrium was wider than a typical corridor and open to the sky, with one end serving as the school's main entry and the other leading to the central courtyard. On either side of this social space were an assortment of classrooms and offices. Almost the entire perimeter of the academic wing was lined with classrooms, but perhaps more interesting were the innermost rooms: a significant portion of them were completely embedded within the building, with no windows and skylights for illumination. Reid followed Nowicki's "School for 1950" in relying on top lighting, but he replaced the prototype's curious plastic bubbles with over 600 rectangular light wells topped with skylights, made from a prismatic glass block developed a few years before at the University of Michigan. Perimeter rooms, unlike the *Forum* project, had full-size windows for added light.

One noteworthy development that permitted loft plans like Hillsdale High School to exist but was largely overlooked in the celebratory publicity given the school—which included an Honor Award from the American Institute of Architects—was the state of mechanical ventilation by midcentury. Hillsdale did not utilize a conventional air conditioner, in the sense that its equipment did not control the air's humidity, but it did provide a continuous flow of fresh air (which could be heated) to the windowless interior classrooms as well as the rooms with exterior windows. The main journal articles explaining the building failed to describe its mechanical system. By this time, architects and educators took for granted that they could create internal spaces regulated by mechanical equipment to the extent that access to fresh air was unnecessary; indeed, the entire notion of the windowless classroom rested on the foundation of an acceptable interior environment. In contrast, just a decade earlier, discussions of ventilation systems had been the norm in articles describing new buildings.

Prefabrication

Loft-plan schools resulted from the search for a means to make buildings quickly and inexpensively in an effort to keep up with surging postwar enrollments. The *Architectural Forum*'s challenge to Nowicki to create a school with the components and standards of an office building arose from this impulse, and it led others to experiment with prefabricated parts and construction systems. In 1961, a team of educators, architects, and manufacturers began work on what would become a prime example of the impact of technology on American school architecture: the School Construction Systems Development (SCSD) program. The SCSD, funded by the EFL and led by architect Ezra D. Ehrenkrantz (1932–2001), was aimed at developing flexible, affordable, and high-quality school buildings with prefabricated parts. This was not in itself a new idea, but the SCSD method was novel. Its creators wanted to meld contemporary production processes and the systems approach to problem solving with architectural-design and educational requirements. By merging design, manufacture, construction, and use into a seamless whole and involving all the participants in the process, the SCSD team hoped to lower costs and improve educational architecture.

In the early years of the 20th century, scientific-management principles had proliferated within American schools; from class schedules to pedagogical techniques to building floor plans, efficiency was the order of the day. During this period of public-school expansion, many cities and states instituted standardized building designs to save costs and improve quality. The federal government offered standardized plans and published books on admirable school designs from across the country. The efficacy of these mass designs, however, was often offset by their uninspiring results, as critics chided the lack of individuality and stripped-down quality of standardized schools. By midcentury, educators and architects started to regard school-building standardization favorably when skyrocketing enrollments caused by the baby boom, combined with a deteriorating stock of existing buildings, necessitated more schools than could be built under contemporary mass-production practices. Standardized building plans were easy to construct and proven successful, especially in rural communities, and standardized parts were becoming more accessible. In England, the postwar situation had been even direr than in the

United States in terms of resources and needs, but educators and architects, working with local and national government representatives, were able to create excellent, affordable school buildings using prefabricated, lightweight metal pieces assembled on the site. One of these, the CLASP system (Consortium of Local Authorities Special Program), was used to erect a demonstration school at the Milan Triennial of 1960 that won high honors, received international publicity, and helped bring English school construction techniques to the forefront.

Ezra Ehrenkranz became familiar with those techniques as a Fulbright scholar at England's Building Research Station. He brought his knowledge back to the United States and devised his own version of the CLASP system, which led to a small group of schools in California with long-span steel-frame structures and no internal load-bearing walls. Ehrenkrantz found that his interests' merged with those of the EFL. With Ford Foundation money, the EFL worked with editors of the *Architectural Forum* to organize a "joint inquiry" into the status of school construction. An assemblage of architects, educators, manufacturing representatives, and bureaucrats brainstormed such questions as: "With all the science, skill, and organizational ability available in the world's most advanced free-enterprise industrial community, should it not be possible to lift the whole discussion of schoolhouse economy to a new plateau? Should there not be a technical break-through?" The group, including Ehrenkrantz, concluded that the development of "prefabricated component systems, so-called Erector sets out of which any number of schoolhouse plans could be assembled," was both feasible and desired ("New Proposals to Cut School Costs" 1961, 111).

This outcome led the EFL and Ehrenkrantz to develop the SCSD and partner with 12 California school districts as a test. The SCSD's creators hoped to redirect the focus of industrial standardization to the school building's components, rather than its plan or appearance. SCSD enlisted manufacturers as partners to develop standardized parts. According to an innovative bidding system, manufacturers were provided with performance specifications created by educators and architects rather than product requirements; they were then free to design the component as they wished. Manufacturers of different parts had to work together to make sure their various products could be used in harmony. As a last step, architects could combine the manufacturers' components any way they wanted. This integrated team process exemplified the systems approach to problem solving that became dominant in the aerospace industry and the military.

The SCSD produced 13 schools in total, with the first completed in 1966, and then turned over the system to the local district architects.

The following year, the EFL and SCSD published an extensive summary of their success. But that success was limited. Overall, the SCSD trial indicated that it did not save time or money over contemporary construction practices and, in some cases, could cost more and take longer to build. But there were some savings in operational costs when renovations occurred to these buildings after a few years of use. The SCSD became the most publicized **prefabrication** initiative in the United States, largely because of the EFL's involvement, but there were other attempts to harness the nation's industrial power for the benefit of public education through the mass production of school-building parts, all with varying degrees of success.

The spirit of investigation that pervaded projects like the SCSD also materialized in more visible aspects of school design like the building's form. Architects continued to explore decentralization and specialization in schoolhouses, with approval from educators who viewed school design as a collaborative process intended to generate uniquely adapted spaces that fused architecture, pedagogy, and curriculum in a common cause. Unorthodox shapes and unusual combinations became conventional in 1960s classrooms and clusters. A late 1960s project that symbolized alternative attitudes toward the American school building, John M. Johansen's L. Frances Smith Elementary School (1969) in Columbus, Indiana, displayed the architect's distinctive vision for the elementary school. The building was erected with the help of the Cummins Engine Foundation, established in 1954 by industrialist J. Irwin Miller as a means to encourage quality architecture in Miller's hometown. The foundation offered to pay architect's fees and a portion of the construction costs of any school or public building in or around Columbus if the client selected the architect from a preassembled list of high-status firms. As a result of this generous offer, nearly 40 pieces of architecture have been created for this town of 30,000 in south-central Indiana by such notable architects as Eero Saarinen, Robert Venturi, I. M. Pei, and Skidmore, Owings & Merrill (SOM). To date, 11 school buildings have been part of the project.

Johansen's contribution was the most unique of Columbus's schools and the most controversial. He conceived the elementary-school building as an upward spiraling cluster plan with nine different levels connected by ramps. The original floor plan featured three clusters radiating outward from a central courtyard. The clusters held the school's classrooms and sometimes larger spaces like a dining hall and multipurpose room. Three basic components made up the school, and each was constructed of a different material to make the disparate functions of the building visible. Those spaces that were communally shared, such as the entrance lobby, administrative offices, dining room, and library, were formed from cast-in-place concrete. The classrooms—which were intended to be flexible with operable partitions—were made with steel frames and faced with corrugated steel. Finally, the ramps for maneuvering between floors passed through tubes made from a concrete shell covered with corrugated steel. These tubes proved to be the most unusual aspect of the project, and Johansen's decision to paint them in bright primary colors added to the playful atmosphere.

Smith Elementary School's design reflected typical school concerns of the time, including prefabrication, flexibility, and easy expansion, but its unorthodox appearance was due in part to the architect's fascination with biological organisms, to the point where he described the classrooms as flower petals and the connecting tubes as stalks. In the experimental atmosphere that pervaded 1960s school architecture, Johansen was not the only architect to explore organic inspirations. John A. Shaver established a nationwide practice in this period with scores of buildings shaped like circles, hexagons, or other unconventional forms. Shaver's Valley Winds Elementary School (1964) near St. Louis adopted the snail's shell as the basis for a circular school with interior spaces arranged as a spiral. The walls' extreme curvature eliminated the need for barriers, giving the spaces an informal quality. Those few distinct rooms were wedge shaped. Far from being a gimmick, Shaver argued that the building enclosed space more efficiently than a traditional form, requiring less exterior surface and eliminating the long corridors that dominated so many school buildings. An early-1970s Shaver school was shaped like a kidney and combined open-plan ideas with the spatial segregation made possible by curved walls. Similar designs by other architects across the country demonstrated that every aspect of the early-20th-century monumental-school building had been subject to manipulation at this point, from its size, bulk, and verticality to its overall form and the shape of its schoolrooms.

Urban Schools

Johansen's attempt to inject levity into school architecture appeared to be successful, with students praising Smith Elementary School and the *Architectural Forum* applauding his "adventure for children," but few others followed his extreme departure from convention. Aside from its sometimes eccentric form, the suburban school seemed to be a solved problem to many architects and educators, with the only design questions left to solve having to do with calculating how many of each kind of room was needed for the amount of students expected. Conversely, urban schools began to receive much more attention in the 1960s than in the past as high-profile projects and spirited debates over the quality of city school buildings came to the fore.

The evolution of schoolrooms, in terms of their lighting, ventilation, and adaptation to curricular and pedagogical changes, took place in buildings of all levels in every part of the country, but the innovations highlighted in this chapter, such as the decentralized finger or cluster plans and the reduced scale, took place almost exclusively in suburbs or rural communities, where land was abundant and school facilities could stretch. City schools told a different story. Larger cities had all participated in the creation of the monumental-school buildings during the early part of the 20th century. As the existing stock of city schools began to deteriorate, by midcentury, educators found themselves in a serious predicament.

Like most aspects of American education, the urban-school situation had racial connotations. By midcentury, the population of the nation's inner cities had begun to change dramatically with the influx of blacks from the rural South and the exodus of whites to the suburbs. Statistics show that the Great Migration resulted in a new demographic map: between 1950 and 1966, 86 percent of black population growth occurred in what was defined as the "center city," and 12 percent affected the "urban fringe," meaning that by the mid-1960s, 98 percent of America's blacks lived in urban environments (Wiley 2011, 37). As a result, urban-school inadequacies were disproportionately felt by black parents and students.

The *Architectural Forum* brought the urban-school problem to architects' attention in its 1949 issue on school buildings, lamenting that "not one new school building worth its cost has been built in the last decade" and specifically targeting New York: "Most of the things that are wrong with New York Schools can be summed up by saying that they are just too big" ("Today's Schools—the Bigger the City, the Tougher the Problem" 1949, 85, 90). Six years later, the journal saw signs of encouragement in New York's postwar school-building program, including experimentation with private architects, compact floor plans, lower ceiling heights, and different-sized classrooms. But even the newest schools faced the same problem: how to make urban-school buildings at human scale?

In the early 1960s, the EFL took on urban-school design. In typical fashion, it organized a group of experts into a conference, with representatives from education, academia, and architecture discussing the planning of urban schools and reviewing a group of proposals from Harvard architecture students. The group singled out two factors that had the greatest impact on school design and construction in big cities, factors very familiar to urban educators but less so for suburban educators: the high cost of real estate and continual but unpredictable population shifts. Although the EFL did not specifically discuss vandalism, its report subtly acknowledged that it was a third consideration. In New York City, for example, the school board pushed school architects to design windows with small-pane glass so that janitors, rather than union workers, could replace the windows in case of breakage.

Among the recommendations made by the EFL and its team of experts were to convert nonschool buildings into schools; to use the space beneath elevated buildings (like Harlem's IS 201) for playgrounds and activities, and roofs as well; to integrate educational spaces with nonschool counterparts like commercial establishments in the same building (called "common occupancy"); and to explore the possibilities of demountable and transportable classrooms. Except for the suggestion to utilize the space beneath a building, none of these were brand-new ideas, and none look too far-fetched in our present educational world, since many of them are now commonplace. One further proposal, however, seemed more desperate than reasoned, and it is difficult to imagine today. The EFL advanced the notion of using **air rights** as a solution to overcrowding. This was a popular tool of urban renewal strategists that involved purchasing the right to build above or beneath existing structures, which could often be had for much less than the cost of actual land, or conversely selling the right to build in the air above existing schools, which proved lucrative in many cases when skyscrapers rose over older school buildings. In the early 1960s, developers and politicians utilized air-rights transactions to erect buildings above highways and railroad yards as alternatives to destroying (or remodeling) existing properties. A conspicuous example of the practice was the Pan Am Building in New York City, erected in the air above Grand Central Station and straddling Fifth Avenue. Some educators were similarly attracted to the concept. School boards in Baltimore and New York explored the possibility of creating entire "education parks"—campus-like clusters of school buildings of all grade levels gathered in a landscaped park—above downtown highways.

Despite the attention from influential organizations like the EFL, the quality of design of urban schools continued to be subpar. Not until 1963 did the *Architectural Forum* express some satisfaction with city school buildings: "For the first time in a great many years, FORUM is able to show a considerable number of big-city schools—both built and projected—that look like fortresses of the mind, rather than penitentiaries of the spirit" ("Meanwhile, an Encouraging Lift in the Design of Urban Schools" 1963, 77). The journal's excitement stemmed from a recognition that forces in school administration, finance, and building construction were combining to elevate the quality of urban-school design, and to prove it, snapshots of new schools or projects from various cities filled over 20 pages following the article. Much variety could be discerned in this presentation, from Edward Durell Stone's flat-roofed, Greek-temple-like PS 199 in New York City to Harry Weese's brick-faced agglomeration of hexagonal classrooms at the Jens Jensen Elementary School in Chicago to SOM's corporate-inspired Harry A. Conte Community School in New Haven, Connecticut. Among those unbuilt projects displayed was Curtis & Davis' future IS 201, a building that the *Forum* praised for its handsome facade and practical solution to the urban noise problem.

The satisfaction with the quality of urban-school design exhibited by commentators like the *Architectural Forum* did not last. By the end of the decade, even the EFL's tone was slightly weary after nearly 10 years of struggling with urban-school issues. "In sum, there is no one way to solve any city's educational problems," wrote EFL president Harold B. Gores, in an essay entitled "The Demise of Magic Formulas." "Everything needs to be tried" (Toffler 1968, 172). Gores was thinking beyond the design of individual schools, but his advice was equally germane to architecture. From the late 1960s through the 1970s, urban-school architecture received continuous attention from architects and educators. A renaissance of urban-school design occurred, spawning a variety of successful and unsuccessful buildings and unbuilt projects that tried to incorporate some of the best aspects of suburban schools while acknowledging the dissimilar environment. What many of these projects had in common was a tendency toward inward-looking floor plans behind thick, solid exterior walls. Unfortunately, sometimes the desire to create strong, visible institutional buildings to serve as community anchors for the surrounding neighborhood overwhelmed the architects' and educators' sensitivity to how those same buildings might be viewed by the people whose children would use them.

Referring to the school building as a "jail" or "prison" is embedded in the folklore of childhood and education. Such talk usually reveals more about children's wrestling match with adult authority than about the building's design. In the case of many postwar urban schools, however, the penitentiary reference was too apt and sprung equally from anger at government institutions and disappointment with defensive-looking schoolhouses. The efforts to save money and protect property by putting fences around schoolyards and screening windows, making them smaller, or even removing them—combined with such unrelated factors as the energy crisis, the move toward better electrical efficiency, and the maturity of concrete as an inexpensive and expressive material—produced a generation of urban-school buildings that were large, bulky, thick-walled, and often very unfriendly looking.

Perhaps the most publicized clash between educators and civilians took place in response to Harlem's IS 201. As mentioned above, the people responsible for commissioning and designing this windowless school were quite satisfied with the results, and the architectural world applauded the final product. But the community had a different, unexpected response. Problems began when the final renderings of the building were unveiled to the public. The school's Parents' Negotiating Committee claimed to have been excluded from the design process and was disturbed by the final results. The building's appearance became a point of controversy as the students' parents viewed the windowless exterior not as a logical design choice but rather as a commentary on the surrounding environment and the condition of their lives. Harlem residents referred to IS 201 by such demeaning monikers as "the prison," "the tomb on stilts," "the warehouse," "the fortress," and "Fort Necessity." Local activists were outraged. Lawrence Neal, educational director of the Black Panther Party, attempted to explain. "The whole life experience of the blacks is one of confinement in the ghetto," he wrote. "To them, their community is a prison, and this is fortified by the fact that society prevents them from moving out. This building confirms their feelings of imprisonment." He also ridiculed the notion that a windowless building could isolate students from the sometimes ugly reality outside. "Harlem is a ghetto. Are they trying to exclude that reality from them?" Neal asked incredulously. "The kids need to face it. They've still got to go outside" (Bailey 1966, 50).

When the $5 million school opened its doors in the fall of 1966, only a handful of the expected 500 students showed up. In addition to feeling marginalized during the design process, parents were outraged by the city's failed promise to integrate the school, so they picketed the building and refused to send their children. IS 201 was intended to be a **magnet school**, drawing students from around the city with its new facilities, experimental curriculum, smaller class sizes, and supposedly higher quality of teaching and equipment. But the board of education's efforts to recruit white students from nearby Queens and the Bronx failed, forcing the integration effort to shift goals. Officials next outlined a plan for IS 201 that would ideally result in a roughly fifty-fifty split between blacks and Puerto Ricans, reflecting the makeup of the surrounding neighborhood. Black activists felt betrayed by the move, arguing that it would not be true integration unless white students made up a substantial segment of the school's student population. Community groups demanded white children be brought in to remedy the situation. When the board refused, a one-week boycott ensued.

The IS 201 episode touched on many problems with American education at the time, including how seemingly innocuous architectural decisions could exacerbate inherent tensions between educators and the public. The architects believed they had made the most of a difficult site in a distressed neighborhood and used architecture to provide the neighborhood with amenities it previously lacked and an atmosphere to maximize student potential. The educators were impressed by the design's implied economy and adaptability to progressive educational practices. The community, however, viewed the building differently. Neighborhood residents, already upset by administrative decisions regarding location and integration, unleashed their frustrations on the building's design—it was something tangible and material toward which they could aim their fury. It also was a building they interpreted differently than its creators. Many urban schools of this "fortress" generation revealed a disjunction between symbolic intent and perceived reality. Angry responses to IS 201, like Lawrence Neal's, implied that the architects must have been middle-class white males with no experience with or feel for the inner city or its inhabitants. Members of the community had no training in architecture and no sense of its historical development. When inner city people saw the forms of these new schools, they were not reminded of houses, corporate offices, small businesses, or any of the other metaphors used to describe suburban-school buildings; the only aesthetically comparable structures in their understanding were jails, penitentiaries, and police stations—institutional buildings with negative connotations.

Miscalculations in the design of urban schools by educators and architects undermined their cause. While suburban schools presented architectural design challenges affected by outside considerations, like increasing enrollments and inadequate financing, the social context for most of these schools was stable. City schools, enmeshed in a more complex web of issues, carried a greater burden. America's cities were crumbling in the 1960s and 1970s as white residents fled to the suburbs to follow jobs and seek more living space. Urban renewal projects, such as the Model Cities Program, used federal money to revitalize decrepit city centers and neighborhoods with an aim toward stopping or even reversing this flow of migrants and increasing residents' participation in local decision making. Advocates recognized the significant role schools would play in such programs; indeed, one of the reasons behind white flight was thought to be the suburbs' reputation for providing better-quality education. So the initiatives devoted to stabilizing and reviving the country's urban areas necessarily included city schools. "For if the school is, in fact, more and more intimately tied to its urban context, then the schoolhouse itself must be seen in a fresh light," claimed the EFL. "It is no longer a matter of mere bricks and mortar but an instrument of social policy—an agent of change" (Toffler 1968, 163).

A community-school movement began to grow in the 1960s and bloomed in the 1970s, with deep roots in American history. Schools had opened their doors to the public almost from the very start, when schoolhouses might serve as a temporary or permanent meeting hall. In the larger urban schools of the antebellum era, the top-floor assembly halls often held members of the public during school exercises. By the late 19th century, architects frequently arranged monumental-school buildings so that the public could enter the auditorium and gymnasium (or swimming pool) from their own sets of doors. In the 1900s, citizens across the country began to realize two important things: that public-school buildings belonged to the public, having been paid for with their tax dollars, and that these buildings could be used to engage the surrounding community in a number of educational and entertainment events beyond their ordinary use for educating children. Various clubs, associations, and organizations lobbied school boards to open the school buildings during off-hours. The resulting programs adopted in most large American cities helped to expand the school's role in society and increase the school building's significance.

Educational historians consider Rochester, New York, to be the birthplace of the organized social-center movement. In 1907, a group of 11 local organizations formed a School Extension Committee that was granted access to public-school property and allocated a small portion of the city's educational budget. The committee organized a series of lectures, dances, shows, concerts, art exhibitions, and dinners and opened school gymnasiums, showers, libraries, and music rooms to the public on a regular basis. Its overwhelming success led to the rapid spread of the social-center idea. Wisconsin passed the first state law authorizing the establishment of social centers in 1911. It provided citizens' organizations the right to use public-school buildings free of charge (Perry 1915, 471). According to contemporary accounts, 71 cities in 21 states had created schoolhouse social centers by 1913, and 16 states had followed Wisconsin's legislative example by 1914. Social centers also received official sanction from such organizations as the National Educational Association, which authorized its own Department on the Wider Use of Schoolhouses in 1915.

All of these extracurricular activities were new. Some wider utilization of school buildings occurred in the late 19th century, but rarely was there an entire system of programs organized on a large scale. This attitude began to change after efficiency advocates argued that the school plant should be used at night and on weekends as well as during the day. For decades, critics attacked expensive urban "palaces" as too costly, especially when they were occupied only a portion of the day, five days a week, and not all year round. The social-center movement's popularity was a boon to advocates for more effective uses of school property. A zealous advocate of this idea was Gary, Indiana, superintendent William A. Wirt, who created an innovative educational system partly intended to increase public use of the school building. Wirt's Gary Plan (also frequently called the Platoon School or Work-Study-Play System) kept students in constant motion by rotating them throughout the building, thus using all of its parts simultaneously. Each different subject in an expansive curriculum was taught in its own room rather than the traditional practice of most subjects being taught in the same room. The school day was broken into periods and the students moved to a different room every hour. Theoretically, the platoon system allowed all schoolrooms to be in constant use throughout the entire day. It also permitted twice as many students to be educated at the same time as the standard school. Further, in an effort to utilize the schoolhouse as much as possible, the system facilitated weekend activities for members of the community. Thus, Wirt's concept of efficiency meshed perfectly with the social-center idea.

The social-center movement affected urban-school architecture across the country. Architects began to think of ways to provide public access and accommodations beyond those needed for the students. The notion of the schoolhouse as a public gathering place influenced more than just the building's plan. Commentators singled out the enlarged auditorium, which was relocated from the top floor to the first floor; public entrances so visitors could bypass classrooms; branch libraries; shower baths; playgrounds; movable furniture in classrooms; and larger gymnasiums as architectural partners to the inclusive schoolhouse. The social-center movement did not directly initiate any of these architectural developments, but the changing attitude toward the wider use of school buildings probably facilitated their adoption by architects and educators.

Neighborhood revitalization in the 1960s and 1970s offered urban-school buildings new roles in the postwar world, but two of those roles revisited the earlier 20th century: the school as civic monument and community center. Urban-renewal advocates argued that the wave of new school construction sweeping through America's cities, propelled by government dollars, provided an opportunity to capitalize on architecture's symbolic value and its social promise. Fine new schoolhouses could become an object of local pride, and because of their size and bulkiness, school buildings were visually conspicuous in the community. The EFL promoted the notion of the urban school as "'neighborhood capital'—*the* significant architectural element" (Ferrer 1964, 2).

Language like this echoed similar statements by educators and architects from the late 19th century, the era of urban schools that were monumental in both size and spirit, adorned in historical styles and symbolically announcing the new role of public education in American society. The circumstances were far different, however, during the EFL's time. The earlier generation of monumental schools was boasting to a public that included many who were skeptical of the need for such schools. In contrast, the 1960s schools often were welcomed by the neighbors as a sign of their politicians' civic investment or, at least, a recognition by the city that they existed. Advocates argued that a single school building in a declining urban area could be interpreted as a "sign of intent" on the part of local government to address its citizens' problems, therefore helping raise morale.

Another important aspect of the new schools was their accessibility to the public, often despite the perceived defensiveness of the building's form. It was in this sense that the schoolhouse could fulfill its role as the "neighborhood capital." Harold Gores—in language that again mimicked reformers from the previous century—insisted that urban schoolhouses become "the people's college, their town hall, their cultural center, their country club, their school" (Toffler 1968, 171). The notion of the school building itself as an investment in the neighborhood had proven itself valid in the suburbs, where neighborhood schools had become centers of social life in addition to centers for learning.

Thus it was not unprecedented for educators to expect postwar urban schoolhouses to serve the same functions for their communities. The "neighborhood capital" or the "cultural center" expanded the school building's role beyond educating children and into the realm of social change; the school as neighborhood center for meetings, rallies, celebrations, or any other noneducational event gave citizens a headquarters for organizing themselves to face the vicissitudes of urban life. In some cases, cities used urban-renewal money to create cultural complexes where the schoolhouse and community center occupied separate buildings but remained conceptually tied by their physical proximity. The most publicized example of this trend occurred in New Haven, Connecticut, where Mayor Richard C. Lee's city government engaged outstanding architects like Perkins & Will, Louis Kahn, and Eero Saarinen to develop marquee school buildings as part of a long-term urban-renewal campaign. The mayor's office initiated this project by engaging Dr. Cyril G. Sargent, professor of education at Harvard University, to conduct a comprehensive survey of the city's existing schoolhouses. Sargent's report was alarming: he proposed the demolition of 14 schools, the abandonment of 3 more, and the construction of 15 new school buildings to take their place.

The report further suggested changes in the structure of New Haven's schools, arguing for a different arrangement than the existing divisions of grades 1 through 6 (elementary), 7 through 9 (junior high), and 10 through 12 (high school).

The city followed Sargent's report to the letter by setting in motion a plan to replace 40 percent of its existing school buildings. Three projects in particular were intended to attract public attention to New Haven's progressive marriage of community revitalization and school reform. Saarinen's firm (Kevin Roche, John Dinkeloo and Associates after his untimely death in 1960) was engaged to design a large high school (Richard C. Lee High School 1964), and Perkins & Will was hired to create a prototype elementary-school building that could be replicated throughout the city. Perhaps the most visible aspect of the project, however, was an assemblage of buildings adjacent to Wooster Square. In the middle third of a square city block, SOM architects Gordon Bunshaft and Natalie de Blois devised a monumental court, grouping three buildings in line—a school, an auditorium, and a library/senior center—with a pinched plaza between them. This kind of scheme, pairing classically inspired structures with a formal arrangement around a plaza, was popular in the architectural world at the time and best demonstrated by New York's Lincoln Center, then under construction.

The largest building of the ensemble was the Harry A. Conte Community School (1962), a simple two-story building with a square doughnut plan and an open-air central courtyard. The elementary school served children from kindergarten through eighth grade and included 26 standard classrooms and a gymnasium and swimming pool intended for neighborhood use. Next to the school, and much smaller, was a 350-seat auditorium connected to the Conte School via an underground passage. The third building, a two-story library and senior center, acted as a gateway to the complex from Wooster Square. All three of these buildings shared similar formal characteristics: rectangular or square outlines, two-story height, flat roofs, and a visible reinforced-concrete structure. In the library and auditorium, the concrete supports formed a modern colonnade, while in the Conte School the vertical and horizontal structural members were extruded from the building's full-height glass walls to block the sun, thereby establishing a grid pattern that revealed the school's modular design and referenced SOM's highly publicized corporate work.

The EFL's enthusiasm about the New Haven school campaign led to a publication, *The Schools and Urban Renewal: A Case Study from New Haven* (1964). Educators in other cities followed suit, drafting their own plans for community-center buildings adjacent to schools to create neighborhood capitals. The main focus of governmental reforms, however, was not directed toward construction of new school facilities or even the refurbishing of existing buildings, although both of those initiatives occurred. Instead, most educators were focused on translating the dreams of President Lyndon Johnson's Great Society into a workable reality for inner-city children. Racial desegregation and compensatory education measures (specific programs intended to redress the gap between urban students and their suburban counterparts, such as remedial-reading training, psychological counseling, and teacher preparation programs) were a greater concern, although the quality of school facilities became implicated in both efforts. During Johnson's administration, such sweeping reforms as the Civil Rights Act of 1964, the Elementary and Secondary Education Act of 1965, and the Demonstration Cities and Metropolitan Development Act of 1966 all brought increased attention and expanded funding to urban education, part of which would eventually trickle down to school facilities. But as the new decade dawned, while some urban-school buildings might have achieved a community status commensurate with suburban neighborhood schools, most continued to lag behind in both quality and adaptation to educational practices.

THE 1970S AND BEYOND

The 1970s

If school architecture can be thought of as improving steadily from the last third of the 19th century onward—in terms of better school design and deeper understanding of children and their social and learning patterns—that progression halted in the 1970s, largely due to the effects of an economic recession and the end of the baby boom. The authors of a popular history of American education described the 1970s as "both a retreat from the conflict and activism of the 1960s, and a period of reassessment and redirection for the nation" (Urban and Wagner 2004, 310). School districts around the country were forced to deal with new realities: they had more school buildings than needed, the existing stock of schools was deteriorating, and funding for new construction or renovation was disappearing as budgets tightened.

A series of events in the mid-1970s stimulated a worldwide economic decline that brought an end to a postwar boom economy that had lasted nearly 30 years. When the United States supported Israel in the 1973 Arab-Israeli War, the Organization of Petroleum Exporting Countries (OPEC)—predominantly comprised of Arab countries in the Middle East—retaliated by declaring an oil embargo on those Western nations that had sided with Israel. The five-month boycott drove the price of oil far higher than previous record levels, and it continued to rise even after the embargo ended. This event combined with changes in global monetary policy to incite an international recession, causing inflation, unemployment, and severe declines in stock and bond markets. In the United States, this occurred simultaneously with President Richard Nixon's Watergate scandal and subsequent resignation and the fall of Saigon, ending the divisive Vietnam War. All of these events conspired to bring about an end to the prosperity that had begun after World War II and carried the United States to its position of economic and military leadership.

The 1970s recession would prove to be the country's worst economic downturn since the Great Depression. Architectural firms were particularly affected. Those designers fortunate enough to remain employed in the depressed economy found less money available for projects, and, in the face of the energy crisis, clients increasingly demanded energy-efficient measures like better HVAC systems and specially treated glass. It was during this period, for example, that the windowless classroom reached its zenith. New school construction nearly stopped, and, for the first time, efforts to refurbish existing structures became a high priority. The federal government became active with such initiatives as the Institutional Conservation Program (sometimes called the Schools and Hospitals Program) of 1977, which supported awareness of energy conservation in school buildings and spurred significant research into other means of saving energy in schools, and the National Energy Act of 1978, which established grants for schools and other institutions willing to incorporate energy-conservation measures. Those schools that were constructed tended to be more compact than in previous decades, with smaller windows and fewer long corridors. School architecture was in a kind of holding pattern: the most popular architectural and educational developments of the 1960s—like open plans, access to the outdoors, community access to schools, movable partitions, house plans, and team teaching—continued unabated, but new ideas (other than in the shape of classrooms or their arrangement within the building) seemed scarce. Architects increased their experimentation with prefabricated components, which proved attractive to administrators struggling with shrinking construction and maintenance budgets, and explored different construction materials. Economy replaced flexibility, which had reigned over the field for years as the guiding idea behind school design.

The recession forced educators to take a hard look at their school systems and adjust their plans for the future. Another factor entering into the picture was the country's decreasing birth rate, which fell precipitously from the late 1950s to the early 1970s before leveling off. As a result, public-school enrollments dropped every year between 1971 and 1984, with a 15 percent decline overall (National Center for Education Statistics 1993). As the baby boom tailed off, many school districts found themselves with surplus spaces. They also tended to defer maintenance during these troubled financial times. Because so many school facilities had been constructed in the previous two decades, this was not an immediate concern when the recession began, but over time, maintenance problems would accumulate, and urban schools in particular suffered. In the midst of the various crises during the 1970s, one positive development that occurred involved the design or remodeling of school buildings to accommodate children with disabilities.

Americans with Disabilities Act

School buildings created to accommodate children with various disabilities are a relatively new phenomenon in the educational world, dating back only to the 1970s and appearing only because of federal government initiatives. Prior to that time, some school districts erected facilities for "special" students, who were segregated from their peers. These facilities ranged from temporary wooden portable buildings to brick or concrete schools imperceptible from any other school building in the district—which is to say that there were few if any actual design accommodations in these buildings to help disabled children get through their school day. Then in the spirit of change that pervaded the 1960s, Congress created the National Commission on Architectural Barriers to Rehabilitation of the Handicapped, whose report led to the 1968 Architectural Barriers Act (ABA). For the first time, buildings were required to be constructed so as to allow equal access to disabled persons—in this case, any facility designed, built, altered, or leased with federal funds. President Lyndon B. Johnson sought to use the federal government as a model for a new generation of accessible buildings with barrier-free designs that could put an end to the "cruel discrimination" against disabled citizens.

Although well intentioned, the ABA's enforceability provisions were weak, and after a few years, it became clear to government officials that the quality of accessible design varied widely in the absence of design standards or oversight responsibility. Congress rectified the problem, using the Rehabilitation Act of 1973 to establish the Architectural and Transportation Barriers Compliance Board (later renamed the Access Board) to oversee ABA compliance and propose guidelines for designing barrier-free federal facilities. By the end of the decade, the board was working on a set of standards, which resulted in the federal government's first comprehensive accessibility requirements, the Minimum Guidelines and Requirements for Accessible Design (1982). The Access Board's influence increased throughout the 1980s, culminating in the landmark Americans with Disabilities Act of 1990 (ADA), a law created to protect the rights of disabled people by banning discrimination against them in the private and governmental sectors. The law extended the accessibility gains of the previous decades, requiring employers to provide reasonable accommodations for the disabled and governments to meet Access Board standards for public places. In particular, the list of public facilities mandated to be accessible included public schools for the first time. Since their authorization, ADA standards have continued to evolve and strengthen. Accessible schools are now ubiquitous in our society, even older buildings that have been renovated for current use and portable or modular structures as well.

The ADA established national design requirements for schools at a time when they were most needed. Coinciding with accessibility concerns in the 1960s was a growing awareness of inequalities in the education of children with mental and physical disabilities, and once again the federal government's involvement was crucial. A major stride toward remedying this iniquity came with the Education for All Handicapped Children Act of 1975, wherein Congress required public schools receiving federal funds to comply with federal requirements mandating equal access for the disabled. As a result of these federal regulations, new design requirements altered existing and proposed schoolhouses to make them more accessible. The key was to remove all barriers, both physical and conceptual. Changes ranged from such small-scale adjustments as new signage and redesigned bathroom facilities to larger adaptations like ramps, elevators, and wheelchair lifts. At a time when critics were castigating the public schools and highlighting the iniquities inherent in the system, designing for disabilities was an educational success.

The 1980s and 1990s

Administrators made few curricular changes during the 1970s as the population wave broke. The ratio of academic to nonacademic courses in high schools remained stable, along with consistent criticism that the public schools were failing the nation's youth by aiming to make them happy rather than teaching them important skills and knowledge. Opponents of the differentiated curriculum argued that its original intentions had been distorted to the point where schools now served as custodial warehouses for children instead of providing academic and vocational training. Dissatisfaction with the status quo bred alternatives like charter schools, private academies, and school vouchers. As these protests grew louder, educators increasingly relied on standardized achievement tests to gauge student learning and measure the system's effectiveness—and they were often disappointed. Overall, the 1970s marked a period of great anxiety among educators and commentators concerned about the quality of American education and fearful that the advances of the immediate postwar years were being dissipated.

The dire situation in America's schools continued until the 1980s when a reinvigorated economy and rising birth rates brought more students and schools. The most significant changes in public education occurred in curricula as a "back-to-basics" adjustment—somewhat similar to the crisis educators faced in the late 1950s after the Sputnik launch—brought more traditional subjects and pedagogical techniques back into the classroom. For example, the educational world reacted strongly to the publication of *A Nation at Risk: The Imperative for Educational Reform*, a 1983 publication by the National Commission on Excellence (NCE). The report condemned the woeful state of American secondary education. Its authors' main critique was that the nation's high-school curricula lacked depth. "Secondary school curriculums have been homogenized and diffused to the point that they no longer have a central purpose," they wrote. "In effect, we have a cafeteria-style curriculum in which the appetizers and desserts can easily be mistaken for the main course" (National Commission on Excellence in Education 1983, 18). The NCE recommended that curricular differentiation—the high-school standard for nearly a century—be abandoned. Instead of trying to offer individualized programs for students based on their interests and talents, schools around the country were encouraged to adopt a uniform academic curriculum for all high school students that emphasized "the five basics" (English, mathematics, science, social studies, and computer science).

This suggestion of a return to 19th-century common-school ideals resonated with both educators and the public. Within three years of the report's publication, 45 states and the District of Columbia had raised high-school graduation requirements, and many others had strengthened math and science requirements. Comprehensive testing occupied a salient role in the new educational scheme as a means to monitor progress toward these goals. "The context of high school education has changed," wrote G. Alfred Hess, describing the new movement. "The focus has shifted from warehousing and managing the behavior of kids to a focus on student learning . . . a new focus on academic performance" (*School Reform in Chicago* 2001, 44).

As educators evaluated their programs in light of *A Nation at Risk* and numerous other scathing critiques, a spike in new school construction began in the late 1980s, a response to the slightly rising population of school-age children and the deteriorating state of existing schoolhouses. The recession-influenced hiatus in school construction, as mentioned above, coincided with decreased efforts to maintain and refurbish those schools that were already in use. But a massive injection of attention and money into the country's school infrastructure helped publicize a nationwide epidemic of aging school buildings. In the late 1990s, Department of Education investigators calculated the average American public school building at 42 years old. The U.S. General Accounting Office estimated that one-third of all public-school students, or about 14 million children, attended classes in structures that needed "extensive repair or replacement" (U.S. General Accounting Office 1995, 2). And just a few years later, the National Trust for Historic Preservation placed neighborhood schools on its list of "America's 11 most Endangered Places" and began a campaign to promote maintenance and renovation over destruction.

Some of the worst school buildings could be found in cities. After an intense period of attention in the early 1970s, urban schools seemed to once again disappear from educators' view. This neglect was surely aided by the fact that as cities continued to lose residents, fewer new school buildings needed to be constructed, in sharp contrast to the continuous demand for suburban educational facilities. It was therefore inevitable that school architecture would reemerge as a topic of concern once the generation of 1970s urban schools began to physically deteriorate or educational changes rendered them ineffective or obsolete. In cities like Chicago and New York, the demand for high school students was so low and funding so scarce that neither city constructed a new secondary-school building between the late 1970s and early 1990s. When educators started building again—even if it was in the late 1980s—urban-school designers continued but reinterpreted many of the common tendencies of postwar schools and clothed them with the materials and symbolic language of the burgeoning postmodern movement.

In 1987, after years of inattention and neglect, much of it related to the city's financial crisis, New York inaugurated a massive capital campaign to construct 189 new school buildings in a decade. It was the first intervention of its kind in over 20 years, and like the previous initiative, its planners relied on nationally prominent architects and firms to provide quality and attract attention. So while the older postwar initiative enlisted Edward Durell Stone, Curtis & Davis, and Charles Luckman Associates for prestigious commissions, for this renewed effort, the board of education used

a limited competition among New York offices to develop a prototype
school building. During a presubmission meeting with architects from
many of these major firms, the board realized it could generate more possibilities with more than one source, so it altered its original intentions and
selected four entrants to each develop an individual prototype. The Prototype School Program produced two versions of a 300-student elementary
school, one by Perkins & Will and another by Gruzen Samton Steinglass;
a 1,200-student elementary school by The Ehrenkrantz Group and Eckstut
Architects; and a 1,200- to 1,800-student intermediate school by Richard
Dattner. All of the various schools contained auditoriums, community
rooms, and prekindergarten classrooms, demonstrating the continuing relevance of school buildings to the surrounding communities. Each design
was modular, and each was repeated multiple times so that the initial campaign produced 13 schools from these four prototypes by 1992.

The prototypes had to respond to traditional urban challenges
relatively unknown in the suburbs, including small, awkwardly shaped
sites—sometimes in close proximity to skyscrapers—and surrounding
high-traffic streets. The architects' solutions favored multistory structures
with highly articulated facades featuring sections of different heights,
materials, and colors and enveloping floor plans that segregated multiple
classroom modules from shared and administrative facilities. All of them
evoked architecture's history and the building's immediate context in some
way. Gruzen Samton Steinglass's schools referenced urban townhouses in
their form, while Perkins & Will gave their buildings an Art-Deco aesthetic to match the surrounding neighborhood. Dattner's school contained
arched windows, string courses, cornices, and references to baroque curved
facades. And The Ehrenkrantz Group and Eckstut Architects employed
gabled roofs and Gothic verticality. Brick- and masonry-clad walls gave
these schools a patina of age and visually distinguished them from the
dominant concrete-and-steel schools of the 1960s.

New York City's approach to new school design can be seen clearly
in a highly publicized school that was not associated with the Prototype
Schools Program. Gruzen Samton Steinglass, in addition to their elementary schools, teamed with Cooper, Robertson & Partners to create the
Peter Stuyvesant High School (1992), the most expensive school building
in the city's history to that point and its first new high-school building in
15 years. The $150 million structure eventually became the public face of
New York's school-building renaissance.

Stuyvesant's monumental 1907 predecessor had deteriorated significantly and could no longer adequately house the operations of the city's
marquee high-school program. In addition to boasting one of the top

programs in the city, Stuyvesant was now a highly selective magnet school for mathematics and science, meaning it would draw top students from the entire public-school system. The site chosen for a new structure was in Lower Manhattan's Battery Park City—one half mile from the World Trade Center—on an awkward triangular lot. Because the school housed nearly 3,000 students and over 100 faculty members and the lot was restricted, the only feasible solution for the architects was to build vertically. Stuyvesant would be a "high-rise school," 10 stories tall in its main block. From the street, the school looked like an amalgam of four to five different buildings, each with a distinct mass and slightly divergent facade treatments—a fashionable contemporary architectural trend. This tendency also helped to visually fragment the mass of an extremely large facility. Despite its appearance, however, the school was a unified whole behind the walls. The floor plan occupied the entire one-and-a-half-acre site. Most of the classrooms were placed in the main, 10-floor linear block, with sports, theater, and other facilities appended. Recognizing the challenges of circulating so many students through such a massive structure, the architects installed "skip-stop" escalators that stopped only on certain floors.

Back to the Future

Some commentators raised concerns of elitism over Stuyvesant High School's seemingly luxurious materials, like the polished granite in the entryway and partial limestone sheathing, but overall the public response was positive. Architectural and educational critics lauded the building upon its opening, citing its multiple science laboratories, five gymnasia and Olympic-sized swimming pool, high-quality auditorium, and beautiful views of the Hudson River from inside. Stuyvesant captured the salient qualities of school architecture that developed in the late 20th century, including a return to monumentality and symbolism and a reliance on historical plan types, both architectural aspects of a broader back-to-basics movement within the American educational world.

As a consequence of the intensive focus on the condition of the nation's public-school buildings, construction escalated to levels not seen since the immediate postwar era. Expenditures rose by almost 40 percent between 1990 and 1997, to nearly $25 billion. During that period, however, an interesting phenomenon occurred: the landscapes of both education and school architecture had changed dramatically, with both educators and architects looking to the past for guidance. A Nation at Risk and similar educational critiques spurred advocates to seek a return to academic school subjects with an emphasis on testing. This approach had repercussions beyond the

high-school curriculum. Concurrently, the fashionable postmodern movement in architecture had made historical styles, materials, and models
acceptable again after being banished during the reign of high modernism.
These two forces combined to produce a new generation of school buildings characterized by traditional ideas, like more formal floor plans, tall
building profiles, multiple facade colors and materials, extensive use of
masonry cladding, and an increased interest in architectural monumentality (although many new schools tended to have smaller student populations). Such qualities tied the fin-du-siècle schools to early-20th-century
precedents rather than postwar experiments. School architect Earl Flansburgh summarized the significant transitions: "Flexibility [in the postwar
era] was achieved by such architectural elements as open-plan classrooms
with operable partitions (suitable for team teaching), and conference rooms
and specific project areas related to clusters of classrooms," he wrote.
"Now, with renewed interest in basic education in mathematics, science,
English, and history, we don't see this interest in flexibility . . . We're
seeing simple interiors, reflecting a basic educational program. Exterior
educational symbolism has replaced interior educational flexibility as a
driving force for academic buildings" (Flansburgh 1988, 102, 104).

Late-20th-century American school buildings combined the monumental and the casual, as if to link the premodernist and high-modernist pasts
of the 1900s and 1950s, respectively. Monumentality showed in large,
well-marked entrances, wide corridors (sometimes two stories high) and
commons areas, and great expanses of glass. Familiar materials like brick
and sometimes wood, brought inside the buildings, helped to offset this
quality, as did the practice of leaving ducts and pipes exposed in the ceilings as a display of the structure's inner workings. Floor plans were more
elongated, less boxlike than in the 1970s, but simpler than those of schools
from a century earlier because the new schools held fewer rooms and no
old-fashioned shop spaces. And campus plans had virtually disappeared—
school spaces once again were gathered into a compact whole. The same
back-to-basics movement that emphasized such traditional educational
methods as testing and core subjects had provoked a return to traditional
architectural ideas as well. Educational reform thus continued to shape
school architecture.

A NEW CENTURY

The 21st century brought few changes to school architecture, at least not
in the initial decades. Most of the considerations taken into account by

school designers and educators were inherited from previous generations: flexibility of classrooms and buildings for different uses, accommodation of nontraditional students, spaces for students to further their social interactions, and so on. School buildings continued to display a wide range of solutions to these challenges. All types of room arrangements developed during and after World War II remained popular: finger plans, loft plans, and the use of central corridors turned into a commons/galleria/agora as both organizing element and social gathering space. The complex forms and mixed use of exterior materials persisted as well. However, some additional concerns arose in response to changes in the larger society. For one, the rapid evolution of microprocessing technology, reflected in Americans' increasing reliance on the Internet, smartphones, and social media, found a favorable audience in the country's educators. Computers became more ensconced in public education, requiring architects to provide more room for IT equipment and wiring. Other than the appearance of such technology in most classrooms (described in Chapter 4), the digital revolution had minimal impact on the basic design of schoolhouses. It did, however, alter school libraries, which continued the evolution into media centers that had begun years earlier.

Showcase Schools

At the end of the 20th century, high-profile "starchitects" began to apply their talents to school design for the first time in decades. Formerly, such famous architects as Richard Neutra, Frank Lloyd Wright, Le Corbusier, SOM, and others almost all tried their hand at schools, and as we have seen, Neutra was instrumental in creating the modern school building. But after the late 1970s, it seems that the nation's most prominent architects and firms either stopped designing schools or did so few that their output was clearly secondary to other building types. The field was left to the school specialists.

This situation changed in the 1990s. The impetus came from a high-school campus produced by the Los Angeles–based firm Morphosis, whose leader, Thom Mayne, would receive the Pritzker Prize—architecture's highest award—in 2005. The Diamond Ranch High School (2000) in Diamond Bar, California, outside Pomona, directed the architecture world's attention toward schools because of its highly regarded creators. Morphosis doubtless satisfied its fans by applying the firm's penchant for sharp, angular, leaning forms and disjointed compositions to a different building type, but upon closer inspection, the school can be seen

Diamond Ranch High School in Diamond Bar, California, designed by Morphosis (2000). Diamond Ranch combined the specialized spaces of modern school buildings with the fragmented forms popular in the late 20th century. It also marked a renewed interest in educational design by high-profile "starchitects." (Library of Congress)

to implement established design ideas that evolved over the course of the century.

The Pomona Unified School District held a limited competition for the design of the high school, which was intended to hold 2,000 students. Morphosis's winning idea involved utilizing a natural slope on the barren hillside site to structure the school's organization. The school's concept was a linear one, running almost straight along the east-west axis. Three terraces, involving minimal intervention into the hillside, formed the platforms for school activities. The northernmost terrace, highest on the hill, contained the football field; the school building proper occupied the center; and the bottom terrace was for athletic fields. There would be 50 classrooms, administrative offices, a library, gymnasium, and cafeteria, with the latter doubling as a gathering space in the absence of a traditional auditorium.

Morphosis dissected the school into independent units strung along a central pedestrian street and embedded some of them into the hill. This resulted in three distinct levels. The lowest level, which contained the school's entry, included administrative offices, access to the gymnasium and cafeteria, and classrooms for grades 9 and 10. On the intermediate level, the classrooms and administrative offices were complemented by a library, science laboratories, and classrooms for grades 11 and 12. The uppermost level included more upper-school classrooms.

The building's forms were angular, aggressive, and made from concrete and corrugated metal. From a visual or artistic perspective, the application of such a deconstructivist formal language to a school building was unprecedented. In interviews, Mayne spoke of the intentional discomfort imparted by the aggregation of forms and how the firm sought to rethink the educational experience. The two were linked in the architect's mind: as a first step toward something new, Diamond Ranch was not supposed to look like a school building. However, despite its late-20th-century image, many of the school's design elements derived from older ideas. For example, the school's program called for division into six different schools within a school. This was achieved by reviving the finger plan for the two-story ninth- and tenth-grade classrooms. Each of the three fingers sprouting perpendicularly from the main street held four classrooms in a line and cantilevered out from that spine. Small courtyards between the fingers broke up the monotony and allowed for small recreational spaces outside the schoolrooms. Further, the architects zoned the school so that the administrative offices, lower classrooms, upper classrooms, and gymnasium/cafeteria areas would be distinct. While the school-within-a-school concept drove some of these decisions, the plan also had its roots in early-20th-century attempts to make school buildings into community centers in the off-hours; thus, the sections that might be used by the public (cafeteria/auditorium and gymnasium) were segregated from the rest of the school and placed near the entry. In this way, Diamond Ranch replicated the monumental high schools designed by William Ittner and others of his era, with their grand auditoria located directly on axis with the main entrance as a way to invite the community in without disrupting the rest of the building.

In addition to the idiosyncratic forms selected for the building, the architectural press focused its coverage on Diamond Ranch's pedestrian street, expressing admiration for the outdoor circulation route as an interstitial space or void torn through the buildings, resulting in a fragmented assembly of forms jutting in and out of the street like buildings from the set a German Expressionist movie. Mayne even commented on his attempt to narrow the street as much as possible so that students would be forced to encounter each other as they moved through the campus. But what he and the architectural critics failed to mention—or perhaps even appreciate—are the deep roots beneath this design choice. The central corridor, acting as a spine for finger plans or simply organizing movement through the school, was almost as old as school buildings themselves. Morphosis did give the main-street idea a new twist by leaving it uncovered, as an open space between buildings, but even the notion of students traveling from one classroom to another outside had deep roots in Southern California history.

Sustainability and Security

Two important new factors emerged in the early years of the century to impact schoolhouse design: sustainability and security. These concerns grew to the point where the "green and safe" school building has become the goal for school administrators and architects, even more so than the historical regard for flexibility, light, and air. A move toward energy-efficient and ecologically sustainable buildings began during the 1960s with the ecological movement; it gained momentum after the 1973 oil embargo and resulting energy crisis. In addition to a number of government initiatives, such as the National Energy Act, the architectural community devoted itself to defining a new policy toward energy consumption. As more products became available to enhance energy efficiency, there was less of a need for such drastic solutions as windowless classrooms.

The American Institute of Architects formed an Energy Committee during the 1970s to study passive-solar design and energy-performance standards. By the early 1990s, it was publishing materials, such as the *Environmental Resource Guide*, to help architects determine the most effective methods for energy conservation. A major step toward developing a new design mentality occurred when the U.S. Green Building Council was founded in 1993. Five years later, the organization launched its Leadership in Energy and Environmental Design (LEED) program, which has affected school design ever since. LEED is a certification process whereby buildings are rated according to their green (environmentally friendly) design, construction, and maintenance. Different levels of certification (such as silver, gold, and platinum) correspond to energy-efficient performance, and the awards have become indicative of a commitment to responsible design.

School architects may have been ahead of their colleagues in terms of energy awareness given the long history of concern for student health and comfortable learning environments mixed with limited budgets that defined school design in the United States. Since the early 20th century, school architects had considered the building's orientation on the site, the size and location of classroom windows, the optimal space per student for proper ventilation and temperature control, and even the relationships between fresh air/natural light versus circulated air/electric light as vital elements of their designs. So what the movement toward energy awareness added to educational architecture was governmental support and the development of better products to aid the effort. Beginning with active- and passive-solar techniques, school architects branched into more ambitious projects and methods that eventually encompassed all of the following by the turn of the 21st century: site, indoor air quality, environmental impact, energy and water consumption, and materials. By the 2010s, new school buildings were among the leaders in energy-efficient architecture.

Another new development in school design already apparent in the early 21st century was the desire for increased security. This impulse was spurred by a number of high-profile incidents of extreme violence in public schools that began to appear with startling regularity. In 1989, a gunman killed 5 students and wounded 32 more at the Cleveland Elementary School in Stockton, California. A decade later, a pair of disgruntled students were responsible for 15 deaths at Columbine High School in Littleton, Colorado. And in 2012, a single shooter murdered 20 first-grade children and 6 educators in the worst act of violence ever recorded at a public school, in Newtown, Connecticut. (It was not, however, the worst in U.S. history: a few years earlier, a massacre at Virginia Tech University resulted in 32 deaths and 23 people wounded.) In the period 2010–2015, there were over 60 recorded incidents of firearm casualties on primary- or secondary-school properties in the United States.

The architectural consequences of these episodes are still being determined at the time of this writing. However, certain patterns of school design have developed in response and become popular. These include controlled access to the building through increased security checks and metal detectors (both began much earlier in urban schools) and greater building openness and transparency in hallways and classrooms. A salient example of the new mentality could be seen at the Sandy Hook Elementary School (2016) in Newtown, Connecticut. In December 2012, the Sandy Hook massacre brought the national epidemic of gun violence once more to the public's attention when a 20-year-old murdered his mother, drove to Sandy Hook, and opened fire with four guns. The gunman killed 20 children, 4 teachers, the school principal, and the school psychologist, and two other persons were wounded. In the aftermath, the community decided to demolish the existing school building—a rather standard 1950s elementary school built around an open courtyard—and erect a new one. Svigals + Partners Architects won the commission for the $50 million structure.

The architects were tasked with creating a school building that would enhance students' feelings of security while being state-of-the-art; they also wanted the result to be a working school and not a memorial. They responded with a finger-plan design organized around an arc-like central corridor backed away from the nearest streets. A main goal in addition to a safe environment was to embed the building in nature as much as possible. On a site almost completely surrounded by trees, the new school sits back from its neighborhood, with one road allowing access and egress. A series of checkpoints, including a surveillance gate, join with a bus loop and multiple parking lots to restrict vehicular access to the building. A further barrier is provided by a creek and rain garden at the foot of the school's facade, which must be crossed by a series of footbridges. Inside the building, increased security is visible if one knows what to look for but subtle enough that the children are unaware. Windows are aligned to offer clear views of the exterior from nearly every hallway or classroom. For further protection, the glass is impact-resistant. Other techniques used by designers around the country include placing the office in a conspicuous location next to the entry, making stairways, hallways, and classrooms visible with extensive glazing, and eliminating dead-end hallways, nooks, crannies, or any other spot in the building where someone might hide. The challenge for school architects now is to find the proper balance between the openness cherished by educators and desired by children with the protections necessary in anxious times.

Like Diamond Ranch High School, schoolhouses of the 21st century reveal a great reliance on principles developed in the previous century. The differentiated curriculum remains despite its many critics, and consequently the school building maintains its decentralization, and corridors and classrooms still form the building blocks of school design. Open and closed plans are both popular. Health concerns still drive school design in part, although they have been supplemented by serious security anxieties. Centralized gathering places continue to proliferate. School designers strive for an even greater sense of informality or casualness than their midcentury predecessors. In a very real sense, the past is always present in American school buildings, in their forms and arrangements, in the same way that the schoolroom stubbornly retains its archetypal shape.

Chapter 3

OBJECTS OF EDUCATION

Schoolrooms and school buildings are not the only material entities encountered by teachers and students during the school day. They are supplemented by a host of other objects and ancillary spaces. Ever since the colonial period, educational objects have aided teachers and students alike, whether in the form of furniture, visual aids, books, or writing implements, as technological advances inspired a steady stream of new information-delivery tools—some of which could be self-operated by the student. Every new mass-communication device of the 20th century found its way into the schools, including radio, motion pictures, television, and, most revolutionary of all, the computer. By the century's end, computers and their software had made a substantial impact on pedagogical techniques in the nation's schoolrooms.

BLACKBOARDS

Of all the equipment used by American teachers over the centuries, perhaps the piece most associated with the schoolroom is the blackboard. The large, rectangular green or black board filled with chalk writings or mathematical problems is as much a symbol of education as anything else associated with the process. Blackboards have a long history of supporting schoolroom activities in this country and continue to serve as a basic component even though their form has evolved in recent years.

The blackboard's ability to capture the attention of numerous students at one time made it indispensable to public schools. Its roots extended far back into the history of Western education, even before educating all children became a priority. The desire to provide students with a convenient means for temporary writing or numerical operations began with the ancient Greeks, who often utilized small wax tablets for such purposes.

During the Middle Ages, the individual slate tablet was introduced. A handheld-size piece of dark slate stone combined with a slate or chalk pencil allowed every student to have a practice surface. Slates were relatively inexpensive and could be wiped clean with a cloth or sponge. Blackboards appear to have been a common tool of French education by the early 19th century—particularly for mathematics—having evolved from larger, wall-hung slates. Their adoption in North America was slower in comparison. Despite the popularity of the slate tablet, there is scant evidence of blackboard use in the colonies. Joseph Lancaster's equipment for monitorial schools included black wooden boards with letters of the alphabet painted on them in white and hung on walls as a means of exposing multiple students to the same lesson, similar to the small, individual cards he produced so that students would not have to share textbooks. There is no indication, however, that Lancaster's boards were erasable.

Prior to the mid-19th century, blackboard use in the United States was sporadic but increasing. The influence of one institution in particular seems to have spurred its extensive implementation—the U.S. Military Academy at West Point, New York. An English-born mathematics instructor there named George Baron, during a tenure beginning in 1801, relied on a "standing slate" to teach the army cadets. This attracted the attention of the academy's administrators, and before long, the blackboard had become a standard tool for the school's geometry courses. Other institutions of higher learning, like Harvard College, also began to experiment with blackboards for teaching mathematics and science. But West Point pioneered a new approach to blackboards, making them a crucial element of the school's recitation program, and the academy's status was such that pedagogical techniques practiced there were followed with great attention by educators around the country (Philips 2015).

By the 1830s and 1840s, educators considered blackboards an essential piece of classroom equipment. Horace Mann, Henry Barnard, and other leading figures all advocated their extensive employment. Boston's educators attempted to place a blackboard in every grammar-school classroom. The city's famous Quincy Grammar School boasted of blackboards in every classroom, three feet wide and two feet from the floor. Not coincidentally, school supply companies began to offer blackboards around this time; by the 20th century, they would become one of the most lucrative products on the market. One source counted at least 59 companies manufacturing blackboards in 1922 (Zimmerman 2009).

The quality and makeup of blackboards changed as they became more popular. From their origins as actual pieces of slate rock or painted wooden boards, alternatives appeared, often driven by the higher cost of slate rock and quality textbooks. For example, Barnard provided a recipe for constructing a homemade blackboard using lampblack dissolved in alcohol, emery powder, and distilled varnish. Liquid slate was invented in the 1850s for globes, but its inventors quickly adapted it to blackboards and applied it to wood, paper, or cloth backings. The liquid form seems to have provided the first opportunities for colors other than black, as green, blue, or gray blackboards now were available. Later in the century, the blackboard continued to prove its effectiveness even as pencils and paper became cheaper and more prevalent.

In the 20th century, the technology improved and manufacturers made chalkboards from chemical composites or porcelain enamel (or even glass). Around midcentury, the whiteboard was invented as an alternative to the blackboard. Whiteboards—also known as dry-erase boards—offered greater visibility without the chalk dust, which created health issues for some teachers and students and can clog and damage some of the sophisticated electronic devices relied upon in today's classroom. The dry-erase boards feature enameled steel, aluminum, porcelain, glass, or chemical laminate surfaces that can be used with grease pencils or special nonpermanent markers and wiped clean. They became fashionable in the American business world in the 1980s, leading to their incorporation in classrooms in the following decade. In the early 21st century, whiteboards became more sophisticated and popular; in their most complex forms, they could be connected to computer equipment to create SMART Boards, allowing teachers to draw, type, present prepackaged lessons, or even search the Internet—or do all simultaneously. In this way, the SMART board recaptured some of the spontaneity of the long-discarded overhead projector. In 2002, the journal *Education Week* reported that digital whiteboards had been outselling traditional chalkboards for at least five years (Borja 2002). Today, the blackboard remains a staple of the classroom at every level, whether it takes the form of the conventional blackboard or the increasingly high-tech dry-erase boards.

DESKS AND TABLES

Over the many years of American education, from the colonies until today, classrooms of all shapes and sizes, however primitive or technologically advanced, whether in urban, rural, or suburban schools, have all depended upon one kind of furniture more than any other—the seat. Students at all levels of education need to be able to sit, at least part of the day, for the long hours of education to be effective, and in our Western culture, that means students need seats of some kind. When combined with desks, seats become self-contained learning stations. In the early years of colonial education in North America, however, neither desks nor individual seats were part of the schoolroom's equipment.

The first seats were puncheon benches, or wooden logs split in half and planed (or not) on one side to flatten the surface, while the other side was roughly dressed. The logs were long enough to accommodate multiple students and stood on legs of some sort, often so high that the youngest children's feet dangled above the floor. Students put their books (if they had any) on the floor under the bench since there were no desks in the early days and used handheld slates or sand tables for practicing their writing or arithmetic. By the 1900s, larger urban schools were likely to have added desks with backless benches to their schoolrooms, while rural schools continued to use benches for the younger students and primitive shelf-like desks, attached to the outer walls, for older ones.

Monitorial schools relied upon long unbroken rows of desks with backless benches, with enough room between them so students could easily and quickly move back and forth between their seat and their recitation circle. An alternative, rarely used in the United States, was the gallery, a structure of bleacher-like seating with each row of desks raised higher than the row in front. Such galleries could seat hundreds of students at once and direct their attention to the schoolmaster (and vice versa), allowing better visibility and control; they were thought to be particularly effective for the youngest children. Galleries had been popularized by Scottish philanthropist David Stow beginning in the 1830s and remained standard in London's infant schools into the early 20th century. Henry Barnard, in his seminal *School Architecture*, advocated galleries for "very small children." But few instances of their actual construction and employment can be found in the historical record.

Over time, a desk surface for each student and a seat with some type of backing proved to be the norm, although this occurred in urban schools before their rural counterparts. The original flat-planked seat and back surfaces slowly evolved into slightly curved components formed from glued strips of wood, as designers strove to make the chairs more comfortable. Despite their superior design, however, many of these seats remained uncomfortable due to their inability to be adjusted. As seats with desks became commonplace, they also grew heavier and more permanent. In the 19th century, mass-produced cast-iron-and-wood school desks appeared. They usually consisted of an iron filigree framework—often curved to give brooms easier access to the floor under the desk—with a wooden desktop and a matching, unconnected seat. For much of the century, the desk was large enough for two students to sit side by side in individual chairs,

Iron and wood combination desks common in 19th- and early-20th-century schoolrooms. Such immovable furniture reflected the formal and discipline-driven pedagogical techniques prevalent in American schools at the time. (William J. Taylor/Dreamstime.com)

although there were longer variations that accommodated more students. Whatever their configuration, both desk and seats tended to be immobile, bolted to the floor in orderly rows and ranks.

The combination desk was by far the most important type of seating for almost a century. Combination desks had a two-piece wooden seat with the desk attached behind the seatback, forming a kind of backward and straightened Z shape. A patent for a combination desk exists as far back as 1859, although some form of seating that employed desks as back support for students on the benches in front of them was reported over a decade earlier in New York City (van Dulken 2006; Anderson 1962). Over time, the wooden desk parts became more ergonomic, components became lighter and easier to assemble, storage compartments were added, and some versions featured a folding seat for better circulation between rows, since the combination desk was intended to be secured to the floor. In the early 20th century, the cast-iron frame evolved into tubular steel and a pedestal variation that utilized a single support each for chair and desk. Most pedestals were adjustable to a few preselected settings, but combination desks remained popular. In a widely read book on school architecture from the 1920s, architect John Donovan depicted three seating prototypes, and two of them were options on the fixed combination desk. As late as 1936, a survey of school furniture manufacturing found that while sales of fixed combination desks were declining, they remained the most popular type of school seating in American public schools (Pinnell 1954).

A mainstay of American education in the first decades after World War II was the universal desk: a lightweight, movable improvement on the combination desk that made each desk and chair pairing into its own unit. Universal desks originally featured a sturdy metal chair with wooden seat and backrest, a storage compartment beneath the seat, and a single support rising up to stabilize the writing surface. Alternative designs introduced plywood, tubular steel, and an open steel cage for storage, considerably lightening the ensemble. Some companies manufactured models that moved the storage compartment beneath the desktop. During this period, the tablet arm seat achieved wide popularity. Its origins stretched back to the 18th-century Windsor writing chairs that appeared in the American colonies before the Revolution. All versions of the universal desk continued to evolve with more comfortable components, such lighter materials as plastic, and adjustable desk heights.

Postwar classroom furniture was thinner, lighter, and movable, to allow for the informal arrangements encouraged by changing educational ideals in the 1950s. (James Leynse/Corbis via Getty Images)

Desk and chair combinations, while an improvement over previous seating arrangements, were not created to be movable. Well into the 20th century, the majority of school desks were attached to the floor in parallel ranks. While this layout obviously enhanced teachers' control over their students and meshed with the lockstep order so prized in public education, it also restricted teachers from reconfiguring their rooms and thus inadvertently contributed to teacher-centered pedagogies. Some educators voiced their opposition to such inflexibility. As early as 1838, Horace Mann recommended movable desks, and such calls became more frequent as the century progressed. Kindergartens adopted informal furniture rather early, but at the grammar and secondary levels, change occurred slowly. The first mass-marketed movable desk, invented by Rochester, New York, principal Samuel Parker Moulthrop, began production in 1905. Moulthrop devised an adjustable and movable chair-and-desk combination—with storage—as a response to the increasing number of vocational and adult programs offered by the city's public schools, which often required larger-sized furniture and alternative room arrangements. From that point on, movable desks became a regularly manufactured item even while interest in them did not become common until the 1940s. By midcentury, all of the leading publications aimed at school architects advocated movable desks.

The postwar active classroom needed furnishings that were lightweight and easy to move or carry. Lightweight metal desks and chairs were in many ways the backbone of 20th-century progressive education. However, these were often merely lighter versions of traditional furniture, capable of being lifted and moved easily in response to changing classroom circumstances. Movable desks with wheels were a different matter. For a time in the 1960s and 1970s, designers intoxicated by the dream of complete flexibility introduced desks, chairs, bookcases, tables, and even room-divider panels with wheels. The EFL funded the Research and Design Institute of Providence, Rhode Island, to develop a line of school furniture to support its pedagogical and curricular experiments. The company produced rolling chairs, desks, carrels, teacher stations, and bookcases, folding and staking tables, mobile divider panels, and even tote trays ("plastic shopping traylike baskets") for the youngest children, all "symbolic of this new portability" (Smith 1971, 96). Especially popular were small carts for carrying building blocks, musical instruments, art supplies, or toy tools. Over time, however, the enthusiasm diminished as mobile furnishings, like other educational experiments, eventually became either absorbed by standard classroom practices as their novelty wore off or discarded. Today, any given classroom in the United States might have numerous rolling or movable pieces, but they are appreciated—if at all—for their convenience, not for any revolutionary new practices they might inspire.

The atmosphere of reform that engulfed American education during the 1960s included recognizing the child's individuality as a substantial component. Unsurprisingly, the same atmosphere that gave rise to independent study, gently guided activities, free play, **teaching machines**, and other child-centered techniques also generated a unique product intended to facilitate these developments: the carrel. Although they might have failed to gain much traction in the educational world, individualized carrels and their close relative, the cubicle, revolutionized office design around the world.

Educators in the mid-1950s began to explore individualized study spaces as a means to supplement large- and small-group activities. These usually took the form of a simple desk with walls attached on three sides to segregate the user from the noise and activity of the room. The notion of an individualized study space actually originated in medieval European monasteries as small, boxlike wooden desks with walls for monks to achieve privacy while copying manuscripts or studying. Once the printing press was invented and books became prevalent, libraries sometimes created a carrel-like space by putting shelves on top of the lecterns used to display books. Educators in the 20th century recognized the value in providing private space once progressive techniques like independent study became popular. The classroom carrel experiment may have been initiated by Walter Cocking, editor of *School Executive*, when he asked Archibald Shaw (superintendent of schools for Scarsdale, New York) and school architect John Lyon Reid to brainstorm a new approach to independent learning on behalf of his magazine. Shaw and Reid conceived and published "The Random Falls Idea," featuring concepts that would become widespread in the ensuing years, like looser class schedules, flexible interior spaces, and the learning laboratory. The latter was a highly technological, individualized study carrel with a desktop, file drawer, typewriter shelf, and various compartments. Cocking then enlisted architects Charles Brubaker and Lawrence Perkins, of Perkins & Will, to further develop the model a few years later with the goal of producing a carrel to serve as "the individual student's studio" ("Space for Individual Learning: The Biography of a Great Idea" 1963, 31). The result was called "Q-Space" (or Quest-Space), a student desk surrounded by three walls that included a small television screen—the most exciting aspect to educators of the time—and contained added space for storage, bookshelves, and a tackboard. The device's creators alleged it would allow students almost complete autonomy while still being connected to broader activities through audio and television connections. As previously unorthodox classroom practices became more common, promotors envisioned Q-Space as a kind of home base for students in addition to its educational attributes. They also recognized its potential for a future that seemed inevitably dominated by audiovisual instruction.

In the early 1960s, the editors of *School Executive*, now named *Educational Executives' Overview*, sought to upgrade Q-Space. They asked Sol Cornberg Associates to modify the carrel so that it could be used for any level of education. A telephone receiver was the most significant addition. After the upgrade, the system was successfully tested at Grand Valley State College in Michigan. In language that revealed the extent to which many educators viewed technology as the future of teaching and learning, an article in the journal described Q-Space's potential: "A sophisticated installation, for example, could supply each student station with the following information services: 'live' or pre-recorded television (closed-circuit, UHF, and VHF transmission), broadcast radio (short-wave, AM, and FM), intramural public address, tape recordings, disc recordings, slides, motion pictures, filmstrips, and microscopic images . . . It is also possible to receive only audio or only video information from films or videotapes" ("Space for Individual Learning: The Biography of a Great Idea" 1963, 39). Despite its creators' enthusiasm, however, Q-Space failed to live up to its expectations and found only sporadic adoption, probably due to cost but also perhaps because of its inflexibility: in requiring students to be tied to one location, it seemed at odds with the growing tendency toward open classrooms and multiple, simultaneous activities.

The individual cubicle appeared concurrently with carrels and movable furniture; in fact, Q-Space was essentially a technologically enhanced cubicle. Cubicles in general are slightly larger than carrels and can contain more space than the desk and shelf found in the latter. They also tend to be modular systems able to combine individual parts in different ways. Cubicles became popular in schools (particularly libraries) but similarly failed to gain the classroom acceptance promoters desired. The first cubicle derived from the German-born *Bürolandschaft* movement described above, when the Quickborner Team's ideas about informal arrangements attracted the attention of the Herman Miller Research Corporation and its president, Robert Propst. He worked with famed designer George Nelson to devise a full set of office furniture intended to be mobile and to enhance productivity. The Action Office system was unveiled in 1964 as an alternative to the office landscape. Its lightweight, movable desks, chairs, bookcases, and tables could be combined in configurations to fit almost any office situation. Propst, however, was not satisfied, and three years later, Herman Miller introduced his Action Office II, which further developed the furniture but added something new: cubicle walls. Each one- or two-person "workstation" in Action Office II included three interlocking panel walls, which could be positioned in different configurations to form a semienclosed space; Propst favored 120-degree angles—resembling a honeycomb—for their combination of privacy and view. Workstation walls were connected to form clusters, an ideal grouping of furniture for open-plan office environments.

Like desks and chairs, school tables evolved rather slowly. In the earliest days of public education, there was little need for tables, except for the specially made sand tables that helped younger children with their writing skills. Rudimentary desks fulfilled all of the necessary requirements for writing, and students did not participate in small-group activities requiring anything larger (or if they did, like such as in the monitorial schools, they stood). Once again, the kindergartens led the way; experienced teachers began to request small tables scaled to these younger children and their informal endeavors. By midcentury, a vast array of circular, semicircular, hexagonal, and trapezoidal tables were visible in the advertisements and articles filling educational and architectural journals. Some of these objects may have been inspired by the growing popularity of the what came to be known as the Harkness table. Philanthropist Edward Harkness had donated almost $6 million to the Philips Exeter Academy in New Hampshire to fund a seminar system of education to replace the school's traditional lecture format, and in the course of implementing the program, a school administrator conceived of a table specifically intended to encourage small-group conversations. The result was an oval table of rather small size with hidden writing tablets that could be pulled out for use by individual students during exams or quizzes. The intimate atmosphere promoted by the Harkness table encouraged a different type of teacher-student interaction suitable for the growing interest in nontraditional pedagogical techniques inspired by progressive educators. The Harkness table stimulated numerous imitators. By the late 20th century, the notion of a small, flexible table for small-group activities led experimenters to create other geometric shapes and variations on the intimate space for interaction engendered by the Harkness table.

Radio

The realm of educational objects has encompassed far more than furniture. Some of the most innovative and influential objects in American schoolrooms were intended to supplement the delivery of information rather than physically support the students. And throughout the history of education in this country, mass-communication inventions have been incorporated into schoolroom practices whenever they appeared in the larger society. Educators' experiments with the tools of mass media began with the radio. Invented in the late 19th century, radio was emerging by 1920 as an immensely popular new form of entertainment and information, and home receivers attuned to the increasing number of AM (amplitude modulation) radio stations increased rapidly. Along with commercial broadcasting stations, institutions of higher education were involved with the medium from the beginning, giving rise to a culture of alternative educational programming. Experimental stations appeared at Ohio State University, the University of Wisconsin, and Iowa State University as early as the 1910s, broadcasting a variety of programs including weather reports and musical recordings. Not long after these tentative beginnings, educators explored radio's potential to deliver material to students. The U.S. Department of Commerce began to issue licenses to commercial and educational radio stations in 1920. Three years later, Haaren High School in New York City became the first public school in the country to broadcast lessons to students via the radio. Later in 1923, California educators transmitted a series of radio programs on state history to rural elementary schools. The Oakland public schools developed courses in such topics as English, geography, literature, history, and arithmetic; each lesson was 20 minutes long, preceded by 5 minutes of music.

Supporters predicted great things for radio education, touting its ability to reach incredible numbers of students simultaneously, and exclaimed that soon the radio would become "as common in the classrooms as the blackboard" (Cuban 1986, 26). The excitement surrounding this new medium can be seen in a 1930 article in the *American School Board Journal* written by Ohio's state high-school supervisor, which listed over 200 organizations, institutions, and stations engaged in radio education (Reese 1930). Radio's potential for educational applications was recognized even by the federal government. At the end of the 1920s, it formed an Advisory Committee on Education by Radio and, in its aftermath, a National Committee on Education by Radio. When FM (frequency modulation) communications were perfected in the 1930s, the possibilities for educational use expanded significantly. In recognition, the Federal Communications Commission (FCC) first allocated a section of the FM frequency band for educational stations in 1938.

Despite these enthusiastic beginnings, radio's appeal was relatively short-lived. Following World War II, some educators already were lamenting radio's limited viability, and the dream of a radio receiver in every classroom receded. The rapid evolution of television and its potential for greater flexibility in subject matter and pedagogy proved insurmountable to radio advocates; by the 1950s, the brief flirtation with radio education was largely finished.

Overhead Projectors

The blackboard's ability to provide greater visibility to large numbers of students encouraged alternative devices intended to achieve similar effects. The overhead projector proved to be the blackboard's closest relative and a staple of educational technology in the 20th century. Its origins date back to the magic lantern, a 17th-century invention that used a light source surrounded by a concave mirror to direct light through an illustrated piece of glass or oiled paper. The image, considerably enlarged, could then be projected on a wall or hung fabric. By the late 1800s, European and American inventors had developed variations of the magic lantern able to project images from a horizontal source. Within decades, these machines were increasingly utilized in science and mathematics classrooms but remained rare overall. A growing interest in audiovisual instruction in the 1920s exposed more educators to the overhead projector's benefits.

A major breakthrough in projector technology occurred in the late 1930s when Chicago's Brunswick-Balke-Collender Company, a manufacturer of billiards tables and bowling equipment, first marketed its "Tel-E-Score" device for bowling alleys, providing bowlers with a quick means of viewing their scoresheet projected onto a screen above the lanes. Shortly thereafter, the U.S. armed forces adopted overhead projectors as an inexpensive and efficient means of training the mass of recruits and draftees during World War II. After the war, they were adopted by instructors at West Point, becoming a standard educational tool there in much the same manner as the blackboard over a century earlier.

America's baby-boom enrollment crisis made reliance on instruments of mass education imperative, and in the years following World War II, the overhead projector found its greatest acceptance and most pervasive usage. Erasable plastic sheets replaced glass slides, allowing teachers to alter the image without having to replace the slide. This proved particularly advantageous in mathematics and science classes, where teachers actively model problem-solving processes. Educators and politicians recognized the overhead's efficacy, spurring the popularity of overhead projectors through legislation, like the National Defense Education Act of 1958 and the Elementary and Secondary Education Act of 1965, which made funding available to schools and teachers for both research on the use of audiovisual equipment and for the purchase of such equipment (Kidwell et al. 2008).

Overhead projectors' flexibility and low cost made them popular in American classrooms for decades. Gradually, however, they were replaced when new technology rendered them obsolete. The first challenge came from document cameras, which used a copy stand and video camera to project a magnified image of an object, text, or transparency onto a screen. Document cameras appeared in the 1970s and found acceptance thereafter; in the 1980s, they were connected—along with overhead projectors— to computers to improve the capabilities of projected images. Subsequent advances in cameras and computers, followed by the invention of digital projectors, sounded the death knell for overhead projectors, although they remain in use in many areas without the resources for superior equipment.

Film

One of the most exciting objects of schooling to enter the schoolroom in large numbers in the 20th century—and to reshape the room in some cases—was the film projector. Celluloid film was another late-19th-century technological innovation. At the time of film's introduction to American schools, it was widely believed to have transformative capabilities for educational pedagogy and curricula. "Books will soon be obsolete in schools," predicted Thomas Edison in 1913. "Scholars will soon be instructed through the eye. It is possible to touch every branch of human knowledge with the motion picture" (Cuban 1986, 11). Edison spoke as an industry insider, who had been actively engaged in producing educational films for schools for years, making him a pioneer in the field. Shortly after the emergence of the first commercial films, ambitious educators saw their possible utility in the age of mass public education. The very first use of motion pictures in a determined manner seems to have been in the progressive Rochester, New York, public-school system in 1910. That same year, however, the New York City Board of Education rejected a similar proposal for their schools due to concerns about the unavailability of inexpensive and portable equipment.

Educators in other regions of the country hesitated to embrace film for similar reasons. Additionally, films and their equipment were expensive and quite dangerous in the presence of large groups of children given film's potential to cause serious fire-safety challenges if not stored and utilized properly. Boston banned all films from its public schools in 1910— simultaneous with the first extensive tests in Rochester—from fear of fire.

Once fireproof projection booths were introduced, however, the public schools' acceptance of motion pictures and the new "visual education" grew quickly, with larger school systems creating special departments to oversee such practices during and after World War I. Over half of the state departments of education had film and related media departments by the early 1930s. The first national organizations for visual instruction and a journal titled *Educational Film Magazine* debuted in 1919. One prominent educator was led to effuse a few years later: "The motion picture is the single most potent educational factor in our present-day civilization" (Orgeron, Orgeron, and Streible 2012, 22).

Film's impact can be gleaned from a review of the period's school-architecture literature. References to motion-picture projectors began to appear before 1910. A leading reference book for architects on school design listed "a large visual instruction room (moving pictures and stereopticon)" as a "requirement" for a junior high school, commenting that "visual instruction [in elementary schools] is to play a larger and larger part of the school curriculum" (Donovan 1921, 73, 94). By the beginning of World War II, the ubiquity of film in schools led one educator to describe it as "indispensable in the modern school" after being used "almost universally for many years" (Hansen 1940, 39).

The popularity of motion pictures and other forms of projected visuals gave rise to a new design problem for school architects—how best to accommodate the projection equipment and provide the proper atmosphere for viewing so that students could receive its maximum benefits. Lawrence Perkins and Walter Cocking's *Schools* illustrated a built-in storage wall for classrooms with a projector unit on a sliding shelf. However, storing the projector proved less of a challenge than adequately darkening the room for it to work. The authors also addressed the debate over the best manner in which to use motion pictures in schools: whether films should be viewed in the individual classroom or in specially designed spaces. Essentially, educators had to choose between convenience and/or an optimum environment. Perkins and Cocking recognized the financial exigencies faced by most school administrators and decided that the best compromise was to do both if finances permitted, while clearly favoring the special-purpose room (Perkins and Cocking 1949). They showed a model depicting one possible solution. Instead of regular classrooms or auditoriums, Perkins's model was a hybrid of the two. He divided a rectangular classroom into three sections. The first, farthest from the hallway door, included the exterior wall and the room's only windows; combined with the middle section, it formed a traditional classroom. The last third, closest to the door, was a projection area, separated from the middle third by curtains. The architect alleged that the projection area's distance from the windows, along with a curtain of proper material, would provide the darkness needed for the films to be seen properly.

Other architects of the era proposed similar adjustments to the individual classroom while trying to avoid the most common (and least successful) solution—darkening curtains over the windows. Architects believed these curtains deficient because they "flutter in gusts of air, block ventilation, and, even when not in use, decrease the daylight in the classroom" (Caudill 1954, 244). The accumulation of dust was another problem with curtains. In practice, however, teachers usually showed films in their individual classrooms, pulling the curtains shut and hoping for the best. Some of the specialty rooms advocated by experts like Perkins were constructed, but they seem to have been more exception than rule.

Despite pressure from administrators, commercial vendors, and educational theorists, teachers remained unimpressed with motion pictures' contribution to the classroom. Although film projectors became a fixture in schools across the country by the 1960s, they supplemented rather than supplanted other forms of pedagogy. As early as 1923, a nationwide survey indicated that a large percentage of the schools regularly used slide projectors, pictures, and exhibits instead of films (Saettler 1990). A decade later, a study of over 300 of the nation's elementary school principals discovered that only 3 percent of them used sound films (while 52 percent used silent films). As educators praised educational film and boasted of its pervasiveness, a survey of teachers told a different story: over one-third of elementary-school teachers, 39 percent of middle-school teachers, and 56 percent of high-school teachers "never" integrated films into their teaching practices. These percentages would decline in the 1950s, but the overall proportion of those teachers claiming to show films "frequently" remained the same—approximately 40 percent for elementary teachers and 20 percent for their secondary-school counterparts (Cuban 1986). Film never achieved the goals of its proponents but was assimilated without fanfare, like movable furniture, and found a place in American classrooms for decades. Reel-to-reel films and smaller filmstrips played a larger part in the routines of elementary and high-school classrooms after the baby boom. But when television appeared in the schoolroom, it made films look difficult to use and old-fashioned by comparison.

Television

Although many educators expressed great optimism for radio's and film's applications to the classroom, they never became as popular as expected.

Television followed a comparable trajectory. Its supporters preached television's myriad uses and benefits compared to radio and obvious superiority over film. But after years of failed trials and confusion over its proper role, television was displaced late in the 20th century by a similar but even more attractive tool—the computer.

Experimental television stations in the United States emerged in the late 1920s during the heyday of educators' flirtations with radio. It was not until a decade later that commercial television networks began to build their own facilities and begin broadcasting primitive content. In the spring of 1939, the National Broadcasting Company (NBC) opened the first network television studio in New York City's Rockefeller Center to coincide with the World's Fair; a few months later, the Columbia Broadcasting System (CBS) began broadcasting from a studio in the city's Grand Central Station. Two years later, the FCC issued the first commercial broadcasting licenses to these stations. Regularly scheduled network programming began in 1947.

Television offered the mass-media capabilities of radio with the added attraction of a visual component. During its infancy, as commercial television began to reach more Americans, educators were quick to devise schemes for integrating it into the nation's classrooms. An article in an educational administrators' journal reported 51 television receivers in Philadelphia public schools in the spring of 1949. This was a rather amazing proportion, given that a year earlier there were only 16 television stations broadcasting around the country, and a tiny 0.4 percent of American households owned a receiver. Other school systems tried out less ambitious programs, often beginning with a single school or with closed-circuit broadcasts. Soon there was a nationwide movement to find an educational role for television, funded by major philanthropic organizations and supported by governments. The year 1952 saw the establishment of the Educational Television and Radio Center (ETRC)—supported by the Ford Foundation—to obtain and broadcast educational programs created by local stations, while the FCC reserved nearly 250 channels for noncommercial educational use. KUHT in Houston was the first educational television station to take advantage of this opportunity; after its lead, other stations followed rapidly.

The remarkable explosion of television happened in the 1950s. The 0.4 percent of American households with a television in 1948 expanded to 83.2 percent a decade later, as television became one of the fastest-growing technological advances in the nation's history. In less than a generation, its status changed from novelty to an integral part of people's lives. Home television ownership reached 90 percent in 1962, the same year that the

U.S. Office of Education created the National Educational Television Library to provide educational programming to the National Educational Television (NET) Network and later to various public broadcasting stations. Additionally, state and regional networks organized as a means of sharing educational television resources.

Despite continued philanthropic and governmental support, interest in television began to wane in the late 1960s. Much of the disenchantment seems to have arisen from teachers' inability (or unwillingness) to include educational television in their lessons. Teachers complained that programming often failed to coincide with course content or that television's lack of interactive potential reinforced the "sit-and-listen" learning environment abhorred by progressive educators. An important 1967 Carnegie Commission on Educational Television report, entitled *Public Television: A Program for Action*, indicated that television was generally utilized as a secondary rather than a primary method of instruction: "Instructional television, like instructional radio and instructional motion pictures before it, lies outside the process, put to individual or occasional use as ancillary material," wrote the authors (Taggart 2007, 118).

Although television sets continue to serve multiple purposes by 21st-century classrooms, their main function changed from potential educational tool to source of entertainment. They were often connected to videotape players (later digital video disc, or DVD, players) to show educational films, documentaries, movies, or other recorded programming. With the adoption of computer monitors and plasma screens, the television became expendable.

Teaching Machines

The story of the teaching machine, or "Automatic Teacher," is an obscure but important chapter in the history of American schoolrooms. Before computers proliferated, teaching machines provided educators with a valuable tool for individualized learning, allowed for an interactive programmed educational experience, and promised to alleviate teacher shortages that plagued the nation during the height of the baby boom.

The dream of educating students through specially designed machines is longstanding. As far back as the late 19th century, inventors began to patent various equipment intended to let students work through lessons at their own pace with feedback about correct and incorrect responses. A wave of efficiency-mania swept through the psychological and educational fields in the first decades of the 20th century, providing fertile ground for such devices. The first true teaching machine can be attributed to Ohio

State University professor Sidney Pressey, who displayed his creation at the American Psychological Association annual meetings in the mid-1920s and eventually received a patent for a "Machine for Intelligence Tests" in 1928. Pressey's machine operated according to a three-step procedure that could be tailored to a variety of subjects: (a) the machine presented a unit of information to the student; (b) the student responded to the information in some manner; and (c) the machine provided feedback regarding the correctness of the response.

In spite of extensive interest from teachers and administrators, Pressey's machines and the ideas behind them remained novelties. Historians generally agree that he was ahead of his time, but the teaching machine failed to be fully implemented in the 1920s and 1930s because its major selling points did not align with educators' desires. Pressey's invention created opportunities for individualized learning on a faster pace with fewer teachers at a time when none of those qualities were wanted or needed. In fact, due to a glut of teachers arising from the Great Depression and leveling enrollment figures, many educators *feared* the devices, viewing them as potential replacements for live teachers in the classroom. Nonetheless, inventors continued to produce variations of Pressey's machine. Over

Students in a language laboratory, 1950s. Beginning in the 1920s, audio and visual machines were introduced to schoolrooms in an attempt to improve student learning through technology. (Universal History Archive/UIG via Getty Images)

100 educational devices were patented in the 1920s. Anecdotal evidence indicates that—like motion pictures—there was much enthusiasm about teaching machines, but few teachers assimilated them into everyday classroom practices.

The early 1960s proved to be the halcyon days for teaching machines, following a resurgence of interest after World War II. The educational climate had changed since the origins of Pressey's machine; baby-boom enrollments (resulting in larger class sizes), a shortage of trained teachers to keep up with them, the continuing influence of progressive pedagogical ideas, and evidence of the success of multimedia educational tools in training military personnel during the war—all helped to establish a more sympathetic attitude toward the devices in the educational world. Added to that mixture was the imprimatur of B. F. Skinner, the internationally famous behavioral psychologist who devised his own version of the teaching machine. Skinner sought to extend Pressey's early experiments, but his own devices took a different approach to the student-machine interaction. Whereas Pressey's machine relied upon students having previous knowledge of the material prior to using the machine, Skinner's adaptation could teach *new* material through a series of small steps, often referred to as "programmed learning."

According to historians, by 1962 nearly 200 companies were making teaching machines or programmed instructional materials, and by the end of the decade, the creation and support of such devices had developed into a $300 million industry (Benjamin 1988; Petrina 2004). A contemporary article recited a litany of these machines: "There are stationary, portable, and collapsible models. Films, colored slides, records, tapes, discs, paper cards, mimeographed sheets, or printed pages may be used to present the programmed materials. To select or write in the answers and to advance new questions or retire them from sight the student may push a button, press a single key or a series of keys, pull a lever, punch a hole, turn a handle, move a cardboard strip, wind a crank, or make a mark on a piece of paper" (Exton 1960, 20).

Literature reviews indicate that the popularity of teaching machines peaked by 1965 and then fell precipitously thereafter. At first glance, it may seem logical to assume teaching machines were replaced by computers, which could perform the same functions and more, but this supposition is incorrect. As explained below, computers did not become a presence in American classrooms until the 1980s. So the demise of teaching machines must have been the result of such other factors as diminished faith in their effectiveness, the emphasis on small-group work that typified so much of the pedagogy in the postwar period, or teachers continued reliance on passive learning or teacher-centered methods.

Computers

Although a classroom without a computer terminal or Internet access seems nearly inconceivable today, the use of computer technology in American education is a relatively recent phenomenon dating back to the 1960s. Educational computers were born of the same post-Sputnik focus on science and technology that excited educators and fueled the space program. Computers began as somewhat of a novelty, considered an upgraded version of teaching machines. Few outside the computer design world predicted their subsequent impact.

In 1959, the PLATO project began at the University of Illinois, marking the first large-scale use of computers in education. PLATO offered students individualized instruction at any of several thousand terminals located on the campus and at several other schools around the state. Each terminal used a touch-sensitive screen and keyboard to relay information to a single central computer. PLATO's accomplishment surely inspired the introduction of computer-aided instruction (CAI) into other schools in the early 1960s. The federal government showed its support for the development of CAI when the Elementary and Secondary Education Act of 1965 included opportunities for schools to receive funding for computer technology. A few years later, the National Science Foundation supported the creation of regional computing networks across the country, linking hundreds of colleges and some high schools. Corporate America saw an opportunity as well, foreshadowing today's educational scene where software giants influence and sometimes dictate the course of public-school curricula. The first computer company to try large-scale educational computing was the International Business Machines Corporation (IBM). It teamed with Stanford University, using grant money from the U.S. Department of Education, to develop the IBM 1500 Instructional System for schools. The IBM 1500 debuted in 1966 in a test that installed equipment in over 30 locations, each of which could facilitate 32 student stations; the stations included a display and keyboard. The system was successful but remained rarely used because it was too expensive for most schools.

In this pioneer era, computers were huge machines that occupied entire rooms and were programmed using punch cards and card readers. A mainframe or central computer was accessed from outposts equipped with terminals. Programming was cumbersome, and remote connections through telephone lines were unreliable. These conditions would change after 1971 when Intel Corporation developed the first microprocessor, which substantially reduced the component parts of a computer to the point where microcomputers or personal computers (PCs) small enough to fit on a desk soon followed. When PCs entered the marketplace, schools became avid consumers. The early 1980s proved to be the tipping point for computer adoption in schools. Statistics showed that nearly 70 percent of public schools had at least 1 computer in 1984, while the average elementary school had 5 and the typical high school owned 13. One year later, the figures had jumped: 82 percent of elementary schools and 92 percent of high schools had at least 1 computer (Cuban 1986).

Those surveys were undoubtedly skewed by the impact of Apple Inc. The company revolutionized microcomputing with its Macintosh PC, which not only included a mouse for easier maneuvering around the display and better graphics, but also came with free software that let teachers easily create interactive material for their students. The Macintosh's success stimulated a response from other computer companies. All of this competition was good for schools because it helped drive down prices and led to continuing advances in educational programming. Teachers relied more and more on computers to supplement—or in some cases, replace—longstanding practices in the classroom. By 1991, studies showed there was one personal computer for every 18 students in America's schools; in 2000, that number had dropped to one for every 5 pupils (Aslan and Reigeluth 2011).

Unlike television or radio, the embrace of computers actually required some manipulation of educational space. Computer terminals (or laptops) take up room, and computer equipment must be located where air circulation, temperature control, and fire safety are monitored. Although personal computers continued to get smaller, eventually leading to variations like tablets and notebooks, their increased adoption often meant finding new space in the schoolroom or school building. Some schools offered computer laboratories specifically intended to house multiple terminals without doubling as regular instructional space, a retreat from the flexibility so prized by educators of the previous generation. Libraries were popular sites for computers, particularly once the evolution of the Internet prompted many school administrators to convert their library into a media center, replacing book stacks with equipment and tables or carrels. In the early years of the 21st century, wireless technology offered Internet access over large areas and untethering the computer from its cables and wires. Educators applauded the opportunities presented by wireless technology, including the return to a freer classroom atmosphere. The conversion came rapidly, as can be seen from the fact that only 3 percent of classrooms had Internet access in 1994 compared to 94 percent a decade later (Aslan and Reigluth 2011). Computers and wireless connectivity are now ingrained in classrooms around the country. For their first half century, computers have immeasurably aided classroom instruction by providing access to previously unimaginable resources.

Chapter 4

ANCILLARY SPACES

The material history of schoolrooms (and their buildings) is incomplete without a review of the ancillary spaces that have supported them. In particular, corridors and lockers have had a long physical relationship with the classroom, sometimes even sharing the same space, while portable schoolrooms have supplemented school buildings for over a century. Since World War II, the distinction between classrooms and corridors has been blurred, perhaps reflecting the continuing decentralization of schoolhouses, as physical and psychological barriers that once separated these areas continue to be challenged. Portable schoolrooms, on the other hand, remain as they were over a century ago: spaces both reviled and applauded for the contribution they make in service to the school, a necessary evil whose ability to adapt to fluctuating student enrollments is well established.

CORRIDORS

Corridors have been essential elements of educational design ever since schoolhouses began to include more than one classroom on a floor. Their obvious function is to allow horizontal circulation within a building, but over time, corridors became valuable multipurpose spaces accommodating a variety of activities, and their physical form became less distinct as circulation and gathering spaces merged toward the end of the 20th century. Along the way, the corridor was often celebrated, like when it anchored certain new types of plan organization, and sometimes denigrated by educators and architects who debated the corridor's necessity and often experimented with alternatives that eliminated long passageways by aggregating classrooms in centralized groups. Whatever their status, corridors and schoolrooms have been intimately linked in American educational history.

The functional possibilities of corridors beyond internal movement were not fully recognized until after World War II. Previously, corridors tended to attract the attention of architects and educators for three slightly overlapping reasons, in addition to their primary purpose of circulating students through the building: their lighting, their place in maintaining student discipline, and their ability to organize a floor plan.

Lighting was an early concern, part of the broader obsession with schoolchildren's health in the mid-1800s. As school buildings grew larger in the days before electric lighting, designers, teachers, and administrators all recognized the importance of finding ways to allow daylight to reach the building's interior spaces. Educators and architects tried to discern the proper width of corridors and the placement of windows to illuminate them. Large banks of windows at the ends of hallways and transom windows above classroom doors were popular solutions.

The first large school buildings were navigable by short interior hallways linking just a few rooms, but their successors—particularly the monumental late-19th-century high schools—relied on corridors to facilitate multiple movements over the course of the day by hundreds or even thousands of students, who often traveled considerable distances between classes. School designers began to incorporate more single-loaded corridors, lining the hallway with classrooms on only one side in buildings shaped like E's or U's or some other alphabet form that provided interior courtyards for light and air circulation. At the same time, the corridor was charged with unifying these growing school buildings into a coherent whole.

In addition to this double duty of facilitating circulation and enhancing health, corridors in the modern schoolhouse became part of the ongoing struggle to maintain order. The long-standing authoritarian mentality that reigned over education considered long corridors a challenge, with their length and angles spawning opportunities for student mischief outside the teachers' gaze. An enlightening article from 1890 is unique in the way it addressed the correlation between architecture and discipline in some detail and in its emphasis on corridors: they are directly implicated in three of the "four chief foes" to school discipline as outlined by the author, an anonymous "Head Master." The author claimed the school architect can either "greatly aid" in the maintenance of discipline through his design or "can render good discipline almost impossible." Poor design can foster a lack of discipline. Examples of poor design include long rows of classrooms connected by a dark, narrow corridor; hallways with sharp turns; and stone paving in the corridors, which enhances noise. The author believed these features could impel students to run down the long corridors, clash at the angles, and bully each other in the dark corners. Disciplinary "foes" like disorder, noise, and bullying, wrote the headmaster, "are chiefly promoted by long, dark corridors. With short, wide, straight and well-lighted passageways, which can be supervised at a glance, they can easily be repressed indoors . . . To meet the fourth evil [indecent writing], corridors should, as before, be few in number, light, and easily supervised; and their walls, as well as those of all lavatories and closets, should be lined with glazed bricks or tiles" ("The Planning of School Buildings" 1890, 81–82).

In contrast to the circumstances described in the article, the outstanding interior feature of the monumental early-20th-century school building was its wide, brightly lit corridors. Besides their disciplinary advantages, health advocates thought these corridors possessed definite hygienic advantages. Tiled walls, curved joints where the floor met the wall, and large windows intended to flood interior hallways with healthy, germicidal sunlight terminated the end of each corridor. Some architects added skylights to this arrangement. The entire school building was transforming into a machine for manufacturing healthy children at a time when progressive reformers forced urban health and sanitation concerns to the forefront of public consciousness. Corridors worked in tandem with larger and better-placed windows and improved ventilation. Alongside its role in improving students' health, there existed a simultaneous reinterpretation of corridors as sites for extending the learning process into nontraditional spaces. The corridor's promise was apparent to people like noted cultural critic Randolph Bourne (1886–1918), who visited Gary, Indiana, in 1915 to view firsthand the celebrated platoon system implemented by William Wirt. (John Dewey's daughter Evelyn had visited the year before and collaborated with her father on a book highlighting the Gary schools, *Schools of To-morrow* [1915].) Wirt's "Work-Study-Play System" was founded on his belief that the traditional school arrangement was inefficient and uneconomical.

Bourne returned from Gary impressed by the system and fascinated by its buildings. In his account of the experience, he described the Ralph Waldo Emerson and Friedrich Froebel Schools (both designed by William B. Ittner) as "architectural creations of unusual beauty and impressiveness." Inside, the hallways some viewed as merely efficient channels for interior circulation or bright, clean spaces of health and discipline struck Bourne differently: he saw their potential for enhancing the educational experience. Bourne praised the "broad halls [that] serve not only as the school streets for the constant passage of the children between their work, but also as centers for the 'application' work, or for informal study. They are so wide that all confusion is avoided, and they suggest to the visitor that they serve the school community in the same way that the agora or the forum did the ancient city." He expressed his desire that schools would "absorb the museums and galleries" as they have absorbed playgrounds—that is, to make them such an integral part of the environment as to seem natural. A nascent art gallery in the Emerson School corridor represented a first step toward fulfilling that goal (Bourne 1916, 23–24).

Bourne's comparison of the school corridor with the Greek agora and Roman forum would prove prescient. Those places were the traditional meeting areas for ancient city dwellers, where citizens could engage in a variety of activities. Over the course of the 20th century, the American school corridor began to take on a similar role. This evolution started shortly after World War II, when commentators promoted a reconsideration of corridors in light of the changing layout of suburban schools. Finger-plan school buildings were a prominent early example of the increasing size and importance of corridors in the decentralized suburban schools. Extended, corridor-dominant arrangements, like the finger and cluster plans, evolved because they were easier to expand than the alphabet or closed forms of earlier schools, especially given the desire to reduce school buildings to the fewest number of floors. Recognizing that students—especially those in high school—spend a considerable amount of time each day walking between classes, educators and architects considered alternatives that would make the hallways more efficient by multiplying their uses. In addition to serving as art galleries or places to display student work (practices sometimes known as "extending the classroom"), other suggestions included converting a portion of the hallway into a sitting area, a small lounge, or a comparable place for gathering. An enlightening example of the new thinking occurred at Oklahoma's Norman High School (1954), a highly publicized project created by two of the leading school-design firms in the country (Perkins & Will and Caudill Rowlett Scott). The architects described the school's main corridor as a combination of circulatory space, locker area, "community center, lobby, administration waiting space, and leisure reading area for the library" (Caudill 1954, 162). To reflect these various activities, the architects labeled the hallway "Student Center." An earlier, unused version of this space revealed even more of an emphasis on the corridor's social potential; the architects had experimented with subdividing the corridor into small social areas or alcoves that could be used by students for conversation, informal eating, or reading. They discarded the idea, but similar attempts by other designers demonstrated the attractiveness of multiuse corridors and the widespread interest in their development.

In the next few decades, corridors factored greatly in the approaches of two divergent groups: those architects and educators who designed decentralized schools that exploded the building's mass, relocating the school's constituent parts into their own spaces or into logical groupings of spaces, and those with a different outlook who sought to banish corridors from school plans as unnecessary and inefficient. For the former, the corridor served an important role in unifying the floor plan by creating a literal and figurative spine for finger plans, such as at Acalanes High School, or cluster plans, as at Heathcote Elementary School. Additionally, architects recognized that corridors provided the best opportunity to bring in sunlight and create pleasant views in school buildings. Consequently, a generation of visually striking corridors appeared in architectural and educational publications, many of them transparent passages full of light from one or both sides—sometimes through colored glass—and overlooking or flanked by small pockets of manicured nature.

Furthermore, these corridors were attuned to postwar educators' desire for more social areas and a less formal atmosphere. Reformers' ongoing attempts to humanize postwar schools—making them less institutional and more inviting and comfortable—enlisted corridors as an essential part of the change. "The typical classroom today is a glass and masonry box filled with kitchen-like furniture. Its surfaces are hard and cold," claimed the EFL. "Nothing yields to the body, is soft to the hand, or warm to the eye. Connected by cavernous corridors of echoing tile and steel lockers, most modern classrooms are sterile and institutional" (EFL 1960, 133). Architects and educators enlisted the corridor to counter such barrenness. They added carpeting or bench seating along the walls, made small areas for plants, and increasingly displayed student work, inspiring quotations, awards and honors, and materials of all sorts on corridor walls. Corridors expanded into larger areas intended to provide space for student socializing, in some cases even forming a lounge with casual furniture. Broad expanses of glass destroyed the enclosed sensation of older school hallways. In addition to larger windows, some architects added skylights over corridors to enhance their light and pleasant nature.

In some ways, this movement to increase social spaces in the building can be tied to the life-adjustment curriculum—which remained in extensive use as the building corridors were transforming—and its emphasis on nonacademic life skills, like the ability to relate to peers. Educators also had available a growing body of psychological studies on children and adolescents, almost all of which demonstrated the importance of peer relations to healthy psychological development. With children's social and psychological needs in the forefront of educators' minds, they looked to school architects to provide gathering areas, and one of the most logical places to do so was in the corridor, a place where interactions already happened all day long.

However, not everyone supported corridor-dominated buildings, no matter how many social opportunities they might stimulate. Contemporaneous with the corridor's evolution into social space was an attempt by opponents to eliminate hallways whenever possible, usually in the name of cost savings but also with the intention of compacting school buildings (especially in the lower grades) to make them smaller and less intimidating. This mind-set would lead to the emergence of the open-plan classroom described above, and its advocates also favored aggregations of classrooms into compact forms with minimal interior circulatory space.

Over time, the relationship between corridor and social space in some schools changed, evolving from a hallway designed for circulation with a few congregating areas added to a large social area (or accumulation of them) through which students could walk to circulate through the building. By the late 20th century, the hybrid corridor/social space was a standard feature of school buildings, particularly at the high-school level. Schools continued to include a central circulation spine, which was often manipulated to add other functions and renamed "Main Street," the commons, the

High school commons area, early 2000s. Commons areas, "main streets," and other large, open, multi-functional spaces appeared in late-20th-century schools, serving as places for informal interactions or group activities in addition to facilitating circulation through the building. (Andy Cross/The Denver Post via Getty Images)

student collaboration space, the galleria, and similar variations. In some cases, the notions were taken more literally than others. Ohio's Fort Recovery Elementary/Middle School (2000), for example, was designed around a main corridor, with the building's plan resembling an E-shaped building like those from a century earlier. However, Fort Recovery's corridor was a Disneyesque Main Street intended to recreate the glory days of the city's downtown: the walls were made to look like assorted storefronts, and lampposts and brick paving added to the ambiance.

Fort Recovery blurred the boundaries between education and commerce, if only aesthetically, but the connection may have been relevant in other ways. The corridor's expansion and centrality led more than one commentator to perceive a resemblance between the late-20th-century high school and the suburban shopping mall. Conceptually the two were often identical: multilevel buildings organized by arranging individual units (stores or rooms) around broad circulation routes encircling a void (atrium or commons area) that provided spatial openness and seating areas, accented with bright colors and small pockets of greenery. A seminal book of the 1980s, *The Shopping Mall High School: Winners and Losers in the Educational Marketplace* (1985), attacked the shopping-mall mentality as it had been applied to the high-school experience, which the authors felt had come to resemble the customer-and-merchant relationship of the shopping mall. The book criticized the secondary schools' abandonment of rigorous, common standards and values in favor of letting students adopt individualized or customized paths. Students became the equivalent of consumers wandering through their high-school years like shoppers through a mall, pursuing their own interests and desires without guidance or oversight, catered to by the merchant/educators who strove to offer something for everyone without imposing judgment about the worthiness of the student's choices. The authors framed the scenario as a case of foundational progressive ideals (e.g., allowing children agency in their education and the ability to follow their interests) run amok. In a brief passage, however, they extended the metaphor quite fittingly to the school building itself: "Between periods students go outside to find their next destination, entering and leaving classrooms as if they were adjacent stores. Another school appears massive and mysterious from the outside, but its architecture looks inward: everything radiates from a lively covered promenade" (Powell, Farrar, and Cohen 1985, 9).

Although this description, lacking the promenade, might apply to any high school from the 1920s on, it identified the obvious similarity between the concept and organization of high-school buildings and commercial shopping malls—not coincidentally two of the larger physical structures common to the middle-class suburban built environment. After the conservative back-to-basics movement attacked the shopping-mall curriculum and successfully established a narrower, standards-based curriculum, students had fewer choices, but the shopping-mall analogy remained an apt description of a popular school-design idea that mimicked the commercial mall's atrium space and circumscribing balcony. Even in the 21st century, some commentators continue to evoke the shopping mall when describing some new high-school buildings.

OUTDOOR CORRIDORS

A new wrinkle in school design became visible in the early 20th century, borne of economic and student health concerns: the outdoor corridor. It appeared first in Southern California, where the mild climate allowed architects to incorporate the outdoors to an extent not considered possible in other regions of the country. As outlined above, architects like Hunt and Grey and William Templeton Johnson developed a regional prototype reliant on outdoor circulation. Journal articles depicting California school buildings, particularly those by Richard Neutra and Ernest Kump, helped spread the popularity of outdoor walkways. By the early 1940s, the practice was being encouraged for schools in other areas, like the Southwest. Coverage of these early efforts tended to focus on the outdoor walkway's ability to reduce costs associated with indoor corridors, both in terms of initial construction and ongoing maintenance and heating/ventilation. The opportunity

A postwar covered walkway added to an early-20th-century monumental school. The outdoor walkway progressed beyond its Southern California roots to become popular across the country in the 1950s. (Library of Congress)

for students to access fresh air and sunlight were contributing factors as educators looked for any chance to make the school environment healthier. Outdoor corridors also meshed nicely with the extended classroom.

A decade later, school specialists like William Caudill regularly noted the increasing popularity of outdoor walkways and even encouraged their use in such non-California settings as the Midwest (arguing in part that outdoor circulation had already proven itself on university and college campuses). School buildings sprouted canopies of sheet metal, canvas, plastic, and other materials to shield walkways as school buildings decentralized and spread across suburban landscapes. Covered walkways were often part of the uniquely American campus-plan school that epitomized the progressive orientation and modernist architecture of the nation's postwar schools to the rest of the world.

Outdoor corridors continued to be popular until the 1970s, when the energy crisis and shrinking enrollments inspired architects to explore compact layouts and energy-efficient schemes. The notion that students needed fresh air and outdoor exposure lost support, and many educators and architects, mindful of energy costs and confident in the quality of artificial lighting, advocated for windowless classrooms and impregnable building envelopes. Designs featuring courtyards, large banks of windows, and sprawling footprints became less frequent as the open, airy 1950s suburban-prototype school evolved into something more material and less transparent. Some outdoor corridors were destroyed when remodeling became necessary. As the campus plan's popularity declined, so did the need for connective hallways.

Safety concerns in the 21st century are affecting school plans in a significant way. Contemporary security challenges prompted by increasing gun violence on school grounds sometimes preclude the design of unprotected exterior spaces, like outdoor corridors, whenever possible. The outdoor corridor has not disappeared, however, and walking outdoors between buildings continues to be a prized aspect of education in parts of the country with temperate or warm climates. Some of the most highly publicized schools of recent years rely on outdoor circulation, like Morphosis's Diamond Ranch High School (2000), which is organized around an open-air pedestrian street that acts as a spine connecting an ensemble of individual structures along a hillside.

LOCKERS

Children who attended school after the mid-20th century are inclined to think of corridors and lockers as intimately connected. In the schools of that era, lockers lined the hallways or were organized into banks in the middle of the corridor or adjacent to it. In larger buildings, such lockers might occupy most of the wall space. For much of the history of American education, however, this arrangement would have been considered very unusual. Instead, schoolchildren used hooks and shelves in small wardrobes and cloakrooms in the days before locker-lined corridors became the norm.

The earliest accommodations for students' belongings were simple hooks hung on the wall near the entry of 18th-century school buildings. These sufficed in rural America for centuries, but in larger urban schools, a different solution was required as enrollments and school sizes both grew. By the mid-1800s, the most common form of personal storage was a separate walk-in room, usually near the entrance to the classroom, called the wardrobe. The wardrobes were simple affairs—small rooms (sometimes only four feet wide) with hooks or pegs along the walls for hanging outerwear and shelves for other items.

A challenge to this preferred solution arose at the turn of the 20th century as architects began to alter the wardrobe by creating open alcoves along the corridors or, in high schools, designating space in the basement as a separate cloakroom. At the same time, educators introduced the wood or steel locker as a means for students to store more of their belongings in a private manner. This led to some debate in the school-design world over the efficacy of lockers versus wardrobes. Edmund Wheelwright, the highly respected Boston architect whose *School Architecture* (1901) was the most comprehensive guide of its time, favored wardrobes, arguing that they saved money instead of the alternative of hanging clothing in widened corridors. Opponents pointed to fire safety and ventilation issues as favoring corridor storage over wardrobes. The debate lingered into the interwar era, when steel lockers in hallways found greater acceptance, in part because promoters linked them to central vacuum systems, bubbling-water drinking fountains (instead of a water bucket and community cup), and other advances intended to promote healthier school buildings and better hygiene.

The locker's hegemony was not complete until after World War II. Even during the postwar building boom, educators and architects had conflicting opinions about the need for lockers. In *Toward Better School Design*, William Caudill offered ten different arrangements of lockers along a corridor to stimulate designers, while holding out hope that architects might not choose any of them. "Certainly the conventional steel locker is not the final answer," wrote Caudill. "The noise and high maintenance connected with these units give evidence there is much more to be desired" (Caudill 1954, 181). He preferred pegs, hooks, and shelves—the old-fashioned solution—and presented more than one case study depicting alternatives to metal lockers. But voices like Caudill's went unheeded as cost considerations made metal lockers the easier solution.

Interestingly, in the 1980s, traditional steel lockers began to disappear from many schools in favor of a return to pegs and shelves. Safety concerns were the main driver, with school administrators worried about rising instances of drugs or weapons being stored in student lockers and lawsuits over the legality of locker searches increasing. A growing reliance on backpacks also tended to make lockers less of a necessity. And age-old complaints about the excessive noise and maintenance problems of metal lockers reappeared. Today, however, architects persist in designing school buildings with old-fashioned lockers lining the hallways because they represent the best solution for student storage issues. Recent advances have led to the development of lockers made from plastic compounds—which supporters say are quieter, more durable, and longer lasting—but this merely represents a substitution of material rather than new alternative. For the foreseeable future, lockers will continue to be an essential component of American education.

RELOCATABLE (PORTABLE) SCHOOLROOMS

Not all schoolrooms have been inside school buildings. The temporary or **relocatable schoolroom** is a relatively unnoticed but integral element of American education's physical environment. Known by many different names, portable classrooms evolved in response to rapid enrollment growth when the nation's school systems swelled in the late 19th century. Despite educators' opinions ranging from preferred option to embarrassing necessity, they have been part of the public-education system for over a century and continue to serve schools in large numbers today. For example, a survey of public-school principals from 2007 reported that the most popular manner of dealing with overcrowding in schools (78 percent) was by using relocatable classrooms (Chaney and Lewis 2007).

Available evidence indicates that portable classrooms first appeared in Milwaukee in the 1890s, the brainchild of C. E. Lammert, whose position was described as either superintendent of school repairs or superintendent of school buildings. Numerous contemporary commentators gave credit to the French for inventing the concept of temporary classrooms in an effort to handle a sudden influx of Parisian students generated by an 1882 mandatory-education law. Lammert's first American portables were simple one-room, wooden-frame structures called barracks, which could be taken apart and reassembled in a different location.

Milwaukee's portable schoolrooms received a great deal of publicity when the St. Louis school system became one of the first to implement them on a wide scale. St. Louis was considered a premier school organization, and its progressive efforts, particularly in the area of school design, were followed with great interest by other educators and architects. William B. Ittner, the city's school architect, helped attract attention to portables by virtue of his status in the profession. After visiting Milwaukee, Ittner devised and published his own version of the portable wooden schoolroom, which undoubtedly helped facilitate their acceptance by skeptical architects.

Other cities were quick to adopt the new technology. Chicago provides a typical case study. In 1904, the board of education's Committee on Buildings and Grounds sent its acting school architect to St. Louis to examine Ittner's portable buildings. By that time, St. Louis students occupied 30 such buildings. The architect was impressed, and after receiving his report, the committee recommended 6 temporary school buildings be erected as a trial. These structures proved so successful that just over a year later, the *School Journal* reported Chicago educators no longer considered portables to be an experiment; 26 structures had been ordered with 12 more recommended by the buildings and grounds committee. Principals of those Chicago schools incorporating portables were described as "enthusiastic" in their praise. By 1919, the city relied on over 300 portables, each seating 48 students (over 14,000 students in total). The board's chief engineer described their typical construction: rectangular, wooden-framed buildings sheathed with galvanized steel, approximately 30 feet long and 24 feet wide, which enclosed one room. Two units could also be placed end to end to expand the interior space. Other than complaints about cold floors in winter and high temperatures in summer, the buildings performed as needed (Howatt and Leis 1919).

Just three years later, the number of students in Chicago's portable structures had doubled to nearly 30,000. Unfortunately, the overcrowding problem was not solved—a 60,000-seat deficit remained in the city's schools. This scenario would be repeated—not just in Chicago but throughout the country—for the next half century, as school districts struggled to accommodate students during a massive immigration influx, World War II material shortages and financial restrictions, and the postwar baby boom. During all of these challenges, the portable classroom's supporters repeatedly warned administrators to remember the temporary nature of these structures and not let them become permanent. These reminders, however, usually went unheeded.

Advertisements and articles about relocatable classrooms began to appear in educators' professional journals at the beginning of the 20th century, and there was significantly increasing interest in them by the 1920s.

Portable classrooms (right), 1920s. Portable, temporary, or relocatable schoolrooms have been a fixture in American public education for nearly 150 years. They are prized by educators for their usefulness in dealing with enrollment fluctuations. (Library of Congress)

Between then and the postwar era, there were few advances in portable-schoolroom design. Most structures remained wooden framed, with various materials used to enclose the space. Architects attempted to balance ease of construction and cost with comfort. Like standard classrooms, light and ventilation were dominant concerns. Some portables began to include bathrooms. Other designers experimented with nonrectilinear shapes or arrangements of multiple structures. Almost everyone involved with portable classrooms believed that one day they would no longer be necessary.

Despite such predictions, portables remain a fixture in school districts in the 21st century. Their peak use came during the 1950s and 1960s. By that time, the assortment of available formats and materials had expanded to include steel framing and aluminum skins, but the basic nature of the portable classroom remained the same. The EFL supported temporary buildings as a cost-effective solution to overenrollment problems, publishing a booklet in 1964 specifically on the topic. It listed four distinct types of relocatable building in contemporary use: "portables," which were single or double classroom buildings that could be moved as a unit; "mobile" units, which were "variations on the house trailer, bus, or truck" and could be relocated the fastest and easiest; "divisible" structures, which

were moved in segments; and "demountable" structures, based on a pan-
eled wall system and easily dismantled into segments for moving (EFL
1964). Architects and educators interested in such structures were urged to
consider not only the materials, lighting, and ventilation of the classrooms,
but also their size, appearance, and relationship to other portable units and
the main school building.

Not everyone was pleased with portable schoolrooms. Some viewed
them as indicative of racial disparities in the nation's urban schools. When
white schools became overcrowded, new facilities would be constructed.
But black students often jammed into older, deteriorating schoolhouses in
unsafe numbers while school officials refused to build more classrooms.
Portable schoolrooms became fixtures on the grounds of predominantly
black urban schools across the nation. Even Chicago's long-standing reliance on portable classrooms eventually sparked an ugly confrontation that
brought the city's racial tensions to the fore. In reaction to continuing overcrowding, the city's superintendent of education, Benjamin Willis, persuaded the board of education to purchase almost 200 more portable units
in 1961. Each of these relocatable classrooms was a prefabricated 20-by-
36-foot mobile aluminum box that could be delivered to the school site and
easily assembled. They included such amenities as air-conditioning (which
most of the city's permanent school buildings did not have), carpeting, tele-
phones, drinking fountains, and bathrooms. However, critics and angry
parents dubbed these structures "Willis Wagons" and began a campaign
against them, claiming their disproportionate use in black neighborhoods
revealed a strategy of racial segregation. Despite their practicality, Willis
Wagons were simply not acceptable to black families who knew of white
schools with empty classrooms just a few miles away. The black community began a campaign to pressure Willis on racial imbalances. The
Chicago chapter of the Congress of Racial Equality contacted the Illinois
School Problems Commission about emerging racial discrepancies in the
city, and a few months later, the National Association for the Advancement
of Colored People argued that Chicago school-board actions impermissi-
bly resulted in separate and unequal schools for black students in the city.
A series of protests and student walkouts in the early 1960s brought more
attention to the problems, resulting in a threat from the federal government to withhold funding if a desegregation plan was not implemented.
But Willis held fast to his neighborhood-school policy until his resignation
in 1966, prompted when the board approved the transfer of some black
high school students to a white school.

Besides serving as a lightning rod for racial inequities, Chicago's battle
over portable schoolrooms brought to light a dire overcrowding situation.

Statistics demonstrated that the need for portables was a major problem around the country. Educators' desperate attempts to keep up with enrollment increases through portable buildings were failing. A 1964 U.S. Office of Education report revealed that despite the average construction of almost 70,000 new classrooms in school buildings over the previous five years, there remained a shortage of 125,000 classrooms across the country. Approximately 2.5 percent of the nation's educational facilities were classified as "non-permanent." In some places, the figures were staggering: 27 percent of all "teaching stations" in Los Angeles's public schools were portable; in sum, the city relied on over 5,000 relocatable structures. By the early 1960s, the Los Angeles school district had adopted this as an official strategy, constructing only 70 percent of its needed seats in permanent buildings and 30 percent in relocatables. At the same time, Houston had over 1,000 portable units, New York City over 300, and one-quarter of the teaching stations in Oakland were not permanent (EFL 1964).

When the postwar population spike began to flatten in the 1970s, and school enrollments became more manageable, portable classrooms retained their place in the educational world. They had proven their usefulness in terms of cost-effectiveness and flexibility, becoming a permanent fixture on the educational landscape. The new century saw the school-age population rise again. Educators were ready for the shift and relied on portable buildings to handle overflows just as they had been in the past. Recent studies indicate that today around one-third of all American public schools include portable or temporary buildings, while the Modular Building Institute claims there are over 260,000 classrooms in relocatable structures (Gonchar 2014). Interest in designing portable classrooms has dovetailed with a larger societal movement among the millennial generation toward mobile structures, "tiny houses," and sustainable building components.

Many of the new generation of portables share common characteristics, not unrelated to their predecessors. Most are single classrooms inside and formed by combining two or more rectangular units (what the EFL called "divisible"). Shed roofs (sloping in only one direction) or butterfly roofs sit atop a simple structure that is often left exposed inside, along with visible ductwork. Exterior cladding is often bright and colorful. Component parts are as environmentally sustainable as possible. Portable schoolrooms have in some ways become leaders in the movement to make school environments green, with energy-recovery ventilators, rainwater cisterns, composting toilets, sensor-controlled LED lighting, hand-pump sinks, and other energy-efficient products.

As we approach the third decade of the 21st century, portable classrooms—which are often nicer and better equipped than their counterparts inside traditional buildings—are no longer unsightly, makeshift solutions to overcrowding problems. Portable classrooms have evolved from primitive, temporary holding pens with little thought given to student comfort to experimental, self-sustainable facilities displaying the most advanced energy-efficient building elements with abundant air and light. Currently, educators and architects are beginning to explore how entire schools can be made from portable or modular structures. Whatever the outcome of these investigations, the simple one-room portable classroom will continue to be a fundamental part of school administrators' repertoire for dealing with oscillating enrollments and unpredictable funding.

EPILOGUE

Today's schoolroom shares many features with its predecessors over the centuries and will likely be comparable to classrooms of the future. Rooms come in various shapes and sizes, with different contents, wall materials, windows, and furniture, but the standard schoolroom is still a rectangular or square boxlike space where students are led by a teacher. Having proven effective over a long period of time, there is no reason to believe this arrangement will change.

Future schoolrooms no doubt will continue to make adjustments required by the latest technology or trend. Already the extremely casual open-office concept popularized by technology companies to take advantage of wireless communications, with comfortable furniture, gaming areas, movable desks, and no walls or offices, has begun to infiltrate public education, and that trend is likely to continue. Virtual-reality space might also be needed either in the classroom or in a separate space, thus reenacting the debate over films in classrooms from the last century.

There have been no profound innovations in classroom design or school planning since the mid-20th century and the appearance of cluster and loft floor plans, unusually shaped buildings, open classrooms, and windowless schools. One can anticipate some trends in school architecture, however, based on contemporary tendencies. Perhaps most important is the certainty that security will become a salient design consideration for new school buildings. The challenge will be to integrate security measures in a natural, sensitive manner so that schools do not become isolated fortresses. Some recent examples of highly secure schools are admirable in their use of trees, plantings, water features, and berms to create buffers in the guise of landscaping. Inside, school buildings will become more transparent for better visibility; undoubtedly the physical presence of security personnel on the interior will increase as well. The distractions created by these open, transparent, casual environments could resurrect open-classroom critiques.

A potential consequence of the enhanced security of future school buildings may be the weakening of connections between indoors and outdoors that have been an essential component of the educational experience for nearly 100 years. The outdoor classroom envisioned by Richard Neutra, William Caudill, and others could disappear in the attempt to restrict the building's access and egress points.

Another change likely to affect schoolrooms and buildings is the continuing advance of energy-efficient technology. Passive-solar panels, energy-recovery ventilators, rainwater cisterns, composting toilets, sensor-controlled LED lighting, hand-pump sinks, and a multitude of other products and materials—some not yet invented—will put school buildings at the forefront of America's alternative-energy movement. Larger school buildings will follow the lead of the smaller relocatable classrooms in becoming sustainable schools. This greening of the schoolhouse will dovetail with the schools' educational mission by allowing students to see energy efficiency in action.

Finally, schools may become smaller in the future if public-school enrollments decline from a combination of slashed budgets and alternative school options, particularly the already popular voucher and charter schools. This contraction could be expedited if more online instruction is combined with less restrictive attendance requirements.

The school building will probably always exist in some form, but the question of whether it will continue to decentralize is debatable. The physical separation of academic, physical-education, vocational-training, and art spaces and music spaces, firmly ensconced in school design for over a century, makes too much sense to be abandoned. An argument can be made that the proliferation of magnet schools since the postwar era continued the school building's decentralization by exploding special areas of study beyond the school building's walls and out to separate locations. This intriguing hypothesis leads one to wonder if the disparate parts will some day contract—like some theories of the expanding/contracting universe—into a more compact form. Given the history of schoolrooms and schoolhouses, it is likely that both physically decentralized and compacted schools will appear equally in the future.

GLOSSARY

Active learning: Learning that occurs when the student is engaged in some activity.

Air rights: Property rights granting ownership of the space above or below existing structures.

Americans with Disabilities Act (ADA): A 1990 federal law created to ban discrimination against disabled people. The ADA required employers to provide reasonable accommodations for the disabled and governments to meet federal accessibility standards for public places, including public schools.

Clearstory window: A window at the highest point of a wall below the ceiling.

Closed-plan building: Closed-plan buildings are compact and inward looking, often in the shape of a square or rectangle, and usually punctured by one or more internal courtyards.

Cluster plan: A variation of the finger plan that breaks down the mass of the school building and spreads it out, often with clusters of classrooms connected to the core of the school by stalk-like corridors.

Common school: An educational system envisioned by 19th-century reformers whereby all children in a given district, region, or even across the country studied a common curriculum under teachers using the same pedagogical techniques.

Comprehensive high school: A high school offering both academic programs and vocational training.

Curriculum: The course of study in a school, comprising all of the required and elective classes.

Dame school: A popular educational alternative before public schools, dame schools were operated by adult women in their own homes.

District school: A popular early school type, particularly in the Northeast and Midwest, which enrolled local students and were funded by combinations of tuition, property taxes, and sometimes a small contribution from the state.

Double-loaded corridor: A hallway with rooms on both sides, in contrast to a single-loaded corridor, which has rooms lined along one side only.

Faculty theory of psychology: The belief that a number of distinct parts or faculties (reason, memory, emotion, etc.) made up the human mind and that each of these faculties could be strengthened—like a muscle—through exercise: a defining characteristic of 19th-century educational theory and pedagogy.

Finger plan: A type of floor plan that decentralizes the school building by separating classrooms from other activities and aligning them in parallel rows attached to a single corridor, like fingers emerging from a palm.

Graded school: Grouping pupils in classrooms by age rather than teaching all levels of students together.

Grammar school: British term for primary or elementary school. Colonial and early republic school systems were often divided into primary and grammar levels depending on the age and reading ability of the student, but the phrase fell out of favor during the 19th century.

International Style architecture: An early manifestation of modern architecture that explored such new ideas in architecture as the free plan, an emphasis on volume and space rather than mass, a preference for light metal or concrete frames and thin walls, and developed characteristics like flat roofs, smooth cubic surfaces, and ribbon windows. The International Style first appeared in the United States in the 1920s.

Interwar period: The period between World War I and World War II (1918–1939).

Junior high school: Created in the early 20th century as an intermediate step between primary and secondary education, junior high schools (also known as middle schools) became popular in the 1920s as a way to alleviate overcrowding in the high schools and accommodate adolescents' special needs.

Kiva (alcove): A small enclosed multipurpose room for children for relaxation or unsupervised activities separated from the main classroom; popularized by British architects David and Mary Crowley Medd in the 1960s.

Life-adjustment curriculum: A new curriculum invented in the late 1940s to address real-life problems rather than provide an academic foundation. Life adjustment shifted the emphasis from learning basic fundamentals, core concepts, and cultural milestones to readying students for everyday life as an adult in a democratic society.

Loft plan: An alternative to finger and cluster floor plans wherein all rooms are centralized under a single roof; inspired by industrial architecture and the concept of a simple steel-framed building without load-bearing interior partitions.

Magnet school: Schools dedicated to specific areas of study, like performing arts or mathematics and science, which draw students from across district boundaries.

Manual training: Manual training developed in the last quarter of the 19th century to supplement the regular academic curriculum by encouraging students to utilize their hands as well as their minds.

Mental discipline: An educational approach emphasizing the training of the mind to think rather than teaching about particular subject matter. Mental-discipline methods focused on repetition and rote memorization.

Monitorial school: Early-19th-century schools that used advanced students as monitors to teach their peers and operated on a rigid system of control. Created in Great Britain by Joseph Lancaster and Dr. Andrew Bell, monitorial schools enjoyed great popularity in the United States before their eventual decline by the 1850s.

Nonbearing wall: A wall that does not participate in carrying the weight of the building.

Open classroom: Conceptually, an approach to teaching and learning that incorporates free movement, informality, and student-initiated learning. Physically, an open classroom is literally without interior walls.

Open-plan building: Open-plan buildings are more varied in shape than closed plans; a school that has an alphabet footprint or any other configuration that alters the square or rectangle is an open-plan building.

Passive learning: Learning where the students receive information from the teacher without engaging in any activity.

Pedagogy: The method and practice of teaching.

Postwar period: The period after World War II ended in 1945. Often more specifically refers to 1945–1973, or the war's end to the energy crisis.

Prefabrication: Making and/or assembling parts of a building in a factory away from the construction site.

Primary school: Also known as an elementary school. The lowest rung on the public-education ladder, usually involving children from ages 5 to 12.

Progressive education: A broad reform movement beginning in the late 19th century that looked to reorganize educational systems, curricula, and pedagogy; in terms of the latter, it emphasized a more active role for children in their education and encouraged teachers to follow children's interests and give them choices.

Recitation: A fundamental component of education until the mid-20th century: the recital or repetition of memorized material upon command from the teacher.

Relocatable (portable) classroom: A freestanding structure holding one classroom and simply constructed, often from modular parts. While many are intended to be temporary solutions to overcrowding problems, a significant number of relocatable buildings become permanent. Currently, they are an area of interest in the field of school design.

Secondary education: The high school.

Shed roof: A roof that slopes in only one direction.

Single-loaded corridor: A corridor with rooms along one side.

Teaching machine: Special devices designed to allow a single learner to proceed through a given topic at his or her own speed, with feedback and programmed investigation. Considered to be the most advanced educational technology of the 1920s through 1960s, teaching machines became obsolete when personal computers entered public schools.

Team teaching: Employing more than one teacher to teach a single class. The team works together as equals and is able to provide more intensive learning experiences to students than a single teacher.

Vocational education: Education oriented toward training students for future employment rather than higher education.

BIBLIOGRAPHY

Akers, William J. 1901. *Cleveland Schools in the Nineteenth Century.* Cleveland: The W. M. Bayne Printing House.

Alberty, H. B., and E. J. Alberty. 1962. *Reorganizing the High-School Curriculum,* 3rd ed. New York: The Macmillan Company.

Allen, Gerald. 1979. "Schools." *Architectural Record* 165:127.

Anderson, Charnel. 1962. *Technology in American Education 1650–1900.* Washington, DC: U.S. Department of Health, Education, and Welfare.

Andrews, E. Benjamin. 1900. "The Public School System in Chicago." *Education* 21:264–69.

Angus, David L., and Jeffrey E. Mirel. 1999. *The Failed Promise of the American High School, 1890–1995.* New York: Teachers College Press.

Aslan, Sinem, and Charles M. Reigeluth. 2011. "A Trip to the Past and Future of Educational Computing: Understanding Its Evolution." *Contemporary Educational Technology* 2(1):1–17b.

Bailey, James. 1966. "Harlem's Besieged Showpiece." *Architectural Forum* 125:48–51.

Baker, N. R. 1910. "School Room Fenestration." *American School Board Journal* 40:5.

Barnard, Henry. 1848. *School Architecture,* 2nd ed. New York: A. S. Barnes & Co.

Benjamin, Ludy T., Jr. 1988. "A History of Teaching Machines." *American Psychologist* 43:703–712.

Billings, John S. 1893. *Ventilation and Heating.* New York: The Engineering Record.

Borja, Rhea R. 2002. "Digital Whiteboards Outsell Traditional Chalkboards." *Education Week,* November 27. Accessed November 28, 2016. http://www.edweek.org/ew/articles/2002/11/27/13whiteboard.h22.html.

Bourne, Randolph S. 1916. *The Gary Schools*. Boston: Houghton Mifflin Company.

Briggs, Warren Richard. 1899. *Modern American School Buildings*. New York: John Wiley & Sons.

Bruce, William C. 1963. "School Architecture 1963." *American School Board Journal* 146:48.

Bruce, William G. 1911. "Some New Schoolhouses in Chicago." *American School Board Journal* 43:24.

Bruce, William George. 1906. *School Architecture: A Handy Manual for the Use of Architects and School Authorities*. Milwaukee: Johnson Service Company.

Burke, Catherine, and Ian Grosvenor. 2008. *School*. London: Reaktion Books Ltd.

Burrage, Severance, and Henry Turner Bailey. 1899. *School Sanitation and Decoration*. Boston: D. C. Heath and Company.

Busselle, Alfred. 1921. "Domestic Quality in School Design." *Architecture* 43:121.

Callahan, Raymond E. 1962. *Education and the Cult of Efficiency*. Chicago: University of Chicago Press.

"Case Study Schools." 1953. *Architectural Forum* 99: 127–161.

Caudill, William W. 1954. *Toward Better School Design*. New York: F. W. Dodge Corp.

Chaney, B., and L. Lewis. 2007. *Public School Principals Report on Their School Facilities: Fall 2005*. Washington, DC: U.S. Department of Education.

Châtelet, A.-M. 2008. "A Breath of Fresh Air: Open-Air Schools in Europe." In *Designing Modern Childhoods: History, Space, and the Material Culture of Children*, edited by Marta Gutman and Ning de Coninck-Smith, 107–126. New Brunswick, NJ: Rutgers University Press.

Cocking, Walter D. 1956. "Secondary School Design since World War II." *American School and University* 27:185–192.

Colby, S. L., and J. M. Ortman. 2014. "The Baby Boom Cohort in the United States: 2012 to 2060." Accessed June 1, 2015. https://www.census.gov/prod/2014pubs/p25-1141.pdf

Cooper, Frank Irving. 1911. "Perils of School House Construction." *The American School Board Journal* 42:2.

"Costly High Schools." 1896. *American School Board Journal* 12:10–11.

Croly, Herbert. 1909. *The Promise of American Life*, edited by Arthur M. Schlesinger Jr. Cambridge, MA: Harvard University Press, 1965.

Cross, A. J. Foy. 1956. "A School Building Is for Learning." *American School Board Journal* 132:27–28, 94.

Cuban, Larry. 1986. *Teachers and Machines: The Classroom Use of Technology since 1920*. New York: Teachers College Press.

Cuban, Larry. 1993. *How Teachers Taught: Constancy and Change in American Classrooms 1890–1990*. New York: Teachers College Press.

Cuban, Larry. 2004. "The Open Classroom." *Education Next* 4(2):69–71.

Cutler, William W., III. 1989. "Cathedral of Culture: The Schoolhouse in American Educational Thought and Practice since 1820." *History of Education Quarterly* 29:1–40.

Darian-Smith, Kate, and Julie Willis, eds. 2017. *Designing Schools: Space, Place and Pedagogy.* New York: Routledge.

Dewey, John. 1959. *Dewey on Education: Selections.* Introduction and notes by Martin S. Dworkin. New York: Teachers College Press.

Donovan, John J. 1921. *School Architecture: Principles and Practices.* New York: The Macmillan Company.

Dresslar, Fletcher B. 1910. *American Schoolhouses* (United States Bureau of Education Bulletin, no. 5). Washington, DC: U.S. Government Printing Office.

Dresslar, Fletcher B. 1913. *School Hygiene.* New York: Macmillan.

Duffy, John. 1979. "School Buildings and the Health of American School Children in the Nineteenth Century." In *Healing and History: Essays for George Rosen*, edited by Charles E. Rosenberg. New York: Science History Publications.

Dwyer, Charles P. 1856. *The Economy of Church, Parsonage and School Architecture, Adapted to Small Societies and Rural Districts.* Buffalo, NY: Phinney & Co., Publishers, 1856.

Educational Facilities Laboratories. 1960. *The Cost of a Schoolhouse.* New York: Educational Facilities Laboratories.

Educational Facilities Laboratories. 1961. *High Schools 1962.* New York: Educational Facilities Laboratories.

Educational Facilities Laboratories. 1964. *Relocatable School Facilities.* New York: Educational Facilities Laboratories.

Educational Facilities Laboratories. 1965. *Schools without Walls.* New York: Educational Facilities Laboratories.

Educational Facilities Laboratories. 1968. *Educational Change and Architectural Consequences.* New York: Educational Facilities Laboratories.

Educational Facilities Laboratories. 1970. *The Open Plan School.* Dayton, OH: Institute for the Development of Educational Activities.

Endemann, H. 1873. "Chemical Examination of the Air of Various Public Buildings." In *Third Annual Report, 1872–1873*, edited by New York Board of Health. New York: New York Board of Health.

Engelhardt, N. L., N. L. Engelhardt Jr., and Stanton Leggett. 1953. *Planning Elementary School Buildings.* New York: F. W. Dodge Corp.

Exton, Elaine. 1960. "Teaching Machines: Fad or Here to Stay?" *American School Board Journal* 141:18–22.

Ferrer, Terry. 1964. *The Schools and Urban Renewal: A Case Study from New Haven.* New York: Educational Facilities Laboratories.

Finkelstein, Barbara. 1989. *Governing the Young: Teacher Behavior in Popular Primary Schools in 19th Century United States.* New York: The Falmer Press.

Flansburgh, Earl. 1988. "Back to Bells and Cells?" *Architectural Record* 176: 100–113.

Gonchar, Joann. 2014. "Modular Classroom Makeover." *Architectural Record* 202:134–140.

Graves, Ben E. 1993. *School Ways: The Planning and Design of America's Schools.* New York: McGraw-Hill, Inc.

Graves, Karen. 1998. *Girls' Schooling during the Progressive Era: From Female Scholar to Domesticated Citizen.* New York: Garland Publishing, Inc.

Gyure, Dale Allen. 2001. "The Transformation of the Schoolhouse: American Secondary School Architecture and Educational Reform, 1880–1920." PhD dissertation, University of Virginia.

Gyure, Dale Allen. 2011. *The Chicago Schoolhouse: High School Architecture and Educational Reform, 1856–2006.* Chicago: Center for American Places at Columbia College Chicago.

Hall, G. Stanley. 1907. *Youth: Its Education, Regimen, and Hygiene.* New York: D. Appleton.

Hampel, Robert L. 1986. *The Last Little Citadel: American High Schools since 1940.* Boston: Houghton Mifflin Company.

Hancock, John. 1882. "The High School: Its Relation to the Lower Grades of Public Schools." *Education* 3:164–165.

Hansen, J. E. 1940. "Better Teaching through Motion-Picture Equipment." *American School Board Journal* 101:39.

Hays, William C. 1917. "One-Story and Open-Air Schoolhouses in California." *Architectural Forum* 27:3–12.

Herbst, Jurgen. 1996. *The Once and Future School: Three Hundred and Fifty Years of American Secondary Education.* New York: Routledge.

Herrick, Mary J. 1971. *The Chicago Schools: A Social and Political History.* Beverly Hills, CA: Sage.

"A High Nest of Hexagons." 1963. *Architectural Forum* 119: 87–88.

"High School Architecture." 1907. *American School Board Journal* 34:8.

Hille, R. Thomas. 2011. *Modern Schools: A Century of Design for Education.* New York: John Wiley & Sons.

Hoffschwelle, Mary S. 1998. *Rebuilding the Rural Southern Community: Reformers, Schools, and Homes in Tennessee, 1900–1930.* Knoxville: University of Tennessee Press.

Howatt, John, and Samuel R. Lewis. 1919. "Construction and Equipment of Portable School Buildings." *The Heating and Ventilating Magazine* XVI: 24–32.

Ittner, William B. 1931. "Forty Years in American School Architecture." *American School Board Journal* 82:49–51.

Johnson, Philip. 1933. "Architecture for School and College Buildings—Period Styles or Contemporary? Modern Architecture for Efficiency." *American School and University* 5:31–33.

Johnson, William Templeton. 1916. "An Open-Air School in California." *Journal of the American Institute for Architects* 4:161–164.

Johonnot, James. 1871. *School-Houses.* New York: J. W. Schermerhorn & Co.

Kaestle, Carl F. 1983. *Pillars of the Republic: Common Schools and American Society, 1780–1860.* New York: Hill & Wang.

Kett, Joseph F. 1977. *Rites of Passage: Adolescence in America, 1790 to the Present*. New York: Basic Books.

Kidwell, Peggy Aldrich, Amy Ackerberg-Hastings, and David Lindsay Roberts. 2008. *Tools of American Mathematics Teaching, 1800–2000*. Washington, DC: Smithsonian Institution; Baltimore: Johns Hopkins University Press.

Kleibard, Herbert M. 1986. *The Struggle for the American Curriculum 1893–1958*. Boston: Routledge & Kegan Paul.

Kleibard, Herbert M. 1995. *The Struggle for the American Curriculum, 1893–1958*. 2nd ed. New York: Routledge.

Kleibard, Herbert M. 1999. *Schooled to Work: Vocationalism and the American Curriculum, 1876–1946*. New York: Teachers College Press.

Kleibard, Herbert M. 2002. *Changing Course: American Curriculum Reform in the 20th Century*. New York: Teachers College Press.

Koos, Leonard V. 1919. "Space-Provisions in the Floor-Plans of Modern High-School Buildings." *School Review* 27:573–599.

Krug, Edward A. 1964. *The Shaping of the American High School*. New York: Harper & Row.

Krug, Edward A. 1972. *The Shaping of the American High School, 1920–1941*. Madison: University of Wisconsin Press.

Labaree, David F. 1988. *The Making of an American High School: The Credentials Market and the Central High School of Philadelphia, 1838–1939*. New Haven, CT: Yale University Press.

Macleod, David I. 1998. *The Age of the Child: Children in American, 1890–1920*. New York: Twayne Publishers.

Mann, Horace. 1838. *On the Subject of School Houses*. Boston: Dutton & Wentworth.

May, Elaine Tyler. 2008. *Homeward Bound: American Families in the Cold War Era*. New York: Basic Books.

"Meanwhile, an Encouraging Lift in the Design of Urban Schools." 1963. *Architectural Forum* 119:77–78.

Miller, Ward I. 1949. "Requirements of the Modern Secondary School." *American School and University* 20:77–85.

Mills, Wilbur T. 1915. *American School Building Standards*. Columbus, OH: Franklin Educational.

Morton, David A. 1971. "Closing Off the Open Plan." *Progressive Architecture*, February, pp. 68–77.

Museum of Modern Art. 1942. "Modern Architecture for the Modern School." Accessed June 10, 2015. https://www.moma.org/pdfs/docs/press_archives /821/releases/MOMA_1942_0063_1942-09-24_42914-57.pdf?2010.

Nasaw, David. 1979. *Schooled to Order: A Social History of Public Schooling in the United States*. New York: Oxford University Press.

National Center for Education Statistics. 1993. *120 Years of American Education: A Statistical Portrait* Washington, DC: U.S. Department of Education.

National Education Association Committee on School House Planning and Construction. 1925. *Report of Committee on School House Planning.* Washington, DC: National Education Association.

"The Need." 1949. *Architectural Forum* 91: 81–84.

"New Proposals to Cut School Costs." 1961. *Architectural Forum* 115:110–127.

Nickell, V. L. 1949. "How Can We Develop an Effective Program of Education for Life Adjustment?" *Bulletin of the National Association of Secondary-School Principals* 33:154.

Nowicki, M. 1949. "Forum's School for 1950." *Architectural Forum* 91: 134–137.

Ogata, Amy F. 2013. *Designing the Creative Child: Playthings and Places in Midcentury America.* Minneapolis: University of Minnesota Press.

Oommen, Vinesh G., Mike Knowles, and Isabella Zhao, 2008. "Should Health Service Managers Embrace Open Plan Work Environments? A Review." *Asia Pacific Journal of Health Management* 3(2):37–43.

Orgeron, Devin, Marsha Orgeron, and Dan Streible. 2012. "A History of Learning with the Lights Off." In *Learning with the Lights Off: Educational Film in the United States,* edited by Devin Orgeron, Marsha Orgeron, and Dan Streible, 15–66. New York: Oxford University Press.

Orme, Nicholas. 2006. *Medieval Schools, from Roman Britain to Renaissance England.* New York: Yale University Press.

Perkins, Lawrence B., and Walter D. Cocking. 1949. *Schools.* New York: Reinhold Publishing Corp.

Perry, Clarence Arthur. 1915. "Recent Progress in Wider Use of School Plant." *Report of the U.S. Commissioner of Education.* Washington, DC: U.S. Government Printing Office.

Petrina, Stephen. 2004. "Sidney Pressey and the Automation of Education, 1924–1934." *Technology and Culture* 45:305–330.

Philbrick, John D. 1881. "Boston Latin and English High Schools." *American Journal of Education* 31:401–444.

Phillips, Christopher J. 2015. "An Officer and a Scholar: Nineteenth-Century West Point and the Invention of the Blackboard." *History of Education Quarterly* 55:82–108.

Pinnell, Leroy K. 1954. *Functionality of Elementary School Desks.* Austin: University of Texas Press.

"The Planning of School Buildings." 1890. *The American Architect and Building News* 27:81–82.

Powell, Arthur G., Eleanor Farrar, and David K. Cohen. 1985. *The Shopping Mall High School: Winners and Losers in the Educational Marketplace.* Boston: Houghton Mifflin Company.

"Public School Hygiene." 1896. *American School Board Journal* 13: 8.

Ravitch, Diane. 1983. *The Troubled Crusade: American Education 1945–1980.* New York: Basic Books.

"Reducing the School Expenses." 1878. *Chicago Tribune,* March 22, p. 4.

Reese, L. W. 1930. "The Radio Takes on Education." *American School Board Journal* 80:39–41, 134.

Reese, William J. 1995. *The Origins of the American High School.* New Haven, CT: Yale University Press.

Reese, William J. 2002. *Power and the Promise of School Reform: Grass Roots Movements during the Progressive Era.* New York: Teachers College Press.

Reese, William J. 2005. *America's Public Schools.* Baltimore: Johns Hopkins University Press.

Rice, Joseph M. 1893. *The Public-School System of the United States.* New York: The Century Company.

Robson, E. R. 1874. *School Architecture.* London: John Murray.

Rogers, A. C. 1956. "Toward an Expressive School Architecture." *The Nation's Schools* 57:81–84.

Rugg, Harold Ordway, and Ann Shumaker. 1928. *The Child-Centered School.* New York: World Book Company.

Rummel, Frances V. 1950. *High School: What's In It for Me?* Washington, DC: U.S. Office of Education.

Saettler, Paul. 1990. *The Evolution of American Educational Technology.* Englewood, CO: Libraries Unlimited.

Schlereth, Thomas J. 1991. *Victorian America: Transformations in Everyday Life, 1876–1915.* New York: Harper Perennial.

School Reform in Chicago: Lessons and Opportunities, a Report for the Chicago Community Trust, August 2001. 2001. Chicago: Chicago Community Trust.

School Survey Committee. 1924. *Survey of Public School System, City of New York.* New York: Board of Education of the City of New York.

"Schools: Fresh Ideas and Long Range Criticism." 1952. *Architectural Forum* 97:101–133.

Schultz, Stanley K. 1973. *The Culture Factory: Boston Public Schools, 1789–1860.* New York: Oxford University Press.

Seaborne, Malcom. 1971. *The English School: Its Architecture and Organization, 1370–1870.* Toronto: University of Toronto Press.

Short, C. W., and R. Stanley-Brown. 1939. *Public Buildings: A Survey of Architecture of Projects Constructed by Federal and Other Governmental Bodies between the Years 1933 and 1939 with the Assistance of the Public Works Administration.* Washington, DC: U.S. Government Printing Office.

Smith, C. Ray. 1971. "The Portable Desk." *Progressive Architecture*, February, pp. 96–97.

"Space for Individual Learning: The Biography of a Great Idea." 1963. *Educational Executives' Overview*, March, pp. 28–39.

"Standardized School House Design." 1918. *The American Architect* 114:559–560.

Stuart, A. T., James Knox Taylor, and Jay J. Morrow. 1908. *Report of the Schoolhouse Commission upon a General Plan for the Consolidation of Public Schools in the District of Columbia.* Washington, DC: US Government Printing Office.

"St. Louis School Architecture." 1904. *American School Board Journal* 28: 8–9.

Taggart, Robert J. 1988. *Private Philanthropy and Public Education: Pierre S. du Pont and the Delaware Schools, 1890–1940.* Newark: University of Delaware Press.

Taggart, Robert J. 2007. "The Promise and Failure of Educational Television in a Statewide System: Delaware, 1964–1971." *American Educational History Journal* 1:111–122.

Taylor, L. O., D. R. McMahill, and B. L. Taylor. 1960. *The American Secondary School.* New York: Appleton-Century-Crofts.

Thirty-Seventh Annual Report of the Board of Education. 1892. Chicago: Public Schools of the City of Chicago.

"Today's Schools—the Bigger the City, the Tougher the Problem." 1949. *Architectural Forum* 91:85–91.

Toffler, Alvin, ed. 1968. *The Schoolhouse in the City.* New York: Frederick A. Praeger.

"Toward Better Schools." 1949. *Architectural Forum* 91:101.

Troen, Selwyn K. 1975. *The Public and the Schools: Shaping the St. Louis System, 1838–1920.* Columbia: University of Missouri Press.

Tyack, David B. 1974. *The One Best System: A History of American Urban Education.* Cambridge, MA: Harvard University Press.

Tyack, David B., and Elisabeth Hansot. 1982. *Managers of Virtue: Public School Leadership in America, 1820–1980.* New York: Basic Books.

Tyack, David B., Thomas James, and Aaron Benavot. 1987. *Law and the Shaping of Public Education, 1785–1954.* Madison: University of Wisconsin Press.

Upton, Dell. 1996. "Lancasterian Schools, Republican Citizenship, and the Spatial Imagination in Early Nineteenth-Century America." *Journal of the Society of Architectural Historians* 55:238–253.

Urban, Wayne J., and Jennings L. Wagoner Jr. 2004. *American Education: A History,* 3rd ed. New York: McGraw-Hill.

U.S. General Accounting Office. 1995. *School Facilities: Condition of America's Schools.* Washington, DC: U.S. General Accounting Office.

Van Dulken, Stephen. 2006. *Inventing the 19th Century: 100 Inventions That Shaped the Victorian Age, from Aspirin to the Zeppelin.* New York: New York University Press.

Weisser, Amy S. 1995. "Institutional Revisions: Modernism and American Public Schools from the Depression through the Second World War." PhD dissertation, Yale University.

Weisser, Amy S. 2006. "'Little Red School House, What Now?' Two Centuries of American Public School Architecture." *Journal of Planning History* 5:196–217.

Wheelwright, Edmund M. 1897. "The American Schoolhouse II." *The Brick-builder* 6:244–247.

Wheelwright, Edmund M. 1901. *School Architecture: A General Treatise for the Use of Architects and Others.* Boston: Rogers & Manson.

Wiley, Amber N. 2011. "Concrete Solutions: Race, Class, and Architecture of Urban High Schools from 1960–1980." PhD dissertation, George Washington University.

Willis, George W., William H. Schubert, Robert V. Bullough Jr., Craig Kridel, and John T. Holton, eds. 1993. *The American Curriculum: A Documentary History.* Westport, CT: Greenwood Press.

Willrich, Michael. 2003. *City of Courts: Socializing Justice in Progressive Era Chicago.* New York: Cambridge University Press.

Winsor, F. 1877. "The Ventilating and Warming of Schoolhouses in the Northern United States." *The American Architect and Building News* 2:327–330.

Zimmerman, Jonathan. 2009. *Small Wonder: The Little Red Schoolhouse in History and Memory.* New Haven, CT: Yale University Press.

Zueblin, Charles. 1902. *American Municipal Progress: Chapters in Municipal Sociology.* New York: Macmillan.

INDEX

About the Author

Dale Allen Gyure, PhD, is professor of architecture at Lawrence Technological University, Southfield, Michigan. He is the author of *The Chicago Schoolhouse: High School Architecture and Educational Reform, 1856–2006* and the essay "Creating Friendly School Environments: 'Casual' High Schools, Progressive Education, and Child-Centered Culture in Postwar America" in *Designing Schools: Space, Place, and Pedagogy.* Dr. Gyure has served on the boards of directors of the Society of Architectural Historians, the Frank Lloyd Wright Building Conservancy, and Docomomo Michigan and is a member of the Michigan Historic Preservation Review Board.